Finningley
Loughton
Edlington
Wadworth
Brauwll
Maltbye
Mysterton
Stockwith
Blyton
Walkringham
Euerton
Pilham
Gringley
Coringham
Beckingham
Gainsbugh
Matterfey
Blythe
Clawarth
Sauby
Springthorp
Hayton
Auston
Sutton
Bole
Knathe
Clarburgh
Barnbye
Gateburton
Retforth
Stow
Radforth
Babworthe
Grove
S. Leuerton
Brampton
Workfop
Ofburton
Ordfall
Trefwell
Elsley
Headon
Gamston
Carbarton
Askam
Bothumfale
Houghton
Burrotts
Warfop
Parlethorp
Walsbye
Edenftow
Kuton
Allerton
Laxton
Wellawe
Rughford
Akring
Knesall
Girton
Agle
Searle
Norwell
Kerfall
Caunton
Bilsthorp
Collingham
Maplebeck
Langford
Eldworth
Kirklington
Muscombe
Winkborn
Kelham
Hockerton
Papplewick
Halam
Winthorp
Barnby
Farnfeld
Hauerham
Beckingham
Oxton
Suthwell
Morton
Rowlesbye
Fenton
Thurgarton
Epperston
Claypole
Calverton
Stubton
Woodboro
Arnold
Dodington
Gedling
Shelford
Wesboro
Houghton
Merston
Nottingham
Ratchiffe
Coulston
Thoroton
Bingham
Aslerton
Bottesworth
Tythebye
Elton
Muston
Edwalton
Cropwell
Redmill
Sedbrok
Codgroue
Althorp
Rodington
Plumtre
Staunton
Slauford
Barrowbye
Bradmere
Keyworth
Coulston
Wulsthorp
Belvoir castle
Harlaxton
Knolton
Widmerpoole
Hicklyng
Croxton
E. Leaks
Wyfhaw
Nether
Knipton
Braunston
Clauston
Broughton
Skillington
Grimston
Sproxton
Dalbye
Prestwowld
Walthim
Stonefbye
Walton
Ragdal
Melton
Barrow
Segrave
Hoby
Thorp Araby
Wiverby
Garthorp
Kirkbye
Friseby
Stapleford
Wimondham
Rothebye
Brokefby
Gaddesbye
Dalbye
Edmedham
Mountsorell

Nottingham, Nobles, and the North

STUDIES IN BRITISH HISTORY AND CULTURE

VOLUME IV

Nottingham, Nobles, and the North

Aspects of the Revolution of 1688

BY

DAVID H. HOSFORD

Published for

The Conference on British Studies and Wittenberg University

by ARCHON BOOKS

Library of Congress Cataloging in Publication Data

Hosford, David H.
    Nottingham, nobles, and the North.

    (Studies in British history and culture; v: 4)
    Bibliography: p.
    Includes index.
    1. Great Britain—History—Revolution of 1688. I.
    Title. II. Series.
DA452.H7   941.06'7   75-19458
ISBN 0-208-01565-5

First published 1976 as an Archon Book,
an imprint of The Shoe String Press, Inc.,
Hamden, Connecticut
for
The Conference on British Studies
and
Wittenberg University
Springfield, Ohio

Printed in the United States of America

To Susanna

Contents

FOREWORD

Studies in British History and Culture was founded in January, 1965, as a joint publishing venture of the Conference on British Studies and the University of Bridgeport; Stephen Graubard and Leland Miles were the Senior Editors, and the New York University Press was printer. The first round of manuscript competition was announced at the Fall 1965 Conference meeting. No one suspected then that more than forty manuscripts would be submitted in the next eighteen months.

From the screening of many readers and editors, one manuscript emerged as winner in the first phase of competition: John Schlight's *Monarchs and Mercenaries*. Professor Schlight's work met many of the ideals laid down by the editors and Conference officials. These ideals include vigorous research, original interpretation, literary grace, and the prospect of interest among scholars in several fields. The editors were especially seeking works which would challenge traditional viewpoints. Professor Schlight's volume admirably fulfilled this last ideal. He assembled impressive evidence to support his thesis that mercenary troops rather than knights-on-horseback constituted a dominant institution in feudal society.

The second *Studies* volume, L. P. Curtis, Jr.'s provocative *Anglo-Saxons and Celts: A Study of Anti-Irish Prejudice in Victorian England*, met all of the foregoing ideals. The third volume was Martin Kallich's *The Other End of the Egg: Religious Satire in Gulliver's Travels.* Professor Kallich's book was "controversial" in the best sense, namely, in its capacity to stimulate reassessment of a major work in English literature. Like his two predecessors, Kallich took a fresh approach to the subject— that is, he attacked views previously held to be unassailable.

Kallich's book was published in 1970. A five-year hiatus then occurred when the University of Bridgeport decided it could no longer fund the monograph series. Fortunately, Wittenberg University volunteered to become co-publisher with the Conference and with Archon Books. The result is that *Studies in British History and Culture* now presents its fourth work, David H. Hosford's *Nottingham, Nobles, and the North: Aspects of the Revolution of 1688*, which continues the high level of research and writing that have characterized the series. As a pioneer work in the study of the revolution in the country, Hosford reasserts an English role in the revolution and provides substantial proof for the contention that the events of 1688 were, in fact, a conservative revolution.

Hosford's study of the revolution of 1688 in the two counties of Nottinghamshire and Derbyshire has broader implications and applications than might at first appear. Nottingham itself was important, for the Princess Anne rode there after her flight from Whitehall. And the fact that there was a rising in the two counties demonstrated the truth of William's claim that he had been invited to come to England. If the role of the Prince of Orange was very large, he did not act in a vacuum. As Hosford demonstrates, the swift changes of policy during the reign of James II had had a scouring effect on local government, so that by 1688 there was very little of it left. A small push, and William brought only fifteen thousand men with him, was enough to topple a state of five and a half million inhabitants. But William did not, and could not, do it all by himself. Hosford is also correct in emphasizing the importance of the peerage in this part of the country, at least. Here they took the lead and it was the Duke of Newcastle who provided almost the only opposition to the conspirators. The gentry and the common people, for their part, were happy to watch the activity of their betters. In this respect the revolution in Nottinghamshire and Derbyshire differs from that at York to the north as well as from the course of events in the main arena to the south. Although the events described here may seem at first to be something of a sideshow, like those in Scotland, they were in fact an essential part of the final victory. Throughout England, and throughout the greater part of the Empire, the overwhelming majority of Englishmen wanted to preserve their institutions from the innovations of James II. It is hoped this interesting study will encourage others to work on the revolution in some other English counties.

Stephen Baxter
Leland Miles
Senior Editors

Acknowledgements

My greatest obligation is to Professor William L. Sachse for introducing me to the intricacies of Restoration history and for his continuing encouragement and assistance in developing this study. I am also particularly grateful to Professor W. R. Fryer who guided my first research efforts in England and whose interest in my work has been a special source of satisfaction. Professor Stephen Baxter and Professor Richard Schlatter both kindly consented to read this book in manuscript and offered numerous suggestions and valuable criticisms. Finally, the late Professor Douglas Lacey helped me over a number of hurdles in interpreting the shorthand entries contained in Roger Morrice's "Entring Book."

I am deeply indebted to the owners of private manuscript collections and to the librarians and archivists in the various research centers and manuscript repositories in which I have worked. I especially appreciate the kindness of those individuals who allowed me access to manuscript materials in their possession: the Duke of Devonshire, the Duke of Rutland, the Marquess of Lothian, the Marquess of Northampton, Earl Spencer, the Earl of Stamford, Lord Kenyon, Sir Fergus Graham, and Lt. Col. John Chandos-Pole. I am also grateful to the Duke of Portland for the use of manuscripts on deposit at the University of Nottingham and the British Museum.

The initial stages of research for this study were made possible by a United States government grant (Fulbright-Hayes Act) and a University of Wisconsin graduate fellowship. A post-doctoral fellowship awarded by the William Andrews Clark Memorial Library enabled me to participate in a seminar in Restoration history during the summer of 1973, and allowed me to draw upon the very substantial resources of the Library. The Rutgers University Research Council provided a grant to cover clerical expenses connected with final revision of the manuscript.

I would like to thank Mrs. Jane Otten and Dean Elizabeth Mitchell for editorial and proofreading assistance. My wife Carla has given unfailing support and help during the writing and revision of this study. Finally, Professor Albert A. Hayden, Managing Editor of the series in which this book appears, has provided invaluable guidance and assistance in readying the manuscript for publication.

D. H. H.

Newark College of Arts and Sciences,
RUTGERS UNIVERSITY

xiv

A NOTE

on Dates, Terms, and Maps

In 1688 England still adhered to the Julian calendar, while most continental states had adopted the much improved Gregorian calendar. At the time of the revolution, the discrepancy between the two systems amounted to ten days. Thus, it was November 5 when the Prince of Orange landed at Torbay according to English reckoning but November 15 in the eyes of most Europeans. Matters are further complicated by the fact that the Julian new year began on March 25 rather than January 1. Accordingly, the Convention parliament assembled on January 22, 1688, from the English standpoint, and on February 1, 1689, as far as continental observers were concerned. Following current practice among historians, English dates are given in conformity with the Julian calendar but with the new year beginning on January 1.

Another potential source of difficulty arises from the fact that students of history lack an agreed vocabulary, and certain terms easily give rise to misunderstanding. The word revolution is used in this study because that is how contemporaries referred to the events of 1688, and posterity has confirmed the usage. However, revolution in the seventeenth century political context essentially connoted a cyclical pattern of change. To most men involved in James II's deposition, the term meant little more than a turning back to the old order, a restoration. It should also be noted that the peerage or titled nobility is sometimes referred to simply as the aristocracy.

Portions of two contemporary maps of England are reproduced as the end papers of this volume by permission of the William Andrews Clark Memorial Library, University of California, Los Angeles. The Philip Lea map (1688) provides substantial detail of the counties of Derby and Nottingham, the innumerable small villages, and some of the more important physical features of the countryside. The John Adams map (c. 1685?) illustrates the larger setting for the rising at Nottingham, with particular emphasis on major towns and distances in central England.

I

THE REVOLUTION AND THE NORTH

JUSTIFICATION for yet another study of the revolution of 1688 is, perhaps, unnecessary. Despite the considerable amount of attention the events of that year have received from serious scholar, constitutional panegyrist, and antiquary alike, no completely satisfactory account of the overthrow of James II can be said to exist. Recent research has done much to discredit the traditional Whig thesis, expounded so ably in the nineteenth century by historians such as Macaulay and Mackintosh and admirably refined in our own century by G. M. Trevelyan, with the result that the glory of 1688 has all but vanished in most contemporary treatments. Important biographical studies by scholars such as Baxter, Browning, and Kenyon and the recent revisionist essay by J. R. Jones[1] clearly demonstrate that the revolution of 1688 can no longer be regarded as a great national movement directing its energies against a Catholic tyrant bent on subverting the constitution and religion of the country. New insights and a better understanding of the complexity of the event have been gained, undoubtedly the most important of which is a clearer recognition of the role of William of Orange. However, many unexplored avenues of research still remain; no new interpretation has yet gained general acceptance, giving rise to many-sided controversies and differing shades of emphasis.

Leaving aside the complex and perplexing question of the effects of the revolutionary settlement on politics, religion, society, and the constitution in general, the points at issue concerning the causes and course of the revolt are in themselves many and varied. Should the revolution be regarded, from the English side, as the rising of an entire people alienated by the misgovernment of their king, or should it be seen as the work of the traditional landed aristocracy?[2] When did William of Orange first determine on armed intervention in England, and what were his motives for adopting this plan of action? Who were the leading conspirators against the government of James II, and what were their objectives? Can the events of 1688 be viewed as a revolution at all, or was it essentially a *coup d'état* engineered by the Prince of Orange in combination with certain segments of the tiny group that formed the political nation?[3]

What factors were most significant in bringing about the rise of an organized opposition to the king, and, even more important, what led the members of this opposition to engage in conspiracy and open rebellion? To what extent can the causes of the revolution be found in public reaction to the religious and governmental policies of James? Did the slogans of the exclusion crisis—Catholicism, French domination, and arbitrary power —again sway opinion, or were the grievances of individual, class, corporate body, or religious group of more consequence? What role should be assigned to the English in what, a generation ago, was regarded as their own revolution?[4] Does acceptance of the assertion that William came to England with his eyes on the crown, and with an army sufficiently large to obtain it, relegate the efforts of his English supporters to secondary importance, or did their planning, organization, and supportive insurrectionary activity contribute substantially to the success of the invasion?

By no means an exhaustive list, these points of controversy are raised merely to underscore the necessity for further investigation and reinterpretation of almost every aspect of the revolution. Perhaps in no instance is this more clearly evident than in the need for a reassessment of the part played by the English in the overthrow of the last Stuart king. It may be fairly argued, on the basis of studies such as Pinkham's, that the rehabilitation of the Prince of Orange as the central figure in the revolution has caused the pendulum of historical interpretation to swing too far. The objectives and contribution of the prince to the inception and success of the revolt cannot be ignored; the danger at the moment lies, however, in discounting too completely the role of the English conspirators. Without their efforts there would have been no revolution just as surely as it could not have been accomplished without the leadership and support of the prince.

One may question, for instance, the motives traditionally ascribed to the seven signatories of the invitation, but to dismiss them as political nonentities engaged in a largely irrelevant act is to misread the strength and significance of the opposition. Even the Whig historians, with their emphasis on the Englishness of the revolution, have failed in many cases to detail adequately the activities of their countrymen in support of William both before and during the revolt.[5] While the limits of the present study will preclude touching on many of the controversies engendered by the events of 1688, two issues of primary importance—the aristocratic nature of the revolution and the English contribution to it—will be central themes. Furthermore, by focusing primarily on the events leading up to and comprising the rising at Nottingham, with reference to related activity elsewhere in the north, a topic will be assayed which has received relatively scant notice.

For the purposes of this study, the term north will be used, as it was by contemporaries, in only a very general sense. The geographical area described by it will be taken to include not only the six counties of the far north, but also the seven counties of the northern midlands, the southern tier of which is formed by Shropshire, Stafford, Leicester, and Rutland. The single survey attempting to describe and correlate revolutionary activity within this region can be found in an article, based almost exclusively on published source materials, by A. C. Wood.[6] Essentially a summary introduction to the subject, Wood's treatment of the rising at York in support of the prince has already been largely superseded by Andrew Browning in his biography of the Earl of Danby.[7] As yet the rising at Nottingham, counterpart of that at York, and its links with other centers of insurrection in the north have not been fully analyzed.

The lack of attention the north has received in most treatments of the revolution is not surprising, for in many ways it represents something of an historical "if." During the early summer of 1688, the seven signatories of the invitation to William lost no opportunity to besiege the prince with advice as to how he should go about the business of invading England. For reasons which will later be dealt with in detail, the conspirators strongly advocated a northern landing along the Yorkshire coast. Had this course of action been adopted, and there is every reason to believe that William at the very least considered it a viable option well into the autumn,[8] the north would have become the center of the revolution.

The English conspirators had made elaborate plans for supportive risings there; focal points of native insurrectionary activity at York and Nottingham were to be triggered by the arrival of William. Instead of the slow accretion of English adherents that marked the prince's progress in the west, there would have been a massive influx of supporters to his standard in the north which would have been followed by a quick march on London. Whether because of the Protestant wind, the advice of his seamen, or a desire to play a lone hand, it was at Torbay rather than in Yorkshire that the prince finally landed his forces on November 5. Already disheartened by news of the false start William had made some two weeks earlier and with all their plans subsequently thrown into confusion, the northern conspirators made no outward move to support the prince for more than a week, and action on a significant scale did not result until November 20.

By that time, attention then as now had become riveted on events in the south. The progress of William's army, news of desertions from the royal camp, petitions by the bishops and peers in London, and the futile and confused activity of James II filled contemporary newsletters and have ever since overshadowed all else in subsequent accounts of the revolution. Those passing references made to the risings in the north in histories of the Whig tradition have described them as but further examples of the universal revulsion of the English from the excesses, religious and political, of James, resulting in massive uprisings in support of the Protestant prince and the liberties and constitution of England. Although not referring to the north specifically, Macaulay best sums up this attitude:

4

Actuated by these sentiments our ancestors arrayed themselves against the government in one huge compact mass. All ranks, all parties, all Protestant sects, made up that vast phalanx. In the van were the Lords Spiritual and Temporal. Then came the landed gentry and the clergy, both the Universities, all the Inns of Court, merchants, shopkeepers, farmers, the porters who plied in the streets of the great towns, the peasants who ploughed the fields.[9]

Recent scholarship touching upon the events of 1688, while rejecting this interpretation out of hand, has generally contented itself with regarding the risings in the north as of limited significance. Arguing that they represent a case of too little, too late, Browning concludes that the supporters of the prince in the north lost their opportunity to exercise any real influence on the course of the revolution by hesitating too long before adopting a decisive course of action. From this standpoint, their efforts on the prince's behalf were of such minimal practical significance that the final outcome was determined essentially by the struggle between James and William. The revolution then assumes somewhat the characteristics of a duel between two professionals, one of whom lost his nerve before the final match.[10]

Neither of these approaches can be considered a fair assessment of the northern insurrections, and it may be argued that the attitudes adopted in many cases reflect insufficient research into the subject. Little time need be spent considering the Whig viewpoint, but the opposing argument merits both attention and some measure of acceptance. It is true that risings of considerable scope, based on careful planning, took place in the north without assistance from or even direct communication with William. At the height of the revolts more than four thousand men were in arms at Nottingham and York, a number which could easily have been exceeded had sufficient equipment, enough experienced officers, and early plans for a rapid march to join the prince permitted wider recruitment of foot soldiers. Moreover, the rising at Nottingham alone counted more than a dozen peers in the van of the movement, including some of the most venerable titles in the north.

The arrival of the Princess of Denmark in that city resulted in fresh accretions of strength, for her presence was regarded as

5

something akin to a stamp of approval on the proceedings. Both at Nottingham and York elaborate systems of finance and supply were established; the militia was successfully raised in a number of counties; regiments were organized, admittedly raw and undisciplined, but of sufficient mettle to permit some of them later to be incorporated into the regular army for use in the Irish campaign; and the royal garrisons in the area either came under the control of the insurgents or were in no position to pose a serious threat. To all appearances a barrier had been raised to James II in an area amounting to almost a third of the country. An obstacle had been placed in the way of troop movements from Scotland or Ireland, of adherents to the royal cause in the northern counties, and of any possible attempt on the part of the king to fall back on the north to regroup his forces for a prolonged struggle with the prince. In the eyes of one observer, the king was caught with his back to the wall, for it was expected in some quarters that the rebels in the north would march on London while William continued to advance in the same direction from the west.[11]

The most significant aspects of the revolution in the north are not, however, to be found in a simplistic catalogue of achievements such as these. The strength of the rebels and their raw levies was, after all, never tested, their sway over the north never challenged, and the mixed motives of the nobles who led them in support of the prince or a free parliament never subjected to the trial of actual combat with the king. Estimates in London and elsewhere as to the unity and size of the northern insurrections were almost without exception much exaggerated. While a strong case can be made for the contributory role played by the insurgents in the north, it would be wishful thinking to maintain that the outcome of the revolution was not essentially determined by events in southern England.

The fact remains, however, that a study of the northern risings is vitally important to an understanding of the revolution because they provide a microcosm from which much can be learned about the aims, organization, and leadership of William's English supporters. Perhaps more clearly than by any other approach, investigation in this area makes it possible to consider afresh the question as to whether the policies of the king had so alienated his people, or a particular segment among them, as

6

to provide sufficient cause for revolt. Moreover, a closer look at the north and the events which led up to the risings there allows a reassessment of the English contribution to the revolution, for there is a real need to redress the balance which has swung so far toward a purely Williamite thesis.

At the outset it must be recognized that the phrase "revolution in the north" is meaningless before the early autumn of 1688. There was nothing inherent in the region, nor were there any special factors relating to the nobles and gentry whose seats of influence were located in the area, which tended to foment disaffection. It would, however, distort the picture to pick up the story at such a late point, since the commitment to open revolt had been made several months earlier. Accordingly, this study includes brief consideration of the earlier years of James II's reign, with emphasis upon those factors clearly contributing to the coalescence, growth, and transformation of opposition to the king into active rebellion. The approach is not strictly regional, for developing resistance to the regime should be understood as a national movement spearheaded by members of the nobility. Although far removed from Nottingham and the north, the one was a direct outcome of the other.

By early autumn, 1688, it is possible, however, to focus on the north as a separate aspect of the revolution and defensible to continue to do so even after the prince's landing at Torbay. While there can be no question that revolutionary activity in the north was greatly affected by what happened in the south, and, indeed, would never have come to fruition if William had not come to England, the northern insurrections saw no direct intervention by either James II or William of Orange. The king was, of course, in no position to send troops into the north to quell the revolts there, and his directives to lord lieutenants, deputy lieutenants, garrison commanders, and municipal officials generally went unheeded or were impossible to implement. William, whether intentionally or not, had little or no communication with his northern allies until well into December and, in the case of the Earl of Danby at York, not until the flight of James had pretty well decided the final outcome of events.

To attempt a study concentrating on the rising at Nottingham alone would, on the other hand, be indefensible, for the revolt there must be linked to its counterpart at York and related movements throughout the north and beyond. Too much can be made of the apparent unity of purpose and direction of these insurrections, but the principals at the two main centers of activity, the Earl of Devonshire at Nottingham and the Earl of Danby at York, were in close communication and their efforts if not their goals coincided with an agreed plan. With few exceptions, activity in support of William's invasion encountered in towns as far removed as Carlisle, Chester, Newcastle, and Northampton can be directly linked to Nottingham and York. Emphasis will, however, be placed on the rising at Nottingham for several reasons, not the least of these being the detailed accounts of events at York already undertaken by Browning and readily available in the published memoirs of Sir John Reresby.

Furthermore, the largely uncharted regions of the rising at Nottingham in some ways offer more interesting and valuable possibilities for a case study. It was not, for instance, dominated so completely by one man as the rising at York was by the Earl of Danby. True, the Earl of Devonshire can be pointed to as a central figure in the events at Nottingham, but the presence of the Whig extremist Lord Delamer, on the one hand, and that of the Tory Earl of Chesterfield, who came in only after the arrival of Princess Anne, provides a full spectrum of religious and political opinion and motive for involvement.

It may also be argued that the role of the nobility in the revolution emerges more clearly here than at York, a statement which at first glance might lead one to suppose that Nottingham was an exception rather than a case in point. Accident of history, dictate of economics, desire for proximity to London, or whatever, the further north one went in seventeenth century England, the more thinly scattered were the seats of the nobility. Yorkshire, despite its enormous size, had considerably fewer peers of sufficient age to become involved in this political upheaval than did almost any of the counties further south. The Earl of Danby perforce had to work more closely with the gentry, from whose ranks he had not so long ago emerged, than the Earl of Devonshire and his associates.

Finally, the source materials available for analysis of the rising at Nottingham are particularly full. Accordingly, the evidence permits meaningful discussion of the extent to which the county community—local issues and local personalities—was influenced by and also helped to shape the national response in 1688.

II

THE NOBILITY AND THE TEST ACT

THE ACCESSION of James II to the throne of England in 1685, if not greeted with joyous acclaim, was achieved with a quiet acceptance that is somewhat surprising in light of the heated passions of the exclusion crisis a short half decade before. The new king was, of course, in an extremely awkward and difficult situation, for he was the first avowedly Catholic monarch to rule England in over a century. Had James been willing to keep his religion a private affair and to exercise some discretion in his use of regnal power, all might have been well. He was, however, driven by the desire to remove the legal disabilities of his co-religionists and may have hoped, perhaps, to bring England back to the Catholic fold.[1] Compounded by a conception of the powers inherent in monarchy not unlike that held by his grandfather, his actions tended to reinforce the fears and prejudices of the upper classes—and to some extent of the entire nation—against Catholicism and the intemperate exercise of royal prerogatives on its behalf.

By the summer of 1688 opponents of the king's policies were to be found in substantial numbers in almost every sector of English society, but it was the nobility which stood at the forefront of the opposition. It was, moreover, a group drawn from among the peers

and scions of aristocratic families that had emerged as an organized opposition and which would be transformed into a treasonous conspiracy during the last months of the reign. Nor should
it be surprising that this proved to be the case. The position of
the aristocracy in English society was such that the rule of James
seemed not only to pose a threat to generally held principles
and prejudices of the politically conscious, but was also regarded
as a particular menace to the pride, property, and privileges of
the peerage. In many instances a deep seated personal hostility
to the king developed as the result of actions that violated the
nobility's presumed right to share in power on the central as well
as the local level of government.

Opposition to the policies of James II was conceived of
largely in parliamentary terms until late in 1687. No one, including James himself, knew that the second session of 1685 would
be the last time parliament would meet for over three years. This
explains both the strenuous efforts of the king to secure adherents
in parliament and the constant rumors, some not without
foundation, that another session or new elections were imminent. More than anything else, James wanted to secure repeal of
the Test Act and penal laws to put Catholics on at least an
equal footing with members of the Church of England, and this
could only be effected by a compliant parliament. On the other
hand, those opposed to the objectives of the king regarded the Test
Act, if not the penal laws, as an effective rallying point and
organized their defenses accordingly.

Frequently overlooked is the fact that it was the House of
Lords which established the frame of reference for this struggle
and that it was the opposition to repeal by a substantial majority
of the nobility which stood as one of the greatest obstacles to
James's attempts to secure a packed parliament.[2] This truth,
unfortunately, is often largely obscured by the welter of events
detailed in so many studies of the period. Regulation of municipal corporations, alterations in both the commissions of the
peace and lieutenancies, and appointment of Catholic sheriffs
are all important in terms of understanding the aims of the king,
the resistance he encountered on all fronts, and the process by
which he managed to alienate those who should have been his
natural supporters. To concentrate on these too exclusively,
however, is to ignore the fact that whatever success James might

10

have had in changing the composition of the Commons, the Lords still stood as an immovable obstruction in his path; amongst its members were those who led the way in opposition and resistance to the king.

In the spring of 1685 James had been quite successful in his dealings with parliament, the most loyal to meet since 1661, but by the time the members had reassembled the following November a sharp reaction had set in. The savage revenge visited upon the west country in the wake of Monmouth's rebellion, the dismissal of Halifax from the privy council where he was known to have spoken up strongly in defense of the Habeas Corpus and Test Acts, the continued enlargement of the military establishment, and, of the essence, the employment of some seventy Catholic officers in the army all indicated the direction the wind was now blowing. Against this background, with news of the revocation of the Edict of Nantes scarcely a month old and the first wave of French Protestant refugees just arriving in England, James did nothing to allay the fears and suspicions of his subjects.[3] Instead, the speech from the throne at the opening of the session was a bold frontal attack. The king asserted his intention of maintaining an enlarged standing army, of requesting sufficient supply for its support, and of retaining the services of those Catholics he had commissioned despite the strictures of the Test Act.[4] Not surprisingly, these pronouncements did much to estrange loyal Tory supporters in both houses and to confirm the worst fears of the small remaining contingent of the first Whig party.

It was in the House of Lords that sharp and unrestrained criticism of the king's open disregard for the provisions of the Test Act gave strongest vent to the feelings of discontent in the country—and presaged as well the leading role of the nobility in the development of an effective opposition. As is so often the case in the later seventeenth century, contemporary accounts of the proceedings of the upper house are both scanty and often confused as to the sequence of events. The weight of evidence, however, points to the Earl of Devonshire, recognized as a decided adversary of the court, as the key figure in sparking the crucial debate.[5] To this end he made a sharp speech in support of the Test Act, while proposing that a day be set aside for a full scale debate. He was seconded not only by the Earl of Angelsey and Lord Mordaunt, both of whom had ties with the Whig-Nonconformist tradition, but also by Halifax and two members of the privy council, the Earls of Nottingham and Bridgewater.

The speech making the greatest impact was delivered by Henry Compton, Bishop of London, longtime ally of the Earl of Danby, and the man responsible for the firm attachment to the Church of England of James's two daughters. Speaking on behalf of the entire episcopal bench, the bishops rising in a body in support of his remarks, Compton stressed that the Test Act stood as the sole bulwark against the flood of Catholicism and that if the present breach of the law were overlooked the kingdom would soon be engulfed.[6] A few court supporters, in particular the Earl of Clarendon, attempted to stem the tide, but sentiment ran so strongly in favor of Devonshire's motion that they dared not press for a division. The king's response was to prorogue parliament, a move which cost him a possible supply of seven hundred thousand pounds.[7]

It is possible, of course, to make too much of this appearance of an opposition among the nobility, in spite of the varied shades of political opinion and the prominence of most of those known to have participated in the debate. The outburst in the Lords was in large part a spontaneous reaction engendered by traditional fears of Catholicism, reinforced in some instances—the Earl of Devonshire and Bishop Compton[8] providing the clearest examples—by longstanding political or personal hostility to the king. The basis had been laid, however, for the eventual emergence of an organized opposition to James's policies, with advocacy of the Test Act providing both the central issue and a common ground about which peers of every political hue could comfortably rally.

Seemingly heedless of possible consequences, James followed up the prorogation of parliament by engaging in the first of a series of purges that were often to add personal grievance to opposition in principle. Undoubtedly this first sweep of the broom was intended merely as a warning and example, for the king had by no means given up hope that his ends could be achieved in alliance with Tory churchmen.[9] But the men removed from office or losing their commissions in the army often owed their position to the fact that they were importantly connected, and James ran the risk not only of alienating the individuals concerned but also of displeasing powerful factions.

The numerous and influential Bertie family, for instance, headed by the Earls of Lindsey and Abingdon and closely connected by marriage with such other peers as the Earls of Danby and Rutland, saw four of its number turned out of office. Little wonder that Charles Bertie, writing to his niece, the Countess of Rutland, was led to comment that the army "proving so unlucky a trade I would not have us bend our heads much to it for the future."[10]

The voices of discontent were stilled neither by the prorogation of parliament nor by the tangible evidence of royal displeasure that followed hard on its heels. In his dispatch of December 21, 1685, the papal nuncio d'Adda commented that formidable opposition could be expected in the Lords in the event of another session, indications of which led James to defer further reconvening parliament.[11] Accordingly, the most effective means for channeling dissent into effective opposition was unavailable, and during much of 1686 it seemed as though no barrier, from personal principle to the stricture of statute, would be allowed to stand in the royal path. In whatever direction dissident contemporaries looked the prospect indeed seemed bleak, with the king holding all the cards.

The judiciary, ever pliable in Stuart hands, rendered opinion in the test case of Sir Edward Hales to the effect that the dispensing power could be validly exercised in regard to employment of Catholics. With this backing James promptly appointed four peers of the Roman faith—including three who had been imprisoned at the time of the popish plot—to the privy council. Catholics or crypto-Catholics were beginning to appear in positions of responsibility in the established church, the universities, and in almost every branch of government. In both Scotland and Ireland power seemed clearly to be passing into the hands of those adhering to the church of Rome. Yet another blow was the creation of the ecclesiastical commission, which was given jurisdiction in any case involving spiritual or ecclesiastical matters, the power to suspend or deprive any member of the clergy, and the authority to regulate the universities and colleges. Some thought this body's first act might be to order a general prohibition of preaching, a severe trial, wrote Halifax, for a people "who generally place their religion in the pulpit, as the papists doe theirs upon the altar."[12]

While nothing so drastic was attempted, the seven commissioners did little to quiet fears when they peremptorily summoned the Bishop of London to appear before them. Long the subject of the king's animus, the occasion of Compton's difficulty lay in his refusal to obey a royal mandate directing that Dr. John Sharp, rector of St. Giles, be suspended for delivering two sermons of an anti-Catholic nature. The actual cause was apparently nothing more than James's dislike of the aristocratic bishop, for the latter seems to have complied, insofar as he legally could, by silencing Sharp until his case could go through the proper channels. Headed by the ubiquitous Jeffreys, the ecclesiastical commission paid little heed to such legal niceties, and Compton was suspended from office, although left in possession of the perquisites of his position. All told, the prosecution and suspension were ill-considered moves. An example had been made of the Bishop of London for daring to offer resistance to royal mandate; but of far greater significance was the fact that his treatment at the hands of the ecclesiastical commission served to enhance the stature of one of the king's most hostile and potentially dangerous critics.[13]

Until the summer of 1686 the king's efforts were largely concentrated on maneuvers to get around the strictures of the Test Act, first by issuing pardons and then by exercise of the dispensing power backed by the authority of the judiciary. But James still had not given up hope that his first parliament could be either cajoled or pressured into complying with his desire for repeal. This represented the keystone of his program and, accordingly, a bold frontal assault on the Test Act was envisioned. The method of persuasion adopted, which had proved eminently successful in dealings with the judiciary, was a series of personal interviews with leading members of both houses in an attempt to secure pledges from each for support of repeal in the next session. Although all who were subjected to these "closetings" were presented with a series of stock arguments against the unfairness of the legislation, the king was doubtless relying on thinly veiled threats about the consequences of royal displeasure.[14]

Among the first to be approached in this fashion were the Earl of Shrewsbury and Lord Lumley, both recent converts from Catholicism. To the surprise of many of their contemporaries, neither was willing to commit himself in advance on the issue, with the result that their commissions in the army were revoked.[15] Lord Maynard and Viscount Newport, the treasurer and comptroller respectively of the king's household, were turned out of office for refusing to pledge their votes. The Hyde brothers, Earls of Clarendon and Rochester, were removed as lord lieutenant of Ireland and lord treasurer and lost as well such secondary but remunerative posts as privy seal and wardrobe. Henry Savile, brother of the Marquess of Halifax, was dismissed as vice-chamberlain of the household; Arthur Herbert, vice admiral of England and master of the robes, met a similar fate. Both peer and commoner alike were put under pressure, and those who tried to dodge the issue by staying away from London soon found themselves approached by an emissary of the king.[16]

The significance of this attempt at a straw vote on the question of repeal can hardly be stressed sufficiently. Neither by threat nor persuasion was James able to line up any considerable body of supporters among the members of parliament. An immediate result was to force yet a further prorogation while other methods of dredging up support were devised which, in turn, antagonized further the opponents of the king's policies. More importantly, the resistance James encountered provided the first substantial outward sign of a parting of the ways between the king and the mainstream of those of Tory outlook, a preponderant majority in both houses of parliament, whose rallying cry to this point had been church and king.

Throughout his reign James continually missed the point that this was a dual commitment and that by his actions he appeared to be forcing a choice between loyalty to the established church and loyalty to the crown. Whether or not it was a groundless fear, men of the time did not believe that mere toleration of Catholics was all that the king intended.[17] This feeling was reinforced by his evident unwillingness to compromise and by the measures of dubious legality and outright arbitrary exercise of authority he used to secure the ends desired. Those of Whiggish inclination might claim that they had foreseen at the time of exclusion what was going to happen, but the church had then appeared to be in a secure position and the call of loyalty to the throne so strong, especially if Monmouth were the alternative, that men on the other side of the political fence had been both unconvinced and repelled.

Now the tide was running in the opposite direction, for James seemed bent on a thorough Romanizing policy and quite willing to indulge in illegal practices to gain his end. Moreover, while refusal to comply with the king's wishes might be based in the first instance on generalized grievances concerning religion and consitutional practice, men were confirmed in their opposition on a very personal level by the summary dismissal from office that resulted from their taking a stand against repeal. Not only did this represent a loss of power and influence in the government for the individual concerned, but in several cases it meant as well the loss of an extremely important source of income. It is estimated that Admiral Herbert alone was receiving three thousand pounds per annum at the time he was dismissed; Henry Savile was in serious financial straits because of the elimination of his official stipend; and the Hydes, exemplars of high Tory sentiment, had considered their well paid appointments an essential source of income.[18]

Finally, this sounding out of opinion among the leading members of parliament was of crucial importance in terms of the emergence of an organized opposition. The issue at stake was clearly defined, and for the first time since the prorogation of parliament in November, 1685, it was possible to gauge on a significant scale the reaction to what James had already done and what he proposed for the future. By forcing men to take a stand and then dismissing all who would not support repeal, the king was proceeding to demonstrate to all concerned just how little enthusiasm there was for his policies. In the circumstances, the appearance in England of the Dutch emissary Everhard van Weede, Lord of Dykvelt, dispatched by William of Orange in early 1687, provided the necessary catalyst for action.[19]

Dykvelt's arrival demonstrated William's very real concern about the state of affairs in England, for information from various quarters tended to be of an extremely disquieting nature to a Protestant prince whose wife stood heir presumptive to the throne. Undoubtedly Lord Mordaunt's quixotic venture to The Hague in 1686 had not been without some effect. Rumors were rife, moreover, that an attempt would be made to divert the succession to Princess Anne if she could be converted to Catholicism. The activities of Tyrconnel in Ireland appeared suspect to say the least; and despite assurances to the contrary by a special envoy from James, the Quaker William Penn, the prince seems to have felt that more was intended by the proposed repeal of the Test Act than appeared on the surface.[20]

William decided, therefore, to send Dykvelt to England nominally as a representative of the States General, but with secret instructions from the prince to sound out the situation on all sides. Dykvelt was to attempt a reconciliation with the king if James could be persuaded to drop his efforts to repeal the Test Act. However, he was also directed to approach Princess Anne, to meet with prominent members of every religious group, and to establish contact with the leading opponents of the king's policies of whatever party or political faction. Should James prove unreceptive to the promptings of his son-in-law, then efforts were to be concentrated on building a coalition whose ultimate objective was to resist any change in the English succession.[21]

To this end a series of meetings was initiated at the town house of the Earl of Shrewsbury. In the words of Gilbert Burnet, who had helped to draw up Dykvelt's instructions, the intention was to "concert such advices and advertisements, as might be fit for the prince to know, that he might govern himself accordingly."[22] Among the principals involved in these sessions were the Marquess of Halifax, the Earls of Shrewsbury, Devonshire, Danby, and Nottingham, Lords Mordaunt and Lumley, the Bishop of London, and Admirals Herbert and Russell. Representing virtually every shade of the political spectrum, the overwhelming predominance of peers in the group attests to the forward position of the nobility in leading the way in resistance to James II. Only Arthur Herbert was descended of family whose ties with the aristocracy were too remote to be of any significance. Both the Bishop of London, uncle of the Earls of Northampton and Dorset, and Admiral Russell, nephew of the aged Earl of Bedford and first cousin of the Whig martyr Lord Russell, were closely connected with titled families of considerable prestige, wealth, and influence.

Information as to others who may have been on the periphery of this group, or who were at least brought into contact with it, is scanty and partly obscured because the broad nature of Dykvelt's instructions necessitated meetings with many prominent figures. Nor is the picture much clearer, at first glance, as to the objectives and methods of this emerging opposition group. In connection with the period when Dykvelt was in England,

Burnet records in his history that those meeting at the Earl of Shrewsbury's house "concerted matters, and drew the declaration of which they advised the prince to engage."[23] Since no document of this description survives, some historians discount the statement entirely and a few, in particular Sir John Dalrymple in the eighteenth century, have concluded that a revolutionary conspiracy was already afoot. Neither view can be accepted as an accurate assessment. The very presence of Halifax and Nottingham in the group provides sufficient assurance that nothing of a revolutionary nature was proposed. At the same time Burnet's comment—his presence at The Hague lending credence to the remark—cannot be passed off too lightly.

Undoubtedly some sort of declaration or statement was brought back to William by Dykvelt. It almost certainly expressed the opposition group's determination to resist attempts to repeal the Test Act and its desire that the prince should also refuse to condone the king's efforts along these lines. Interestingly enough, Dykvelt carried back at the same time a letter from James II urging his son-in-law to take the opposite stand, a move which soon elicited from William a negative response hedged with a disclaimer of sympathy for any type of religious persecution.[24] The most important point to be made, however, is that the coalescence of the leading opponents of the king, Dykvelt's mission bringing things to a head, resulted in the formation of an essentially parliament-oriented opposition group.

The latest prorogation had put off the possibility of a third session until November, but the "closetings," the first steps in the attack on Magdalen College, and the issuance of a declaration of liberty of conscience on April 4 suspending operation of both the Test Act and penal laws, gave every indication that James had no intention of altering his course. Determined resistance seemed necessary; opposition to repeal of the Test Act provided an obvious and viable line of defense acceptable even to the majority of the Dissenters.[25] Certainly the Prince of Orange, reassured through Dykvelt as to the Protestantism of Princess Anne, could have wished for no more.

The evidence points to the fact that the English opposition concentrated its hopes and efforts on the House of Lords. It is to this group that one may reasonably attribute the three contemporary estimates of the probable vote of each peer on the question of repeal, two of which found their way to The Hague and the third into the hands of Louis XIV.[26] The earliest of these surveys of the peerage, dated convincingly on the basis of internal evidence to the latter half of May, 1687, would seem to have been drawn up by Lord Willoughby, son of the Earl of Lindsey and one of the four Berties dismissed from command in the army in 1685.[27]

The existing copy of this list in the Dutch archives contains the names of some 161 adult peers, including the bench of bishops, of which it was thought that twenty-two would be barred from taking their seat in the upper chamber because they were adherents of the Roman faith. The formidable resistance expected to the revocation of anti-Catholic legislation can be seen in the estimate that eighty-five of the remaining peers would refuse to support the king on this matter, while only thirty-five were suspected of favoring repeal and some nineteen were of wavering or unknown position. The information summarized in this document is, of course, an admixture from a variety of sources—the results of the closetings, hearsay, previous political and religious leanings, and direct contact. In many instances, however, subsequent activity at the time of the revolution confirms the basic accuracy of the estimate.

Of considerable interest is the fact that opponents of repeal included Whigs and Tories, with no attempt to distinguish between the two, titles that were both old and new, and peers of every rank from every part of the country. Moreover, the probable date of compilation, the departure of Dykvelt from England less than two weeks later; and the very existence of the list at The Hague make it tempting to infer that this document found its way to Holland in the hands of William's emissary. Should this have been the case—and it must be emphasized that Lord Willoughby was intimately connected with the Earl of Danby, a leading figure in the opposition—it would lend further credence to the conclusion that the group meeting at Shrewsbury's had sent the prince a declaration about standing firmly behind the Test Act. In this connection the list presumably would have served to reinforce arguments against the likelihood of James's effecting repeal and would have given the prince some idea of the massive opposition it would encounter.

Willoughby's list is undoubtedly somewhat optimistic as to the number of lords who would appear if parliament met and the count of those who would stand firm against repeal if a division were taken. But in combination with the other two estimates of aristocratic sentiment it clearly substantiates the contention that an overwhelming majority of the peerage could be counted as opposed to the policies of James II. Furthermore, even among the relatively small body of nobles generally considered adherents of the king were those, the Duke of Ormonde and Lord Churchill providing the most obvious examples, who were in the long run to prove unfaithful. Although no corresponding government estimate can be offered in evidence, contemporary references to the necessity of redressing the balance in the upper house by a massive creation of new peers further confirms the obstacle presented by its recalcitrant members.[28]

Interestingly enough James either did not dare or was wise enough not to contemplate forcing the issue about seating Catholic peers in the Lords before repeal was effected, and it would appear that his intent was to raise various pliant members of the Scottish and Irish nobility to gain the needed votes. Whatever stir resulted from such new creations, the royal prerogative was clearly sufficient to double the size of the upper chamber if necessary,[29] even though a compliant Commons obviously had to be secured before steps were taken to alter the Lords. Here it may be fairly argued that the stand of such a substantial proportion of the nobility against repeal was far more influential in thwarting the king's desires than the threat of obstruction when parliament was convened.

Having already embarked upon a program to remove from central administration, household, and army posts those who refused to pledge support for repeal, James turned his attention to the lord lieutenants in the summer of 1687.[30] Because of the tremendous influence they could wield when new elections were held, it became most important to be sure of these men once parliament was dissolved. Among the first to be ousted from their lieutenancies were the Earl of Shrewsbury in Stafford, Viscount Newport in Shropshire, and the Duke of Somerset in the East Riding of York and Somerset. Here the king was tackling those he already knew were disaffected, for Shrewsbury and Newport had earlier been ejected from posts in the army and household as a result of the "closetings," and Somerset had sinned by

20

obstinately refusing to participate in the formal court reception of the papal nuncio d'Adda. The dismissals of the Earl of Rutland in Leicester and the Earl of Derby in Lancashire and Cheshire, however, seemingly resulted from nothing more than their refusal to pledge a favorable vote in advance.[31]

The weeding out process was quickly accelerated in early October when the three questions were drawn up for submission by the lord lieutenants to all deputy lieutenants, justices of the peace, leading members of the gentry, and the municipal corporations in each county. Essentially aimed at determining which men were willing to support the king's efforts to secure a House of Commons amenable to the repeal of anti-Catholic legislation, this attempt at a national straw vote among the politically conscious broke down in many instances at the first link in the chain. Numerous lord lieutenants simply refused to act or went about their task in such a fashion as to negate the possibility of positive results.

The Tory Earl of Northampton, who had already indicated unwillingness to promise his vote in advance, told a meeting of the Warwick gentry that, while he felt compelled by the king's command to put the three questions before them, he had no intention himself of giving a favorable reply.[32] For this bit of candor Northampton was summarily removed from office and replaced by the Earl of Sunderland. Bolder still, the Earl of Scarsdale, first gentleman in waiting to Prince George of Denmark and commander of a regiment, refused even to go down to Derbyshire to put the questions. He, in turn, was dismissed from his lieutenancy and his regiment transferred to the Duke of St. Albans. Some indication of the attitude of Princess Anne and her husband can be gleaned from their refusal to remove the earl from Prince George's entourage until the king had made an issue of the matter.[33]

An embarrassing situation arose in Staffordshire as a consequence of the king's falling all over himself to secure Anglican backers of repute. Upon Shrewsbury's dismissal from the lieutenancy there in August, Lord Ferrers was appointed—despite a previous promise to the Catholic Lord Aston—because the king interpreted an expression of loyalty by Ferrers as meaning full support of his program. Confronted with an order to test the sentiment in his county, however, Ferrers declined to act, although he coupled his refusal with a statement that he personally favored repeal. This was insufficient as far as James was concerned, and Ferrers, having held office for less than three months, found himself replaced by Aston.[34]

These were not isolated cases: Aubrey de Vere, the impoverished but proud twentieth Earl of Oxford, "tould the King plainly he could not persuade that to others which he was avers to in his own conscience"[35] and consequently lost the Essex lieutenancy and command of a regiment of horse. The Earl of Gainsborough was removed as lord lieutenant of both Hampshire and Rutland, governor of Portsmouth, and from the honorific but profitable position of keeper of the New Forest, having paid some five thousand pounds only a few months before for the last two appointments.[36] The Earl of Bridgewater resigned his lieutenancy in Buckinghamshire; in addition, Viscount Fauconberg in the North Riding of Yorkshire, the Earls of Burlington in the West Riding, Abingdon in Oxford, Dorset in Sussex, Pembroke in Wiltshire, Thanet in Cumberland and Westmorland, and Winchilsea in Kent either resigned or were dismissed outright. The death of the Earl of Plymouth conveniently cleared the path in Worcester where the Catholic Lord Carrington was appointed in his stead.[37]

Relatively few men seem to have done what they were supposed to do right away. The enigmatic Earl of Lindsey, the Catholic Earl of Peterborough, the Earl of Rochester desperately clinging to his pension, and the Catholic Viscount Molyneux, who replaced the Earl of Derby in Lancashire, complied immediately, but they were not an impressive lot. Others counted as among the king's most loyal supporters, such as the Dukes of Newcastle and Beaufort and the Earl of Bath—responsible for nine counties among them—procrastinated as long as possible before they were pushed into action. The Duke of Norfolk despite the failure of attempts to secure his reconversion to Catholicism retained the lieutenancies of Norfolk, Berkshire, and Surrey. He took evident satisfaction in reporting to the king that those willing to comply could all have travelled up to London in his coach without straining his horses in the least.[38]

Although almost without exception couched in the most loyal terms, the response made to the three questions in other parts of England was just as overwhelmingly negative as that reported by

Norfolk. Every history of the revolution dwells at length on the significance of the replies, but a point of importance not to be overlooked is the lead given by the nobility. In the first place, the lord lieutenant exercised a sort of natural predominance in his county derived from a base of landownership, custom, and local association.[39] Taken in combination with the almost uniformly Tory outlook of these men—in no small part the result of planned and careful manipulation of appointments in the reign of Charles II—their reluctance or outright refusal to put the three questions cannot but have encouraged plain speaking by the gentry. The issues at stake were clearcut in the eyes of even the most parochial country gentlemen, and it was common knowledge that the dismissal of the lord lieutenants of so many counties was a direct result of the refusal to comply with the king's directive.[40] In the second place, there is a distinct possibility that the small group of aristocrats at the head of the opposition movement may have given the gentry an even more direct lead, although no conclusive evidence can be adduced along these lines.

It has long been recognized, however, that the replies made to the three questions were generally so stereotyped as to indicate some sort of organization behind them.[41] The hand of the opposition leaders is apparently in evidence, for it should be noted that they were in contact with like-thinking members of the gentry, especially those who had served in previous parliaments.[42] There is also some indication that various lord lieutenants not of their group were at least sounded out if not actually encouraged to take a strong stand.[43] The very fact, in addition, that a French envoy was able to secure a copy of a list concerned with the opposition of the peerage to repeal would seem to indicate that it was being circulated with a view toward influencing replies to the three questions. Certainly copies of one or another of the lists of peers had found their way into the provinces. When Viscount Molyneux posed the three questions at a meeting of the Lancashire gentry, one of the men present subsequently noted that "the nobility have already been tried, and have answered, 88 negative, 27 affirmative, 19 dubious."[44]

In light of the methods adopted by James, what countermeasure could have been more effective—or had better chance of success—than a concerted effort to secure uniform replies to the three questions that expressed both loyalty and adamant refusal to derogate the very functions of the House of Commons by pledging votes in advance? The knowledge that a majority of the peerage thought the same way, reinforced by concrete examples of those who gave up office to avoid compliance, must have emboldened some who otherwise might have agreed for fear of standing alone. At best, the success of a project of this sort might deter the king from further action; at worst, it would reveal the overwhelming determination of the political nation to give James no assistance in the matter of repeal. No longer would this question be a matter of conjecture; even those moderates who approved the ends, at least regarding repeal of the penal laws, could openly reject the means with assurance that their neighbors felt the same way.[45]

Although it might be argued that James II owed his throne to the rejection of the exclusion bill by the House of Lords in 1679, he seems to have regarded the peerage with a jaundiced eye and was, unlike his brother, most sparing of new creations.[46] Such an attitude is not surprising in view of the independent and often critical stance adopted by a number of influential nobles within six months of the beginning of the reign. But at the same time it must be pointed out that it had taken little longer for the peerage to develop a real feeling of discontent about the way it was treated as a class. Whether attention was focused on the central government, the royal household, the army, or subsequently on county and local administration, and whether the appointments being considered were functional or sinecures, it appeared to the aristocracy that its members were being pushed out of their rightful inheritance to make room for Roman Catholics and more compliant appointees of dubious distinction. Circumstances such as these pointed to the fact that the king had little respect for the nobility as a class, for their traditional functions and position in society, or for their privileges.[47]

There was, moreover, a grievance of considerable substance in its own right affecting the economic interests of the nobility. University fellowships, commissions in the army and navy, benefices in the church, and offices in every branch and at almost every level of government were considered to be freeholds, which in many cases had cost their possessors good money. Now James was removing men without the slightest regard for their vested rights if they refused to bow before the pressures exerted on behalf of his religion.[48] Property rights, freeholds, franchises, and the virtual monopoly on political offices held by the Protestant nobility and gentry, which it has been suggested was becoming ever more concentrated in the hands of the former and their connections, were being threatened by the king's disregard of the Test Act and his drive to secure its repeal. Nor was this purely a question of prestige and power, for the trend in the later seventeenth century was for titled families to draw an increasingly large proportion of their income from just such sources.[49]

There was also no way to determine how far James might be prepared to go, and it may be proposed that many thought that the idea of property itself was under fire. While the ecclesiastical commission had stopped short in the case of the Bishop of London, for instance, there was no reason to expect it to do so in the future in view of the precedent set at Magdalen College. What were the prospects of private patrons with livings in their gift, or indeed of incumbents, when it became known in the spring of 1688 that the Bishop of Durham was about to put a modified version of the three questions to the clergy of his diocese?[50] The sentiments expressed by Lord Willoughby in 1688 cannot be dismissed as pure rhetoric: "it was the first time any Bertie was engaged against the crown . . . but there was a necessity either to part with our religion and properties, or do it."[51]

By the autumn of 1687, the grounds for opposition to the king were clearly considerable; injustices to individuals and groups had raised up a host of personal enemies and had done much as well to alienate even larger sectors of society. The attitudes and reactions of political elites other than the nobility—the Anglican gentry, the clergy of the established church, the moderate Dissenters, the lawyers—fall beyond the pale of this study. However, disquiet about the trend of royal policy touched almost all elements of the establishment, and this reservoir of discontent provided the basis for hope that the king could be stymied in his efforts to secure a compliant parliament. Opposition lists indicated a strong majority in the House of Lords against repeal, and the returns from the few counties making immediate response to the three questions showed that it would be extremely difficult to do overly much with the Commons. Otherwise, as Halifax noted in his newly published *A Letter to a Dissenter*, it was more or less a case of waiting for "the next probable revolution." James was neither a young man by the standards of the age, nor in particularly good health, and next in line for the throne stood an Anglican daughter married to a Calvinist prince.

III

THE ROAD TOWARD REVOLUTION

STUDENTS of history have generally regarded Mary of Modena's pregnancy as a crucial turning point in the reign of James II. Although not confirmed publicly until two days before Christmas of 1687, rumors concerning the queen's condition had spread far beyond court circles by mid-November. Those opposed to the regime felt no immediate panic, for the queen had a long history of miscarriages and still-born children. Nevertheless, the possibility of a male heir to the throne or diversion of the succession to a daughter brought up as a Roman Catholic still carried with it far reaching consequences. More than ever James became an old man in a hurry. Buoyed up by the hope that his work might not be undone after his death, he also faced the need to effect a permanent settlement of affairs to forestall problems in the event his successor was a minor. Less than ever could the Prince of Orange accept a role which cast him as the nominal head of a parliamentary opposition. The crown on which he had long counted for his wife seemed to be slipping from reach.

News of the pregnancy also had a profound effect on the character of the English opposition, which was by force of this event to evolve within the matter of a few months from a constitutional movement into a full-fledged conspiracy. The Test Act had previously provided a convenient and acceptable rallying point for James's enemies, but retention of the Test was, after all, merely a stopgap defense aimed at constraining the king from yet further excesses. Real relief from the grievances under which the nation lay was not to be expected until the next reign, although it might be hoped that the Prince of Orange, as husband of the heir presumptive, could influence James to mitigate his policies somewhat. In essence William had been the only person to whom the opposition could look for assistance and encouragement. For his part the prince had been sufficiently concerned about the state of affairs in England to give countenance to the movement. Nor could this cease to be the case with the knowledge of Mary of Modena's pregnancy; self-interest on both sides dictated a strengthening rather than a weakening of the relationship.

As most histories of the revolution recount, tentative negotiations between William and the opposition leaders began in April of 1688. It was not until the last day of June, however, that the "immortal" seven subscribed their ciphers to the invitation the prince had demanded as a precondition to his active involvement. Evidently William had not counted on this delay,[1] but it took considerable time for the thinking of a majority of the opposition leaders to swing around to accepting a proposal that amounted to nothing less than participation in an act of treason. What was being proposed was not something that could be decided overnight; it represented a radically new departure. William was demanding the kind of commitment that a group of reasonably politic and moderate men could contemplate only in desperation, and it may be fairly argued that those of more conservative inclination could not construe the situation in those terms until early June.

By that time the second declaration of indulgence had appeared, the petition of the seven bishops had resulted in their prosecution for seditious libel, and the worst fears for the future had been confirmed by the birth of a Prince of Wales. The grievances giving rise to general opposition to the king among the political nation were both substantial and cumulative in effect, but it took this direct attack on the church and its leaders and the seeming end to any hopes for a Protestant succession to bring matters to a head. Some of the group with whom Dykvelt originally met—Admiral Russell, Henry Sidney, the Earl of Devonshire, and Admiral Herbert[2]—probably inclined toward seeking William's intervention much earlier. On the other hand, others of even greater weight—Danby, the Bishop of London, Lumley, and the Earl of Shrewsbury[3]—were unlikely to have entertained serious thoughts before early June about such a course of action.

By then the trend of events, soon further confirmed by the trial of the seven bishops, paved the way for adoption of a plan which could win general acceptance only when circumstances seemed to preclude any other satisfactory solution. Even so the Earl of Nottingham withdrew from the conspiracy at the last moment, basically for reasons of conscience,[4] and Halifax rebuffed tentative overtures in such a manner that the split between the marquess and the opposition, first apparent in April, received its final confirmation.[5] The temptation is, of course, to attribute the longest life possible to the conspiracy against James II, and evidence is certainly available to indicate that the idea of a direct confrontation between the king and his son-in-law had been in the air for quite some time on both sides of the North Sea. As a practical alternative, however, it could not have had much appeal to William before the spring of 1688,[6] and it is extremely unlikely that the opposition had given it serious consideration until the end of May or the first weeks in June.

Describing the fevered public indignation aroused by the trial of the seven bishops, the imperial ambassador reported that the affair was commonly regarded as the beginning of a revolution.[7] While hindsight makes such an observation appear far closer to the truth than the envoy could possibly have realized, it is extremely doubtful that even the signers of the invitation viewed the situation in such clear-cut terms. The dispatch of the invitation may be interpreted as the first overt act of rebellion, but it was William rather than his English supporters who foresaw that the wheels of revolution had thereby been set in motion. In fact, there is no evidence to indicate that the conspirators as a group were thinking at the outset about dethroning James II, nor is it likely that any design to assist the prince would have succeeded had it been presented in that light. Forced to turn to William as a last resort, the participants in the plot against the government seem to have given little thought to the possible consequences of the proposed rescue mission. The onrush of events, the supportive groundwork necessary for the success of the invasion, and the prospect of regaining influence and office diverted the seven from any careful consideration of what the ultimate settlement resulting from their efforts might entail.[8]

At this point one can detect quite clearly the development of two parallel tracks in the movement against James II. William obviously needed and encouraged his English supporters, but without doubt he had every intention of exercising ultimate control over the movement for his own ends. Those ends included, at the least, securing a freely elected parliament which could reasonably be expected to swing England into the anti-French camp and insist that the Prince of Wales be raised a Protestant. At the most, William envisaged the desposition of James and transferral of the reins of authority into his own hands.[9] For their part it is apparent that the seven signatories regarded the whole project as essentially an English affair. Of necessity the prince would play a primary role at the beginning, yet the plans they submitted to The Hague at the end of the summer indicated that they expected to exert considerable control over the course of events.[10]

Such would seem to be the reasoning behind the suggestion that William come over with a large fleet and a small army, and the whole question as to where a landing was to be effected can be viewed in much the same way. Every effort seems to have been made to stack the cards in favor of a northern descent either at Bridlington Bay or in the Humber estuary below Hull, although the southwestern coast was mentioned as an alternate site. Admitting that disaffection with the government of James II was rife in both sections of the country, the English conspirators argued that the aftermath of Monmouth's rebellion had been such that people in the counties involved would hesitate to join the prince's standard.[11] Further, Yorkshire and surrounding areas were said to be well stocked with horse for dragoons and carriage, provisioning the army there would present no difficulties, and the road system would facilitate a rapid and easy march on London.

Central to any understanding of this strong advocacy of a northern landing is the realization that if the seven signatories of the invitation had a collective power base it was in the counties of the north. That this should be the case seems largely an accident of history and basically a minor point, since four of the conspirators did not come from the area. But the fact remains that the Earls of Danby and Devonshire, the two conspirators with the greatest political reputation, were men of considerable influence in the counties of York and Derby respectively. To a lesser extent the same held true for Lord Lumley in the county of Durham.

There was, then, advantage to a landing along the Yorkshire coast. Immediate support and assistance could be expected from three of the foremost opponents of James and, indeed, they jointly committed themselves to raise the north whenever William should arrive. Another positive feature of this plan from the English standpoint was that it would put this powerful trio of peers in a position to influence if not totally control the management of the entire affair. In fact, if William were to follow the advice of the conspirators and bring over only a token land force, the movement against James would become almost exclusively an English undertaking. The prince would provide little more than a convenient rallying point, with his fleet standing off the coast as a safeguard against French intervention.

Just how clearly the group of seven understood the purport of their counsel is uncertain, but there can be no question that the Earl of Danby, shrewd and ever ambitious, had a firm grasp on the possibilities of the situation. His voice seems to have been the dominant one when the proposals for the prince were being drawn up, and clearly he sought to cast himself as William's principal advisor and, perhaps, as arbiter between princes.[12] Given the circumstances, however, Danby was out of his league. He and the other conspirators were thinking of the invasion in terms of activity on land, while William's naval advisors were unanimous in pointing out the possible dangers of landing on the east coast of England given the stormy weather and the lack of good harborage.[13] Above and beyond the specifics of the situation, Danby's calculations were still a rather pathetic exercise in futility. He either misunderstood William's motives for agreeing to undertake the expedition or failed to assess properly the strength of character of the man with whom he was dealing.

Clearly the prince had specific objectives in mind by the summer of 1688, and he was unlikely to allow one or more of his English supporters to cast himself in the role of power broker. On the other hand, there is also little doubt that William needed and desired substantial support and assistance from the English upper classes. His invasionary force may well have contained many expatriates who could be paraded to the fore once a landing had been made, but a sympathetic response and the physical presence of a portion of the landed aristocracy were necessary additional ingredients for success. The north offered these on an organized basis, despite drawbacks of a different nature. No such assurance could be forthcoming from the southwest where the seven principal conspirators had neither local power bases nor strong family connections.

The promise of immediate support in the north may well have been the decisive factor in shaping William's response to the seven. Certainly the gist of the story, as recorded by Burnet, indicates that the prince had resolved to land his expedition on the Yorkshire coast as a result of the conspirators' strong advocacy of this strategy.[14] In communicating this decision to his English allies, William almost certainly gave warning that circumstances beyond his control might make it necessary to put down elsewhere. He seems, however, to have promised that in any event some sort of assistance in the north would be forthcoming.[15] Thus it is not surprising to find that the plans of the prince's supporters fastened almost exclusively on the expectation that he would arrive in the north or that a secondary task force would come with men, money, arms, and instructions.

As plans for the invasion developed, the English conspirators were immediately concerned with the recruitment of other men of prominence willing to give active assistance in the movement against the king. The process of sounding out individuals to determine whether they were willing to engage in the project was a ticklish business, but James had unwittingly done his best to create an atmosphere in which it was possible to expect benevolent neutrality if not a promise of support. The Earl of Nottingham and the Marquess of Halifax, each of whom had a general idea as to the direction in which events were moving, provide clear-cut examples. An even more striking instance is revealed in the correspondence between the Earl of Danby and the Tory Earl of Chesterfield in the early autumn of 1688.[16]

Although Chesterfield was a staunch Anglican much concerned about the danger of the church's position and the general direction of James's policies, he was still a member of the privy council, albeit an inactive one. He was, in addition, very much a man of principle in a rather rigid and narrow sense. Yet despite this background, Danby openly broached the subject of the projected invasion, outlined the plans for northern risings in conjunction with the arrival of the prince, and sought to enlist Chesterfield in the movement. Just as the Earl of Nottingham had ultimately decided he could not violate the oaths he had taken, so Chesterfield chose not to engage on the grounds of conscience. There is, however, absolutely no evidence to indicate that he felt it necessary or even desirable to take steps to counteract the conspiracy.

Clearly the king's position was precarious indeed if Chesterfield and Nottingham, men who should have been his natural allies, represented the best that could be expected from the Tory-Anglican nobility. Furthermore, the relative security of the conspirators as they attempted to broaden and extend their base of support becomes obvious as well. Yet for every individual who left some trace of contact with the circle of principal conspirators before William arrived, there are many more whose precise relationship and connection with the original seven is obscure. Chesterfield might predict success for the movement against James, but the dangers of participating in the project must have appeared all too real to those involved. One can only suppose that much of the material valuable to the historian met the fate of the Duke of Ormonde's papers, burned by a cautious wife after he deserted the royal army for that of William.[17]

An unfortunate by-product of the Whig interpretation of the Revolution has been the tendency to place too much stress on its non-partisan or bi-partisan nature. One can, of course, easily attach too much significance to the Whig and Tory labels, and the Earls of Danby and Devonshire provide an obvious example of prominent men from both traditions working together effectively. Yet even in this instance it is worth noting that an important purpose of the first assignation of these two men in the north—a meeting held on the neutral ground of an inn at Whittington, Derbyshire, halfway between Kiveton and Chatsworth—was to effect a formal reconciliation. Both men had long been political opponents, and Devonshire, then a member of the Commons, had attacked Danby with particular violence when the latter was impeached in 1678. Obviously the two had been associated to some extent during the year preceding the revolution, but Devonshire seems to have felt the need to avoid possible friction and misunderstanding by acknowledging that he and the Whigs had falsely maligned Danby's character.[18]

In general, men of similar political views and outlook tended to cooperate more comfortably than those who had previously stood on opposite sides of the political fence. The fact that Devonshire and Danby meshed together as well as they did during the northern rebellions is the exception rather than the rule, and in no small part must be attributed to Danby's rather pragmatic approach to the whole game of power politics. This is not to say that it was impossible to subordinate partisan differences in order to promote William's coming, but tensions existed, especially over the largely undefined question of final objectives, and they became marked indeed once it appeared that the movement against James was succeeding with results unexpected among some from the Tory quarter.

It is also clear that differences in political convictions and differences in political associations played an important role in determining who was to approach whom when it came to expanding the circle of men privy to the conspiracy. Trust and confidence in the person who broached the subject of supporting the prince's projected invasion were ingredients as essential as strong conviction concerning the justice of the cause. As much as the conspirators might maneuver to stay within the letter of the law, their intent was treasonous even in the limited sense of forcing the king to summon a freely elected parliament. For a displaced roundhead of Lord Delamer's ilk to have approached the Earls of Chesterfield and Nottingham,[19] for instance, would have resulted in disastrous consequences for the project, while a man of Danby's credentials could do so with relative impunity.

One can see this process of like attracting like working itself out most clearly in terms of the circle of conspirators associated with Lord Churchill, who was one of the most important recruits added to the ranks of those supporting the projected invasion. His credentials had been established with the opposition during Dykvelt's embassy in 1687, when he had acted as an intermediary between Princess Anne and the Dutch envoy. It is likely that he remained at least on the fringe of the group of leading opponents of the king thereafter. Apparently he was approached in connection with the invasion plan at a fairly early date, and it is obvious that by mid-summer he had committed himself to lend active support to the movement.[20]

The significance of Churchill's part in the conspiracy is twofold, although it is usually painted exclusively in terms of his position as a ranking army officer and the commander of the king's forces at Salisbury. Certainly his role in promoting support for the prince among a considerable circle of army officers was to be of importance in establishing forces at work within the military that would impair its effectiveness and morale in any confrontation. This was a project undertaken in conjunction with Colonel Charles Trelawney and General Percy Kirke,[21] both men of previous loyalist reputation, and was directed toward enlisting support among men of similar outlook. Through his brother-in-law Colonel Charles Godfrey, Churchill may also have been linked to the Rose Tavern club, which included a group of Whig oriented officers and ex-officers presided over by Lord Colchester.[22]

Much more crucial, as far as the risings in the north are concerned, was Churchill's connection with and influence in the household of Princess Anne. According to Burnet,[23] Churchill undertook not only to join the prince himself but also to assure that both Anne and her husband would do so as well. Nor does this appear to be a figment of the good bishop's imagination. As every history of the revolution records, Prince George deserted the king by pre-arrangement the day after Churchill crossed the lines at Salisbury.[24]

In Anne's case the evidence points to the fact that her flight from London in late November to join the northern insurgents was not a matter of prior planning. There is little question, however, that the princess was initially favorable to William's project. More than almost any other leading participant in the revolution she seems to have entertained serious and lingering doubts about the legitimacy of the Prince of Wales.[25] She sincerely believed, in addition, that the Anglican church was in danger, and her conversations with Clarendon in the autumn reveal that she was totally out of sympathy with her father.[26]

While the letter Anne managed to dispatch to William in mid-November indicated some indecision as to whether she should withdraw from the Cockpit, a part of the palace at Whitehall, it is clear that she was prepared to do so and that her husband and Churchill expected her to follow such a course of action.

There is, then, every indication that Churchill served as a central figure in a circle of men privy to the conspiracy against James II long before William landed at Torbay. It was a circle marked by strong connections with the household of the Prince and Princess of Denmark and one which included numerous scions of aristocratic families who were often ranking officers in the army. Among the more notable individuals drawn into the movement against the king through this connection were the young Duke of Ormonde, commander of a regiment brought over from Ireland and the newly installed chancellor of Oxford University; the Duke of Grafton, natural son of Charles II and commander of a regiment of foot; Colonel John Berkley, commander of a regiment of dragoons; Lord Drumlanrig, son of the Duke of Queensbury; and Lord Cornbury, son of the Earl of Clarendon and lieutenant colonel of Churchill's own regiment.[27]

Looking at the composition of this group, the significance of similar political orientation in terms of the enlargement of the conspiracy becomes even more apparent, for all the men involved in it were Tory in outlook and loyalist by tradition. Obviously the attention of this circle was directed primarily toward testing sentiment in the military establishment and approaching individuals there who might be likely to favor the prince's design.[28] Despite the fact that its links with the Williamite movement in the north were largely indirect, this group is an important example of the tendency toward uniformity in political outlook within individual groups preparing for the prince's arrival. Furthermore, in at least two instances the Cockpit circle was the apparent device which brought into the plan political associates and family connections with a direct role to play in the north.

Although proof positive is lacking in the case of the Earl of Scarsdale, one of the dozen or more nobles who participated in the rising at Nottingham, circumstantial evidence would seem to point in that direction. Given the plan for a northern landing, Scarsdale was an obvious candidate to be brought into the scheme because of his influence in the county of Derby. He was, moreover, likely to be receptive to the idea since his opposition to James's policies had cost him the lord lieutenancy of Derbyshire, command of the Princess of Denmark's regiment of horse, and his position as Prince George's groom of the stole.[29] On the other hand, Scarsdale's politics were poles apart from those of the Earl of Devonshire, while he was intimately associated with the household of the Prince and Princess of Denmark. These facts, combined with his role during the Nottingham rising, make it likely that the earl was initiated into the conspiracy through the Cockpit circle, quite probably during the summer when he was in London.[30]

The Earl of Derby is a second example of a Tory peer drawn into the plans for the northern risings by the men associated with Lord Churchill. Commanding considerable local influence in Lancashire, and to a lesser extent in Cheshire, Derby was apparently first introduced into the plot in mid-October. James summoned him to London then to replace the Catholic Viscount Molyneux in the lieutenancies of those two counties.[31] By that time the possibility of Dutch invasion was common knowledge, as was the general reluctance of the upper classes to accept at face value the seeming change of heart this threat wrought in James. Generally an indecisive man,[32] Derby evidently spent most of his time in town consulting with friends and associates as to what he should do. These men were obviously very much involved in the plans for William's expedition, for they advised him to accept the commissions offered on the grounds that as lord lieutenant of both Cheshire and Lancashire the earl would be in a position to use the militia in support of the prince.

Unfortunately, the record of the earl's activities at this juncture, kept in the form of a diary by his trusted associate Roger Kenyon,[33] makes no mention of specific individuals consulted. In light of Derby's Tory orientation in politics, however, the Cockpit circle would seem to be the most plausible point for his entry into the movement against James. The timing of his visit to London further strengthens the case. By mid-October the leading participants in the scheme, with the exception of men connected with Churchill, had long since either joined William or withdrawn into the country. Most important, a chance reference to the fact that among the peers Derby approached was one to whom he was related makes the Cockpit circle even more likely. The earl was the Duke of Ormonde's brother-in-law, and there are numerous indications of his dependence upon Ormonde during the revolutionary period.[34]

On the basis of the advice Derby received in London, he eventually established contact with Lord Delamer, whose influence rivaled that of the Stanley family in Cheshire,[35] in order to coordinate efforts in the northwest in anticipation of William's arrival. Delamer, who had thrice spent time in the Tower on charges of treasonous complicity with Monmouth, tended toward aristocratic republicanism. While it is no surprise to find Delamer in the vanguard of those actively opposed to James, the question arises as to when and by whom he was initially brought into the scheme. His relationship with the men who had advised Derby to contact him is also a riddle, in view of the general thesis that supporters of the conspiracy tended to organize in subgroups reflecting their traditional political associations.

The crucial role of Henry Compton in recruiting support for the movement against the king emerges here.[36] Because of his position in the church hierarchy, the prominence of his family, and his political background, the bishop was ideally suited for the task. Largely as a result of his suspension from office at the behest of James, Compton had become firmly established in the national mind as a man of Protestant principle, resolutely opposed to the direction royal policy was taking. In conjunction with the loyalist tradition of the Compton family and of the bishop himself,[37] this made his credentials impeccable whether he was dealing with Whig or Tory. In the final analysis, he was the only man among the original seven conspirators who could easily gain the confidence and trust of others no matter what their own beliefs or political persuasion.

Especially in the case of the Tories, such a combination of attributes was to be an important factor in the success of the English side of the revolution. The Bishop of London, more than any other single individual, symbolized the futility of the loyalist doctrines of passive obedience and nonresistance. His contribution to the development of the conspiracy was already considerable, not only as one of the signers of the invitation but also in connection with such events as printing the petition of the seven bishops. It was only natural, therefore, to find him playing a central role in the expansion and coordination of the conspiracy against James as it developed in the early autumn. His commitment to the cause, seen largely in terms of securing Protestantism, was unwavering. In a very real sense he stood above faction and partisan loyalty to the extent these created difficulty in bringing men together in the project.

Compton's contribution to the revolution in this respect is very clearly revealed by his activities when he journeyed into the north during the latter half of September.[38] Danby, Devonshire, and Lumley had all withdrawn separately into the country some weeks before to organize and make plans. One may suppose that the bishop left London not long after the three remaining signatories of the invitation—Shrewsbury, Russell, and Sidney—departed for Holland. The essential purpose of his mission was to enlarge the circle of men privy to the projected invasion, but he also served as a communications link among the various groups already preparing for William's descent and possibly transmitted news from The Hague.

The timing of Compton's journey seems to have been determined by the expectation that William would make his landing in early October.[39] This made it both imperative and somewhat less dangerous to expand the circle of peers and gentry committed to take up arms and raise men when the critical moment arrived. Presumably the seven had already decided before leaving London to use Nottingham and York as the focal points for rallying supporters of the prince, information which may have been a part of the "full scheme of advices"[40] that Shrewsbury took to Holland. Certainly this would seem to be the case, for what is known about the arrangements which Compton concluded would indicate that plans had previously been formulated on this basis. In fact, it is worth noting that the peers approached earlier—the Earls of Chesterfield and Nottingham and the Marquess of Halifax—were not only important on the national stage, but also had local influence in the region surrounding William's probable line of march south.

The information available indicates that Compton first went into Bedfordshire. There he approached the Earl of Bolingbroke, a man generally opposed to the policies of James yet unwilling to engage in direct action against the king.[41] The bishop then moved on to Castle Ashby, the family seat of his nephew, the

39

Earl of Northampton. There he was apparently joined for a family conclave by the Earl of Dorset, related to both the bishop and Northampton by marriage.[42] Both Dorset and Northampton had long been associated with the opposition, but it is impossible to determine whether the subject of the prince's expedition had been broached previously. In any event, they agreed to support the project and to join the Earl of Devonshire at Nottingham whenever the prince should land. Compton's success in this respect was evidently matched by commitments from others in the vicinity, including the Montagus of Horton, Lord Grey de Ruthin, and the Earl of Manchester.[43]

Within a few days at most, the bishop moved further north, securing a promise of support from the Earl of Stamford in Leicestershire if Lord Delamer were to come into the scheme. The Earl of Rutland proved too circumspect to be drawn into the movement directly; but in Nottinghamshire, Compton had no difficulty in winning the adherence of Sir Scrope Howe of Langar, a man whose association with the opposition dated back at least as far as Dykvelt's embassy in 1687. Howe's commitment was especially important. He was a leading Whig in the county and could be counted on to neutralize partially the efforts of the ultra-royalist Duke of Newcastle. The bishop then went into Derbyshire to meet with the Earl of Devonshire, the pivotal figure in the plans for the impending rising at Nottingham. Thereafter Compton conferred with Lord Delamer in order to coordinate the latter's activities with those of Devonshire, although there may already have been some preliminary contact between these two peers.[44]

While the record is not entirely clear, it seems likely that the bishop also visited the Earl of Danby in Yorkshire before returning to London. Given Danby and Compton's close association during the events of the revolution, it was only to be expected that the latter would try to make contact in the north. It may also have been necessary to do so in order to communicate news from The Hague and information about the others involved in promoting the northern risings. However, the bishop does not seem to have participated in the second meeting between Devonshire and Danby at Ribston Hall, the family seat of Sir Henry Goodricke.[45] Very little information about this meeting survives, but if Danby's recollection of the event is to be trusted, it was at this time that specific arrangements were worked out concerning the risings at Nottingham and York. Much depended, obviously, upon the circumstances surrounding the prince's landing, but insofar as planning was possible it was determined that Danby should move first in the hope of surprising the governor and garrison at York since Nottingham was an "Open Town."[46]

The assignation at Ribston occurred on October 1, and it is likely that Compton had already begun his return journey to the capital by that time.[47] There would have been little reason to remain in Yorkshire long; to have done so might easily have resulted in unwelcome attention and awkward questions. As it was, Sir John Reresby, governor of York, received a report that the meetings between Danby and Devonshire were cause for suspicion and ought to be investigated.[48] Besides, Compton had done all he could to assist the Williamite movement in the north by enlarging the circle of conspirators, serving as a communications link among them, and helping to coordinate the specific arrangements for the rising at Nottingham. London was to be the bishop's station during the invasion period, and he needed to return quickly if he were to be available as a resource to Princess Anne.[49]

The bishop had surely made a contribution of very considerable importance in the recruitment of men prepared to assist the Prince of Orange in his undertaking. It is most unlikely that any of the other principal conspirators could have approached peers of such differing outlook as Lord Delamer and the Earl of Rutland or the Earls of Stamford and Northampton, with less risk of exposure, or that anyone stood a better chance of success in influencing young peers like Grey de Ruthin and Manchester to gamble with their futures. Compton's importance as a link between political traditions can probably be seen as well in the establishment of a working relationship between Delamer and the Earl of Derby. The bishop had, of course, visited Delamer in the north, and information as to the latter's intentions appears to have been passed on to Derby through Compton's contact with the Cockpit circle, which in turn brought the earl into the scheme in mid-October.[50]

The Bishop of London's contribution notwithstanding, the basic pattern of expansion of the plot against James was by contact between men of similar political outlook, which is reflected in what little is known about Devonshire and Danby's contribution in this respect. Unfortunately, Devonshire was very careful to leave no trail of evidence that might compromise him or his contacts. The fate of his friend Lord Russell in 1683 doubtless made him doubly cautious, and it is next to impossible to detail his activities in terms of recruiting support against James.[51] He must have been as busy in Derbyshire and surrounding areas making preliminary contacts with those he could trust as Danby was to the north, but just how far he went with this process is unknown. There is little point in trying to read the history of the rising at Nottingham backwards in this context, since the bulk of the participants came in after the earl had taken up arms and put out a declaration.

Browning makes an interesting surmise, however, when he reasons that part of the purpose behind Devonshire's trips into Yorkshire in early October was to make contact with prominent Whigs in the area with whom Danby had no close ties.[52] The fact that Devonshire was joined there for a time by Thomas Wharton, the eldest son of Lord Wharton, serves to confirm this conjecture.[53] When or by whom Wharton was brought into the conspiracy is unknown; but he was actively associated with the disaffected group of army officers and ex-officers meeting at the Rose Tavern, collected a large store of arms at Winchendon, and ultimately joined the prince in the west.[54] Had the plans for a northern descent materialized, his family's traditional base of influence in the north and strong ties with Nonconformity would have been important. Accordingly, it is not unreasonable to suppose that Wharton was approaching men unsympathetic to Danby and their mutual Bertie relations as well as coordinating strategy with Devonshire.

In Danby's case one can see even more clearly the pattern of expansion on the basis of similar partisan affiliation in conjunction with factors such as family connection and geography. Although his attempt to bring the Earl of Chesterfield into the project had been rebuffed, Danby more than offset this failure by recruiting the support of other prominent men of Tory-Anglican background. Perhaps his greatest success was in winning the adherence of the numerous Bertie clan to which he was related by marriage. Among the family members joined with him in the movement against James were his brothers-in-law, Charles Bertie and the Earl of Abingon, and his nephew, Lord Willoughby, son of the Earl of Lindsey and a figure long associated with the opposition.[55]

Others brought into the scheme by the earl before William arrived included John D'Arcy, grandson of the Earl of Holderness and third party to the meeting between Danby and Devonshire at Whittington;[56] Sir Henry Goodricke, a leading figure among the Yorkshire gentry whose country home was a center for Danby's activity; and, quite probably, Lord Fairfax of Cameron and Captain Christopher Tankard, both men of influence among the gentry of the West Riding. Just how widely Danby spread his nets is difficult to determine. Complex political maneuvering on the county level brought him into contact with many of the gentry in October, and some could have been initiated into the plot against James. However, considering the list of just those men known to be associated with Danby in advance of William's landing, the basic uniformity of their political outlook and background is immediately apparent.

There simply is not enough evidence to analyze the developing conspiracy against the king with any precision, yet it is possible to trace certain definite connections and to suggest other likely combinations. Almost everything points to the emergence of a series of subgroups in which there was a basic consistency in political viewpoint. Essentially there was a Tory-Anglican orientation among Danby's associates and in the Cockpit circle. The same is doubtless true in terms of a basic Whig outlook among those working with the Earl of Devonshire, the Earl of Stamford, or Thomas Wharton. Bridges existed between Tory and Whig groups, with Bishop Compton playing an important role in this respect. Family connection was also a moderating factor, since Thomas Wharton was in consultation with his Bertie relatives,[57] and the Whig Charles Godfrey, Churchill's brother-in-law, may have been the link between the Rose Tavern group and the Cockpit circle. The importance of geography emerges clearly too. Excepting those of the seven signatories who joined William in Holland and the army plotters, contacts were limited almost exclusively to men who had some power base or local influence that was important in terms of the plan for a northern landing and subsequent march on London.

IV

SOME LOCAL BACKGROUND

THE EMERGING opposition and its transformation into a conspiracy against James II has thus far been considered largely as a national phenomenon, with emphasis on the role of the nobility. But with the development of plans for risings at Nottingham and York to coincide with the landing of the Prince of Orange, some attention must be devoted to the northern setting. Danby and others of the seven had, after all, stressed the general disaffection in the north as an important factor in favor of William's launching his invasion there, and significant insurrectionary activity took place even after the prince made a southern descent. None of this would have happened had the environment been totally hostile to the Williamite cause. Yet little effort has previously been made to determine whether any special circumstances contributed to a revolutionary situation in the north, or, indeed, to analyze the impact of James II's policies there.

The attention of most historians has generally focused far too narrowly on London and the actions of the central government. One is reminded in nearly every study of the revolution, for instance, that the clergy in the capital almost without exception refused to read the second declaration of indulgence. But what of the clergy in the provinces? Or, to cite but two other examples, what was the reaction in given localities to the regulation of municipal corporations and alteration of the commissions of the peace? Essentially, an assessment must be made of the king's attempt to undermine the independence and autonomy of local communities and groups, to methodically subordinate local interests to the center.

In the final analysis, county boundaries are largely meaningless in any study of the risings in the north, or even specifically of the rising at Nottingham, which drew supporters from well over a half dozen surrounding shires. However, a satisfactory analysis of the impact of James II's policies on the local level throughout the midlands and north would require a massive study far beyond the scope of the present undertaking. In the circumstances a sample of reasonable proportions can be made by examining background events in the county of Nottingham, the center for one of the two major northern risings, and in the neighboring county of Derby, which initially provided a substantial proportion of the men taking up arms at Nottingham and which was also the Earl of Devonshire's primary base of local influence.

By the autumn of 1687, systematic intrusion into local affairs had become a keynote of the king's campaign to secure a pliant parliament. Regulation of municipal corporations represented the most important aspect of this policy, since exclusion had taught that control of the boroughs was a necessary prerequisite to control of the House of Commons.[1] Compared to the twenty-one boroughs in Cornwall returning men to Westminster, neither Nottinghamshire—with six seats divided among the county town, Newark, and East Retford—nor Derbyshire—where the county seat alone was represented—offered much scope for securing a large block of court supporters. Nevertheless all four of these municipalities were subjected to royal interference during the year before the revolution, and Nottingham was forced to surrender its charter for the second time in less than a decade.

Of the four boroughs in question, only Nottingham was of sufficient size to be numbered among the more considerable centers of urban population in seventeenth century England. Reliable estimates for the period are, of course, difficult to make, but it appears that the town had something on the order of six thousand inhabitants at the time of the revolution, while the nearby county seat of Derby was considerably smaller with less than four thousand residents. Comparatively, Newark was a relatively modest town numbering perhaps twenty-seven hundred citizens, and East Retford, with a population of seven to eight hundred, was a village much smaller than the neighboring communities of Worksop, Mansfield, and Southwell.[2] Similarly in Derbyshire there were a number of towns of moderate size, such as Bakewell and Chesterfield, which had no representation in parliament, although the citizenry was carefully cultivated at election time because of their votes as freeholders in the county.[3]

Despite its relatively small size in the modern frame of reference, Nottingham easily ranked within the top dozen cities of the period, and in the northeastern portion of the country it was surpassed only by York, which was declining in importance, and possibly by the rapidly expanding town of Newcastle. A bustling, prosperous center of trade and manufacture,[4] its strategic importance should not be overlooked, for the bridge over the river Trent there formed a link in one of the principal lines of internal communication between the two great divisions of England.[5] From the standpoint of geography and population, Nottingham was an obvious choice as a center of supportive activity for an expedition landing along the Yorkshire coast. Moreover, its political history in the 1680's made it unlikely that the citizenry would be totally hostile toward the prince's project.

Nottingham's first taste of royal regulation had come early in the aftermath of the exclusion crisis when the Tory Duke of Newcastle, the county's lord lieutenant and a figure of very considerable local influence, engineered the surrender of the borough charter in 1682. Although it is quite possible to view the whole question of municipal regulation in broader terms than mere reaction to Whig excess,[6] there can be little doubt that the strength of Whig sentiment in the common council, supported by such prominent members of the local gentry as William Sacheverell, Sir Thomas Parkyns, and Richard Slater, made it seem desirable that action be taken. Not that Newcastle and his mayoral protege, Gervas Wylde, found the going easy, since the council was almost evenly split between opposition and loyalist members.

46

Given the rough and tumble of local politics during exclusion, the questionable tactics used by the court faction were not exceptional; but the immediate consequence was the Whig refusal to recognize the validity of the new charter issued by Charles II. There followed a very confused period in municipal government when the two factions each held elections in 1682 to choose officials for the ensuing year according to the provisions of the charter they regarded as operative. For a time Nottingham was treated to the spectacle of two mayors and two pairs of chamberlains and sheriffs along with the attendant popular disturbances flaring up between supporters of both sets of officials. Acting upon directions from London, the Duke of Newcastle finally managed to impose some semblance of normality, with the Whigs closed out of the corporation entirely. Their demise as an effective political group was completed less than two years later when twenty-two opposition leaders, including burgesses and their supporters among the gentry, were successfully prosecuted for riot in connection with the disturbances following on the municipal election in 1682.[7]

The new charter granted by Charles II did not differ radically from the old one, except for the fact that two influential officials —the recorder and the town clerk—were henceforth to hold office only during royal pleasure.[8] It did, however, make a clean sweep of the Whig opposition in the corporation by naming all members of the common council as well as the other officeholders for the borough. Traditional election procedures were to apply subsequently as vacancies occurred, but the fact that appointments to the council were for life ensured that power was effectively concentrated in the hands of the court party.

Such an arrangement worked very well indeed in terms of promoting the election of men of acceptable Tory mold to parliament in 1685,[9] but difficulties began to emerge once James launched his sustained drive to secure repeal of the penal laws and Test Act. In Nottingham as elsewhere, the breakdown of the alliance between the crown and men of Tory principle was clearly revealed by the response made to the three questions. Despite the endeavors of the Duke of Newcastle to elicit favorable answers, the best the mayor and aldermen could promise after a week's reflection was to try to secure the election of "two Loyal Persons"[10] whenever a new parliament should be called.

Every effort was made to frame the reply in terms as diplomatic as possible, but vague assurances of the sort made were obviously reflective of the fact that the Tories and "high church"[11] men installed in office by Charles II had been pushed to the point where they could no longer be relied upon to carry out the wishes of the monarchy.

By this time, however, the machinery had already been established in London to deal with those municipal corporations which could not be depended upon to influence the selection of candidates favoring the principles of the declaration of indulgence. Taking the form of a commission of regulation headed by the ubiquitous Jeffreys, the task of altering the personnel of local governments on the basis of reports received from a network of local agents was well under way by the end of 1687. The connecting links between Nottingham and the commission were Timothy Tomlinson, the corporation's solicitor, and Caleb Wilkinson, a Dissenter who was soon to be installed as a member of the common council. Their recommendations, in combination with advice elicited from others knowledgeable about the situation, brought forth the spate of orders in council descending upon the corporation in the early spring.[12]

The result of these illegal mandates was a clean sweep of all local officials, including the mayor, the entire common council, sheriffs, coroners, chamberlains, and town clerk.[13] Not even the personal intervention of the Duke of Newcastle on behalf of one of the individuals involved was of assistance, for the commission had found the removals "requisite for His Maj[es]ties Service at this time."[14] Unfortunately, very little is known about most of the men named in the directives from London to fill the vacancies created, but apparently they were drawn from the Nonconformist community.[15]

Almost the only person among the new appointees who had previously figured prominently on the local political scene was John Sherwin, the mayor named to replace Gervas Rippon. The juxtaposition of these two men is interesting, for Rippon was Church of England and a notable court supporter in the early 1680's, while Sherwin was a Dissenter and had numbered among the leaders of the opposition then. Both were relatively wealthy men whose interest in borough politics was a natural by-product of their standing in the community.[16] That Rippon

48

should be dismissed at this juncture is not, in the circumstances, very surprising, but the appointment of John Sherwin in his stead presents the curious picture of one of the more vociferous opponents of the crown in the reign of Charles II now willing to work hand in glove with James.

As J. R. Jones has pointed out,[17] cases of Whig collaboration with the Stuart monarchy in the last two years before the revolution were not particularly rare. Even James was politic enough to realize that court supporters and Catholics alone were far too few in number to carry the day once it had become clear that most men of Tory-Anglican sentiment would not assist in repeal of the penal laws and Test. The first declaration of indulgence had, of course, been a bid for the support of the Dissenters and their sympathizers, a large element of the group that had come together earlier under Shaftesbury's leadership. Some strict Nonconformists accepted this proclamation at face value and were willing to cooperate accordingly, although even the Quaker William Penn seems to have had mixed feelings on the subject.[18] In the case of collaborators of Sherwin's ilk, some further consideration must be made of their motives for agreeing to work with their old opponent.

Generally speaking, there can be little doubt that self-interest and the calculated gamble that James might succeed in his plan to remove the religious and political disabilities of the Nonconformists persuaded some to join his camp. A plausible variation of the argument from expediency would explain Whig collaboration in terms of the wish to supplant local rivals, those loyalists who had firmly entrenched themselves in power during the royalist reaction. Certainly there is every indication that rivalry between the two political groups had been bitter in Nottingham, and the fact that the dubious measures used to dish the Whigs were common knowledge cannot but have added to the desire to turn the tables.

Yet it would be dangerous to attach too much weight to this line of reasoning, since only two of the councillors voting against surrender of the charter in 1682 were returned to office with Sherwin, and one of these subsequently refused to serve.[19] In the main, the more prominent members of the old opposition party, men like William Greaves whose election to the mayoralty had been quashed by the surrender, stood aside for the duration.

As already noted, however, Sherwin was a man of a more extreme and activist bent than most, which is reflected in the leading role he played in the disturbances surrounding the local election just after the surrender of the charter.[20] Accordingly, it is quite possible that he should be numbered among those urban collaborators who came to accept James because he had broken with the traditional power structure and because he advocated a program of reform legislation that was similar in some respects to Shaftesbury's.[21]

Also to be taken into account is the possibility that the king had a hold over Sherwin resulting from the heavy fine levied against him when he was convicted of riot in 1684. In cases of a similar nature, the guilty party was often allowed to post a bond for the amount due, which was then retained by the government as a guarantee of future good conduct. This was, of course, precisely the tactic adopted in an attempt to secure the Earl of Devonshire's acquiescence to royal policy after he was fined thirty thousand pounds upon conviction for a minor misdemeanor in 1687; and the same may have been true in the case of William Sacheverell, one of the most active Whigs in the Commons during exclusion and among the gentry associated with Sherwin in the alleged riot at Nottingham.[22] Although the court's strategy backfired disastrously in Devonshire's instance, leverage of this sort presumably worked to better effect with men of lesser stature whose social and economic position was less secure.

On the whole, however, it seems much more reasonable to conclude that a man like Sherwin was willing to collaborate because he subscribed to elements of the king's program as he understood it. That this should be the case is not surprising, for many of the issues that concerned a Devonshire or a Danby had little relevance on the local scene, and even the dilemma royal policy posed to the leaders of Dissent would have had limited impact. The urban collaborators were quite frequently "men of restricted ambitions and limited mental horizons. They were absorbed in the little worlds of their own communities, and many stood to gain financially from the possession of municipal office."[23] Once office had been accepted there was a strong tendency to overlook events that were generating increasing fears among other sectors of the community.[24]

Unfortunately, Sherwin's death in the early spring of 1688 precludes any determination of the limits of his willingness to cooperate, but there is nothing in the stance of the other members of the corporation to indicate hesitation to comply with royal directives before William of Orange landed. Much more important to these men was the fact that they were largely dependent on the central government for continuance in office. In normal circumstances their religious beliefs would have disqualified many of them from membership in the corporation. They lacked a strong base of support within the community given the method by which office had been obtained and, in the instance of at least one of the more prominent new aldermen, there was even no history of previous connection with Nottingham.[25] Their position was isolated indeed.

The question of opposition to royal policy aside, the dubious distinction of appointment by illegal mandate to a government operating under a charter of questionable validity was obviously sufficient cause to make most men of standing shy away from the new regime. Some of the loyalists displaced by the orders in council evidently went further. It is apparent that the new members of the corporation were soon confronted with legal challenges to their authority, to say nothing of pure obstructionism. In this respect the situation differed little from that of other corporations throughout the country, and by the time advice was sought in London the central government had already turned to the use of *quo warranto* proceedings to settle the problems attendant upon the replacement of duly elected officials with men of more favorable disposition.[26]

By May arrangements for the forfeiture of the charter granted to Nottingham by Charles II seemed well in hand, and the attention of the corporation was turned to the question of the provisions of the new charter to follow. A number of changes were suggested by the common council as a whole, but these were concerned mainly with technicalities except for one obvious bid for popular support in requesting restoration of a traditional fair.[27] Much more indicative of the insecurity and isolation of the new appointees was the proposal apparently emanating from George Langford, Sherwin's successor as mayor, and elaborated upon by Nathan Wright, the deputy recorder who was negotiating the terms of the new charter in London, to limit the franchise for the election of corporation officials to current members of the common council.

Whether or not Langford had the backing of the common council in suggesting this change is not clear. Of more importance is the fact that, less than a month later, the mayor had reversed himself and was making every effort to secure retention of the traditional election procedures.[28] The most plausible explanation of this sudden change of heart is that some hint of what was intended had leaked out and caused such an adverse reaction—perhaps compounded by the turmoil surrounding news of the arrest of the seven bishops—that it was considered too risky to proceed further. Nor was it really necessary to do so, since the deputy recorder had sent word from London that the new charter would contain a provision reserving the king's right to remove any official and then nominate a successor. There is nothing to indicate, however, that this reversal in position was the by-product of any growing opposition to the king among the members of the corporation. Rather, it would appear that they were fearful of adding to their unpopularity by advocating the limitation of traditional rights, which now seemed unnecessary since the court would be able to deal directly with any problems resulting from the election of unacceptable officials.[29]

As it took shape in the summer of 1688, the rough draft of the new charter was a very satisfactory document both from the standpoint of the central government and the members of the corporation. The government had effectively tightened its control over the borough and its handpicked officials, and they in turn stood to benefit from a much more secure legal position. But the advantages expected by Langford and his associates in this connection never materialized because of a series of muddles in securing final judgment against the old charter. Just what went wrong is unclear, but the *quo warranto* of Nottingham never reached the court of the king's bench during the trinity term, and action was still pending in mid-October when James reversed the process of regulating municipal corporations.[30] Since the king could not legally grant a charter until the old one had been forfeited, the situation became very confused when a new charter was delivered to the common council on September 29, the traditional date of municipal elections.

What emerges most clearly at this point is the desire of Langford and the other officials to retain office while avoiding any action that might subsequently leave them open for prosecution. There was, however, neither the desire nor the possibility of totally ignoring James's new charter, especially since it reappointed for the following year the same slate of officials installed by the orders in council that spring. Accordingly, the mayor and his associates managed to secure their election in the manner prescribed by the charter of Charles II, presumably because the majority of those entitled to vote dissociated themselves from the proceedings. Then, a few days later, they went through the motions of swearing themselves in under the terms of the document issued by James.[31]

The cautionary tactics adopted by the corporation were to stand them in good stead in the months ahead. This was largely due to the fact that the king's proclamation of October 17 restoring municipal charters and officials removed since 1679 did not apply to Nottingham, which was one of thirty-four boroughs exempted from the general provisions of this directive.[32] Even after the charter issued by James was determined to be worthless, Langford and the others remained the duly constituted officials of the town as a result of the election they had conducted under the provisions of Charles II's charter.[33] Accordingly, in the last weeks before William of Orange landed, Nottingham was an exception to the general pattern which saw the transfer of power in most corporations from royal appointees to those displaced at one time or another since the exclusion crisis.[34] Continuity rather than chaos prevailed, but the advantage to the central government as the time of crisis approached was to be limited.

A prime consideration in pursuing a policy of regulation had been, of course, the hope of securing a pliable House of Commons by influencing the selection of members chosen by municipalities. Despite the fact that the franchise in parliamentary elections was particularly wide in Nottingham, the influence of well disposed officials could be considerable, the more so since the common council claimed the right of creating burgesses and thus adding to the electorate.[35] Yet the ability and disposition to maneuver in the political arena was a far different thing from lending concrete assistance to James's government once it was known that William's supporters were planning to use the city as one base for their activities in the north. Whatever the legal technicalities of the situation, the members of the corporation were in too isolated a position to do much more than try to look out for their own interests. While the opposition of the displaced loyalists had been relatively muted thus far, partially because of the Duke of Newcastle's influence, hostility was not far below the surface. Furthermore, as already noted, there were a good many men of the old Whig connection who had shown no inclination to collaborate with the king, and even within the group installed in power by royal mandate two men were to defect from the ranks in October.[36]

At best the corporation's base of support had been limited to the Dissenters who constituted a not inconsiderable strand in the population. Indications are, however, that the moderate Nonconformists in Nottingham as elsewhere were drawing back from the temptation of alliance with the monarchy to secure removal of statutory disabilities, and that indeed there was fear that they might be tempted to join those following William's standard.[37] Of necessity, therefore, the primary consideration of the members of the corporation became one of maintaining their own positions, which, in turn, meant doing nothing that might later redound to their discredit whichever way events should turn.

Nottingham's importance as a city of considerable size and wealth, as well as its prominent place in the plans for the northern risings, give particular importance to its political history prior to the revolution. Furthermore, the relative wealth of available source materials permits detail in treatment that cannot be matched in the case of the other two parliamentary boroughs in Nottinghamshire. However, the pattern of royal regulation followed in Newark and East Retford generally approximated, with some variations, that of the county town. Quite possibly because they had returned court supporters during exclusion, pressure to secure surrender of the charters of these two municipalities came late in the reign of Charles II. Whatever the reason for delay, neither corporation was granted a new one until after James had ascended the throne. The result was that the documents in question, unlike the charter received by Nottingham in 1682, contained a provision enabling the king to remove any official by use of orders in council.[38]

Again unlike Nottingham, the generally loyalist complexion of the two town councils apparently necessitated little or no tampering with the personnel of the corporations at a time when the king was still hopeful of working through those of Tory orientation. On the other hand, the replies made to the three questions in the autumn of 1687 indicate the same unwillingness to support James's program which was found among men of similar political and religious outlook throughout the country.[39] Unfortunately, the records of the borough of East Retford do not survive for this period, but there is evidence that royal mandates may have resulted in the displacement of at least some of the town's officials in the summer of 1688.[40] Certainly this was what happened in the case of Newark where orders were received directing removal of the mayor and five aldermen and nominating more pliable men to fill their positions.[41]

Why the remaining Newark aldermen were not displaced is unclear, for they constituted a majority on the town council and were able to nominate and elect one of their number to succeed the king's appointee as mayor in September, 1688.[42] Willingness to cooperate with royal desire on the question of repeal, possibly a by-product of self-interest and pressure exerted by the Duke of Newcastle, is the obvious answer; and it would seem to be confirmed by the favorable report made by an agent of the commission of regulation in the same month.[43] However, there was apparently no hesitation in reverting to the old charter and personnel of the corporation once James issued his proclamation to that effect in October, for the records of those present at the mayoral nomination in the following April indicate the participation of all but one of the displaced aldermen and none of those put in office by royal mandate.[44] Presumably the same pattern holds true for East Retford, so that in both town governments a group of men was returned to power just before the revolution who were unlikely to be favorably disposed toward the king.

In the politics of Derbyshire, the county town figures particularly prominently, since it represented the only avenue to parliament besides the county delegation itself. The records of the corporation do not survive for the period, but other sources make it evident that the central government applied much the same measures to Derby as elsewhere. The first step in the process of municipal regulation was made in 1681 when the corporation's charter was surrendered and a new grant procured from Charles II. As in the case of Nottingham, the new charter wrought little change in the constitution of the borough and was intended to do no more than eliminate the influence of a hostile faction on the common council by appointment of a full slate of court supporters.[45] No evidence remains to indicate serious difficulties in securing surrender, but the relatively early date at which pressure was applied to the corporation was doubtless a consequence of the fact that its representatives, Anchitell Grey and George Vernon, had supported exclusion.[46]

Derby was not again disturbed until the last year of James II's reign when, presumably on the basis of the reports of agents for the commission of regulation, a little more than half the members of the corporation were displaced by orders in council and successors nominated.[47] Although momentarily expected in light of what was happening elsewhere, no further alteration of personnel was undertaken for the simple reason that the remaining appointees of Charles II were far more concerned with retaining office than in offering opposition in principle to royal requests. An interesting reflection of this fact can be seen in the split that developed between the old and new members of the corporation when word reached them in April that *quo warranto* proceedings had been threatened. This was the obvious step for the crown to take in order to tighten its hold over the town by grant of a more restrictive charter, but what may seem surprising is the willingness of the old loyalist faction to cooperate with the king and to make a voluntary surrender. The primary purpose in adopting this stance was to please, but there was shrewd cunning involved as well. If judgment were rendered in favor of revocation, cause would have to be shown and this, it was feared, would provide easy legal justification for the removal of the rest of the old council men.

Actually, the reports on the state of affairs in Derby transmitted to the Earl of Huntingdon, lord lieutenant for the county, indicate that regulation had been undertaken on the basis of misinformation.[48] Not only were the remaining members of the corporation installed by Charles II ready to cooperate in surrendering the charter, but a number of those who had been displaced, including the former mayor Leonard Sadd, were reputedly willing to support such a maneuver.[49] On the other hand, those appointed to office by James refused to countenance such a proposal when it was formally entertained at a council meeting, and by one means or another they were able to stave off immediate action.

Just what went wrong from the royal standpoint is difficult to determine, but apparently the central government relied too heavily on the reports of its own agents and too little on the advice of men intimately acquainted with the local scene. In simplest terms the new appointees, such as mayor Ralph Brough, had been willing to make promises they had no intention of keeping in order to secure office. Essentially these men were using to their own advantage the king's desire to find urban collaborators among the Nonconformist community. The results were no more satisfactory than at Leicester where Sir Henry Beaumont considered additional regulation essential, "since it is plain there is false brothers with fanatics."[50]

Rumors that any new charter would limit voting rights generated a considerable adverse reaction among the citizenry in Derby as it had in Nottingham. However, the focus of discontent was centered on the parliamentary franchise, which was relatively wide,[51] rather than on the method by which town officials were selected. In the opinion of George Vernon, a member of the local gentry and a creature of the Earl of Huntingdon, the opposition to surrender had grown to such proportions by mid-summer that even among the burgesses who had initially favored such a measure none still dared to do so. Moreover, further regulation of the corporation was not expected to help, since Vernon was convinced that no one would take office until the matter had been resolved.

The pressure of popular sentiment against surrender was reinforced by several of the local gentry, ranging from the Whig oriented Anchitell Grey, uncle of the Earl of Stamford, to the loyalist John Coke, who offered contributions to defray the charges of defending the charter. Despite the best efforts of Vernon and Huntingdon to swing opinion around, the common council not only resisted but also proved obstructionist on the issue of supporting court approved candidates for parliament when it appeared that there would be an election in the autumn. The reports made by the king's agents in September indicated that Vernon and John Coke were likely to be chosen, and Coke was not at all the type of representative the crown wanted.[52] Moreover, if Vernon's own assessment of the situation is reliable, his chances for success at the polls were poor, for a number of corporation men were actively promoting the candidacy of Robert Wilmot to stand in combination with Coke.

Unfortunately, the detailed source materials relating to the situation in Derby do not extend beyond mid-September, so that little can be said about the last weeks before the revolution. Vernon's candidate for mayor, alderman John Cheshire, whose tenure in office stretched back into the reign of Charles II, was successful in the Michaelmas election of corporation officials, but what this might have boded for the future in the normal course of events is impossible to determine. Presumably, however, the proclamation issued by James in October resulted in the restoration to office of all members of the corporation previously displaced by royal edict. Of necessity confusion and resentment must have been endemic, and in terms of the approaching crisis the crown gained neither friends nor advantage from the situation.

In the final analysis the same holds true for all four boroughs in the two county area. Regulation theoretically gave the king a much tighter hold over the municipal corporations, but in actuality the problems attendant on the process bred discontent, disruption, and, in most places, isolation of town officials to such an extent that their prime concern became retention of power. This, coupled with the restoration of men earlier removed from office in Newark, East Retford, and Derby, meant that cautious neutrality was about the best that London could expect once the risings in the north in favor of William of Orange were under way. Even if the revolution had not occurred, however, it is by no means clear that the policy of regulation would have produced acceptable parliamentary delegates. In part this reflects the failure of James's hopes for an alliance with the Dissenters, and in turn it suggests the need to consider the religious background in the two county area.

While the overwhelming majority of the people in the region conformed to the practices of the Anglican church, it is also quite apparent that there were elements in these two shires which might have been expected to welcome the king's attempts to secure repeal of statutes creating religious and political disabilities. Reliable information as to the proportion of the population whose sympathies lay outside the Anglican establishment is difficult to come by, but all indicators point to the fact that the Dissenters were quite numerous in both counties, particularly in the county towns. In both instances the Presbyterians were the predominant group, but in Nottinghamshire their lead over other Nonconformist sects, such as the Independents, Baptists, and Quakers, was a good deal less clearcut than in Derbyshire.[53]

Considering the religious proclivities of the king, the question of Catholic recusants must also be taken into account, despite the fact that they represented only a tiny proportion of the total population. As far as can be determined, the few Catholics in Nottingham were centered upon the households of a handful of the lesser gentry, men such as Sir Edward Golding, George Willoughby of Cassal, and perhaps three or four others who had remained loyal to the old faith. In Derbyshire, however, the followers of the tenets of Rome were considerably more numerous, but even in this county, where the proportion of Catholics was considered relatively high, the total number was probably something less than a thousand persons. Here again, most of the recusants were to be found in small colonies centered on the estates of members of the gentry whose links with the Roman church had never been completely severed.

Once James had been deserted by the Tory-Anglicans over the question of repeal, he took the obvious alternative and attempted to put together a coalition of court supporters, Nonconformists, and those Catholics who deemed it safe to enter the public limelight. A crucial step in this process of creating a political counterweight to the old loyalist establishment was the issuance of the first declaration of indulgence in the spring of 1687. The record of addresses of thanks presented to the king by Nonconformist groups in both Derby and Nottingham indicates initial enthusiasm for freedom to worship and relief from prosecution. However, a strain of disquiet and doubt emerged at a fairly early date, and some felt that repeal of the penal laws and Test Act should be accompanied by provision of other statutory security for the Protestant religion.[54]

The first reaction of the Anglican church in the area is, unfortunately, much more difficult to gauge. One may surmise that there was little outspoken opposition among the Derbyshire clergy given the fact that the Bishop of Lichfield was always counted among the waverers on the episcopal bench, if not in a class with the Bishop of Chester.[55] In Nottinghamshire, on the other hand, the influence of the dean and chapter at York—no successor having been appointed after Archbishop Dolben's death in 1686—was clearly exerted in the opposite direction. During a visitation at Southwell just following the appearance of the declaration, clergy, churchwardens, and members of the gentry were treated to a sermon focused on the church in danger and the need for constancy to preserve it from attacks by "papists" and "fanaticks." Even more telling was the final charge in which the churchwardens were enjoined to continue making presentments of Catholics and Dissenters within their parishes notwithstanding the king's declaration.[56] While it cannot be claimed that the tenor of these remarks necessarily reflected the views of the Nottinghamshire clergy or their parishioners, the attitudes expressed may have fostered a more open opposition to toleration than could be found in the neighboring dioceses of Lichfield or Lincoln.

But the real test of the Anglican clergy came with the order in council of May, 1688, directing that the second declaration of indulgence be read in every parish church. In a very real sense the provincial clergy had something of an advantage as they wrestled with the problem, for their brethren in London had almost unanimously refused to comply some two weeks earlier. Yet even with this example very much in mind, the decision was not always an easy one to make. Refusal to read the declaration implied rejection of much of the church's teaching on the subject of obedience to royal will, and there was also the threat of disciplinary action or worse in a diocese like Chester, where the bishop demanded strict adherence to the council's directive. On the other hand, there were the pressures of public opinion, a spate of pamphlets on the subject, and, perhaps most important, the often less than subtle promptings of the Anglican nobility and gentry.[57]

Specific information is lacking as to the record of the clergy in Derby and Nottingham on the days appointed for reading the declaration, but it seems safe to assume that the proportion of those refusing to do so was as overwhelming as it was in other parts of the north.[58] Even in Cheshire, where diocesan pressure for compliance had been strongest, only a handful of priests fell into line. Elsewhere in the area those who cooperated with the royal mandate were apparently limited to a few isolated instances of men whose patrons favored the king's policies, and the penalty paid was virtual ostracism by the rest of the clerical community.[59]

Generally speaking, the second declaration of indulgence is also a convenient point to mark a parting of ways between the king and the mainstream of Dissent, and at the same time the emergence of an entente between the leaders of Nonconformity and the moderate Anglicans. Certainly this would seem to be the case in the two counties under consideration, although there is considerable danger in attempting to generalize about Dissent as if it were a monolithic entity. At the very least some differentiation must be made between the smaller sects, such as the Independents and Baptists, and the larger strand of Presbyterians, especially those known as "church Presbyterians."

The church Presbyterians were occasional or semi-conformers, who kept the letter of the law by attending Anglican services on Sunday mornings and then gathering for their own meetings later in the day. This practice was, of course, by no means unique to the two county area, and essentially it represents one element of the Nonconformist response in the difficult years following exclusion.[60] In the town of Derby the church Presbyterians were apparently quite numerous, while contemporary estimate put the "vigorous" or strict Dissenters at a minority of one hundred fifty out of some four hundred burgesses in the Nonconformist community.[61] It may be suggested, in turn, that the relative strength of the church Presbyterians had an important impact on the political history of the borough, which reflects the increasing fears generated among moderate Dissenters by the direction of the king's policies.

Unlike Nottingham,[62] even after Dissenters had been added to the corporation in the spring of 1688, no address of thanks was returned for the king's first declaration of indulgence. Frequently such addresses were not spontaneous; forms for the purpose, requiring nothing more than the addition of signatures before being dispatched to London, were submitted to many municipal corporations and clergymen by friends of the crown. Since an agent of the Earl of Huntingdon used this tactic at Leicester, it is quite possible that the common council at Derby either refused or made an unsuitable response to a similar approach.[63] Whatever the case, the corporation made only the most sparing of replies to the second declaration and that only after George Vernon had exerted his utmost influence. Furthermore, when it came time for the town to offer congratulations on the birth of the Prince of Wales, Vernon was not only frustrated in his hopes that the Dissenters would make amends by proposing a fulsome response, but found that some were even unwilling to sign the congratulatory address produced for the occasion.[64]

These factors, taken in combination with the refusal to surrender the borough charter, suggest that the new appointees in Derby were moderate Dissenters or church Presbyterians. The desire for power, hopes of profit, and local concerns were sufficient to allow these new men to accept office, but like their counterparts in the Leicester regulation, they were unwilling to collaborate fully with the crown.[65] This was not, however, true of the strict Dissenters at Derby; they still had their eyes fixed upon the immediacies of the situation in the borough and their desire for religious liberty. They were the ones desirous of yet a further regulation of the corporation in their favor, and they could also be counted on to support parliamentary candidates who favored repeal and were generally acceptable to the court. But the tendency among the Nonconformist mainstream was to back away from alliance and cooperation with royalist collaborators. By late summer this trend was reflected in the support church Presbyterians were giving to the candidacy of the Tory John Coke in combination with the moderate Whig Robert Wilmot, a man generally sympathetic to Dissent but not approved by the crown.[66]

Since occasional conformity was a prerequisite for political participation before 1687, it is safe to assume that the church Presbyterian was not uncommon in Nottinghamshire. In fact, the Duke of Newcastle may have been making oblique reference to the phenomenon when he stated, in response to a request for names of prominent Dissenters, that "there is no Gentleman but such as goes to Church, and heares Common Prayer."[67] Information about moderate Dissenters or church Presbyterians

62

in the borough of Nottingham is less readily available than for Derby. However, the relative success of the regulation at Nottingham would seem to indicate that the strict Nonconformist element figured more prominently there. The new members of the corporation were willing to go a great deal further with the crown without becoming entangled in worries about the ultimate consequences.

Although it is not possible to document in detail the shift in attitude among Nonconformists in other parts of the two county area, it is only reasonable to conclude that the result was much the same as in most other sections of the country.[68] A few of the less politic Nonconformists, in the main those drawn from the strict wing of Protestant Dissent, were still able to credit the promises of king and court. Most, however, had swung around to the conclusion that a Catholic monarch was not to be trusted; with considerable reason, fears had arisen that toleration secured in this fashion was likely to be self-destructive. While the second declaration of indulgence in itself cannot be considered sufficient cause for this about face, it was obviously an important factor in the process and as well provides a convenient checkpoint for determining shifts of opinion.

As an immediate cause of the petition and subsequent trial of the seven bishops, the declaration is also significant in that it leads to a situation affording a glimpse of the feelings of the common people on matters of religion. Here the widespread prejudice of the English against Catholicism is revealed once again in the wild celebrations and bonfires that followed upon the acquittal of the bishops. Certainly both Nottinghamshire and Derbyshire were as much caught up in this rather formless outburst of Protestant enthusiasm as any area, and from the county seats to the tiniest agricultural hamlets celebration was the order of the day when the news arrived from London. The authorities were virtually powerless and, at times, unwilling to do anything. Even the ever dependable Duke of Newcastle drank the health of the seven, although for form's sake he threatened his tenants at Norton with eviction when complaint was made of their bonfires.[69]

Popular sentiment had reduced the complex issues of the day to variations on the old theme of Protestant versus Catholic. While the touchstones are missing that would allow a more precise determination of the feeling of the common man later in the autumn, the almost uncanny quiet that settled over England when news of William's projected invasion came out would seem to indicate that the situation was still regarded in the same light.[70] Most people viewed the prince as the Protestant savior, and his coming was not something to be feared or actively resisted.

The essential point in considering elements of the religious background in the two counties is much the same as that made in connection with the survey of municipal corporations. With some variations, what happened did not differ significantly from the overall patterns and trends which historians have already traced for the country as a whole. Certainly the proportion of Dissenters was high in these two shires, and in the case of the county of Derby there were also a considerable number of recusant families among the gentry. From this standpoint the king's program of securing religious toleration might be expected to have considerable appeal, but more significant in the long run was the parting of ways between the mainstream of Nonconformity and the monarchy. Once some allowance has been made for differences in diocesan policy, the attitudes and reactions of the Anglican clergy are similar to those elsewhere in the country.[71] It is impossible to make any conclusive generalizations about popular sentiment from a religious standpoint, except to emphasize that a very basic anti-Catholic bias was prevalent in both counties.

All this, of course, can be accurately treated as preparing the way for the coming of the revolution, and more specifically the rising at Nottingham; but at the same time it cannot be considered exceptional when compared to the rest of England. It was the question of the preservation of Protestantism in all its forms that secured the neutrality or passive support of the bulk of the population during the contest between James II and the Prince of Orange. And it was, moreover, a manifestation of the concomitant fear of Catholicism that was to lead to the mass hysteria and mob action of the Irish night, which swept through Nottinghamshire and Derbyshire with particular intensity. Even in a limited political sense, James II's efforts to create an alternative power structure were unsuccessful; the revolution simply swept the attempt away.

V

The County Community

In Restoration England, political institutions, the law, the church, the militia, and national as well as local administration were all more or less operated by and for the benefit of the upper classes and their connections. Not unnaturally the disruption of this arrangement by James II was a prime cause of disaffection, and any consideration of the background to the rising at Nottingham must include some treatment of the impact of the king's policies on the nobility and gentry of the area. The geographical limits of the two county area used here as a case study present some difficulties in this respect, since shire boundaries often had little relevance to the spheres of influence of many peers and more substantial members of the gentry.

The Earl of Rutland, for instance, had his principal residence and concentration of properties in Leicestershire, yet his attitudes and activities in local politics were of importance not only in that county but also in Lincoln and Derby. The same is obviously true for the Duke of Newcastle, whose influence in Nottingham and Northumberland should not be allowed to obscure the weight his opinions carried in portions of Derby and the West Riding of Yorkshire. On a lesser scale, one can point to a man like John Coke of Melbourne, whose estates gave him a political base in both Derby and Leicestershire.[1] There were among the titled aristocracy, however, a dozen peers whose estates and family connections gave them a considerable degree of influence over society and politics in the two county area, although clearly its extent and exercise varied a great deal.[2]

Taking matters as they stood at the commencement of James II's reign, the political background of these nobles ranged from moderate Whig to ultra-royalist, with most falling someplace among the moderate Tories. The Earls of Devonshire and Clare were the only ones in the group whose stance during the popish plot and exclusion crisis placed them among the Whigs, but neither had numbered among the more extreme elements of the old Country party. Others, the Earl of Kingston and Lord Lexington, had been too young to make a mark in the politics of the early 1680's, and—given the force of the royalist reaction —it is not surprising to find both initially settled on the loyalist side of the fence during the parliamentary election of 1685.[3] Within a relatively short period of time, however, these two peers became disillusioned with the trend of events under James. Lexington apparently resigned a commission in the army in protest, and separately they were to spend most of the reign travelling abroad. Neither returned to England in time to be in any way connected with the risings in the north, although both were back soon enough to participate in the crucial proceedings in the Convention Parliament when they cast their lot with William's most open supporters.[4]

The basically Tory-Anglican orientation of the majority of those remaining—Halifax, Rutland, Scarsdale, Chesterfield, and Ferrers—needs little comment, except to emphasize that men of this ilk formed the dependable backbone of the loyalist reaction in the last years of Charles II. From this standpoint there was little to distinguish them at the outset from the two ultra-royalists, the Duke of Newcastle and the Earl of Huntingdon,[5] since basically it was events after 1685 that were to test how far men were prepared to go with the crown. The only man of the twelve who has left no trace of political involvement is Lord Byron of Newstead Abbey, who must have been something of a recluse since he was rarely even included in the commissions of the peace for Nottinghamshire.[6] Whatever the case, he did have a vote in the Lords. Apparently somebody in the Williamite faction eventually took cognizance of this fact when the going was rough in the Convention Parliament, managed to persuade Byron to make an appearance, and influenced his vote on matters of substance.[7]

Excepting the extreme of aristocratic republicanism, the dozen peers under consideration represent a fair sample of the full range of the political spectrum. But it was the large group of Tory moderates who, in normal circumstance, could have been expected to give solid and dependable backing to the crown. This they were prepared to do in 1685, and as long as this was the case the rumblings of discontent and political activities of the old Whigs were unlikely to be of much effect. Within three short years, however, the king's base of support among the loyalist aristocracy was almost totally dissipated as opposition to royal policy boiled up, basically over the symbolic question of repeal of the penal laws and Test and then reinforced and compounded by what was regarded as a sustained attack on the political power and influence of the nobility.

The Earl of Devonshire was, naturally enough, antagonistic toward James from the very first; the same is presumably true about the Earl of Clare, although lack of specific evidence makes it difficult to speak with certainty.[8] As already noted, the Earl of Kingston and Lord Lexington, both relatively young men without fixed political commitments, veered away from support of the king at an early stage, despite initial loyalist inclination. Even more to the point, however, is the case of men like Halifax and the Earl of Chesterfield. These peers clearly merit the label of Tory and their importance on the national political scene, especially in the case of Halifax, should not be allowed to obscure the fact that they were men of consequence in Nottingham and Derbyshire respectively.[9]

Both were cautious and essentially conservative elder statesmen (Chesterfield lived in semi-retirement because of gout) yet at differing times each was approached on the matter of the prince's projected invasion. While neither was to engage, their refusal was basically a declaration of neutrality, which gives clear indication that alienation from James among the loyalist nobility had reached a dangerous stage indeed. This becomes all the more obvious in light of the fact that Bishop Compton had deemed it safe to approach the Earl of Rutland in the autumn to ask his support for William and that yet another Tory peer from the area, the Earl of Scarsdale, had been brought into the project by those in the Cockpit circle at an earlier stage.

The extent if not the degree of opposition to royal policy among the nobility in the two county area is revealed in the lists of 1687 projecting the probable vote of each on the question of repeal. Of the twelve men concerned, nine were generally believed unwilling to comply with royal desire. Lord Byron, as might be expected, was listed as undeclared, and only the Duke of Newcastle and the Earl of Huntingdon were adjudged favorable.[10] Mention of this is made not to stress the obvious, but rather to focus on the difficulties James faced in terms of local administration. Tampering with the personnel and charters of the corporations was expected to give the crown influence over the boroughs, but as a first step in securing control over society and politics in the counties the king had to have men in the lieutenancies upon whom he could rely absolutely.

In this respect Nottinghamshire seemed to present little trouble since the ultra-royalist Duke of Newcastle was lord lieutenant, although even he seems to have gone through a momentary phase of unease at the trend of events in early 1688.[11] Unfortunately, the duke's pre-eminence in the county (a by-product of his rank and extensive estates) and his general subservience to royal wish were not matched by a corresponding capacity for carrying out his responsibilities in a crisis situation. A rather shallow, querulous, and self-important individual, Newcastle's talents were far better suited to the intricacies of local political intrigue than to making efficient arrangements for coping with the threat of insurrection and invasion.[12] Be that as it may, his influence in Nottinghamshire combined with his pliability in terms of royal policy ensured that James would rely heavily on the services of the loyal duke, especially since the extent of his deficiencies as a leader did not emerge clearly until too late.

The situation was somewhat different in Derbyshire. There the lieutenancy had been wrested from the leading noble family, the Earls of Devonshire, during the royalist reaction and placed in the safe Tory hands of the Earl of Scarsdale. Given Scarsdale's inflexible opposition to repeal, James subsequently found him an unsatisfactory tool for his purposes. The result was the appointment of the Earl of Huntingdon—an uncompromising royalist who could be depended upon to accept governmental policy—to the lieutenancy of Derby as well as that of Leicester, where he replaced the Earl of Rutland. The choice was not an ideal one in a number of ways, and it points up the problem the king faced in trying to find suitable candidates for office among the nobility.

In the first place, Huntingdon lacked the stature and standing of men like Scarsdale and Rutland. This was particularly true in the case of Derbyshire, for insofar as the earl had a traditional sphere of influence, it lay to the south in Leicester.[13] Difficulties in this respect were compounded by the fact that he spent almost no time in the north, relying heavily on hand-picked deputies such as George Vernon, who were simply unable to give efficient and effective implementation to directives coming from London. The fault was not really Huntingdon's for as an active privy councillor, member of the ecclesiastical commission, and commander of a regiment of foot, the demands on his time in London virtually precluded active involvement in the affairs of his lieutenancies. On the other hand, the king had little alternative but to employ the earl given the unwillingness of other peers in the area to cooperate with royal policy and the need to appoint lord lieutenants not completely lacking in local connections and influence. But the difficulties arising from an absentee lord lieutenant were clearly apparent at the outbreak of the revolution, since the counties of Leicester and Derby were perforce left to their own devices when Huntingdon was ordered to join his regiment at Plymouth.[14]

The overwhelming opposition to James II among the nobility associated with the two county area is also reflected in the attitudes of the greater part of the gentry, although a precise determination of the sentiments of such an amorphous group is difficult indeed. The first true test of opinion within this class came when deputy lieutenants and justices of the peace were confronted with the three questions. As one might expect, the Duke of Newcastle acted promptly in this matter so that the replies from Nottingham, apparently garnered in early November, 1687, were among the first received by the central government.[15] The results were less than encouraging, despite the fact that many of the men questioned tried to avoid giving umbrage by hiding behind noncommital phrases.

Only Viscount Chaworth (Irish peerage), generally regarded as the foremost commoner in the commission of the peace, openly vented his feelings by giving a strong negative response coupled with a declaration that he would exert every effort to secure retention of both the penal laws and Test.[16] Of the other eleven men examined at this time, however, only one made a positive reply indicating full willingness to comply with royal policy. The promises of the others to promote the candidacy of loyal persons whenever a parliament should be called amounted to a diplomatic refusal. Nor should it seem surprising that a greater number did not follow Chaworth's lead, for almost all had been hand-picked for office by Newcastle over the years, were under considerable personal obligation to him, and obviously were seeking a reasonable way out of the dilemma posed by ducal pressures and the dictates of conscience.[17] It is interesting to note that some may have tried to avoid the whole problem by absenting themselves, for there were a half dozen deputies and justices out of the county when the questions were put.

Because of the Earl of Scarsdale's refusal to act, the three questions were not presented to the deputy lieutenants and justices of the peace in Derbyshire until January, 1688, when the Earl of Huntingdon made the only recorded visit to the county in his capacity as lord lieutenant.[18] At least as summarized in the report submitted to London,[19] the replies generally reveal a more bold and open opposition to James's policies than is apparent at first inspection of those from Nottingham. Doubtless the trend of events on the national scene, especially news of the queen's pregnancy and the spectres thus raised, in combination with the dismissal of Scarsdale and information and rumor about what the gentry in other areas was doing all contributed to this outspokenness.

Twenty-two men were included in the report—some had been examined and the positions of others were well enough known to make this unnecessary—and of these fifteen registered clear opposition to the concept of repeal. Seven made a favorable response, but while this figure may seem high, it should be noted that one of the number, Arthur Warren of Toton, Nottinghamshire was the same man who had already made the only

70

positive reply in his home county. Even more important, however, is the fact that some time earlier James had begun commissioning deputy lieutenants and justices who did not conform to the Anglican church, and four of the remaining six who supported repeal can be definitely identified as Roman Catholics.[20] So that despite the threat of dismissal hanging over their heads, only two, or three if Warren is counted twice, of the regularly constituted officials of the county stood ready to assist the king in his project. Furthermore, contemporary comment indicates that the three men in question were thought to be of no considerable interest.[21]

The purge in the lieutenancy and commission of the peace that followed was thorough indeed, and at least on paper the transformation had been completed in both shires by February, 1688. Some indication of the scope of the attempted revolution in county leadership can be gleaned from the fact that in Nottingham only one deputy lieutenant in ten had held a commission the year before, while in Derby all seven were new appointees.[22] Little is known about the single holdover in Nottingham, Sir John Molineux of Haughton and Teversall, except that he was in London at the time the three questions were put.[23] It may be presumed, however, that he made a satisfactory reply to royal agents there, and the same is probably true for two others absent at the same time, John Moore and Thomas Markham, both reputed Catholics who had been added to the commission of the peace.[24]

As might be expected the new men in both lieutenancies included a high proportion of Catholics—almost half can be definitely identified as such—but what is surprising in the case of Nottingham is the very substantial number of Whigs put into office. Sir Scrope Howe, William Sacheverell, Richard Slater, and Richard Taylor had all been leading protagonists of the Whig party in the shire, two had numbered among those prosecuted for contributing to the riot in the county town in 1682, and it is clear that as a group the loyalist establishment continued to regard them as a public menace throughout the last years of Charles II. Moreover, the new commission of the peace for Nottingham, representing almost a complete change in the slate of justices, included several other local Whigs such as Charles Hutchinson, John Thornaugh, John White, and George

Gregory.[25] The information is lacking for a precise tracing of the pattern in Derbyshire, but the inclusion of Anchitell Grey among the deputy lieutenants and men like John Maurwood and Samuel Saunders in the commission of the peace indicates representation of elements of the old Country party.[26]

The very composition of the new commissions, including as they did members of the gentry of political substance as well as Roman Catholics,[27] might at first seem to give lie to the contention that most gentlemen stood in basic opposition to James. Certainly it does lead to the realization that care must be used in assessing the implications of the replies to the three questions, which were, after all, directed almost exclusively at those Tory-Anglican squires who held the reins of local power. In the area under consideration, the question emerges as to whether the king had found a workable alternative to the loyalist establishment in the form of a Whig-Catholic alliance. As implausible as this may sound, such a combination might have tipped the balance in Nottinghamshire—reputed to be the most "factious" county in the country—where the possibility of Whig victory at the polls seems to have been avoided only narrowly in 1685.[28]

A clear distinction must be made, however, between those who may be labelled moderates or extremists on the basis of their activities during exclusion. In the former category were men like Sir Thomas Parkyns of Bunny and John White of Tuxford, who had numbered among the Whig supporters in the charter imbroglio of 1682, but who thereafter moved to the right as the royalist reaction proceeded. If approached at all, these men remained aloof from any temptations that may have been placed in their path as James's agents sought allies on the local level. The same is true of Sir Scrope Howe of Langar, who as late as 1683 was still advocating the merits of the Duke of Monmouth, but who had cooled off sufficiently two years later to take an official hint to drop his candidacy for parliament and to have arms seized during the panic following the Rye House plot returned to his possession.[29] While Howe was actually issued a commission as deputy lieutenant in 1688, there is no evidence that he ever acted, which is hardly surprising given his involvement with the growing opposition to the king.

However, among the fairly large extremist wing of the old

Nottinghamshire Whigs, there seems to have been little reluctance to accept office. In turn this required promises of support for repeal; yet if the situation in Leicestershire is any guide,[30] the new officials insisted on qualifying for office in the manner prescribed by law. Essentially, these men were taking advantage of James's need for collaborators simply in order to dish the loyalist establishment. This is not to deny that many of them desired repeal of at least the penal laws by due parliamentary process, but it is to stress the strong element of partisan bitterness that had crept into local politics during exclusion and the royalist reaction that followed.[31]

Accordingly, a temporary marriage of convenience emerged between the crown and certain Whigs. More than a half dozen men and perhaps double that number—such as William Sacheverell, Richard Slater, and John Thornhaugh—actively engaged in the business of the lieutenancy and commission of the peace and continued to do so into the autumn of 1688. Furthermore, given the generally positive attitude of the Duke of Newcastle as well as specific evidence in one instance, there is every reason to believe that the Roman Catholics receiving commissions were active also.[32] As a consequence the transformation of county administration in Nottinghamshire was better perfected than almost anywhere else in England. Even so, a far greater portion of the gentry stood opposed to what had been done and the reasons for doing it, while the dependability of those Whigs who chose to collaborate was certainly open to question.

The situation was quite different in Derbyshire. There loyalist sentiment had reached a fever pitch among the gentry in the aftermath of exclusion, and the overwhelming majority of this class was of Tory outlook.[33] Moreover, those men who had retained something of a Whig orientation in politics were often of more moderate inclination than many of their brethren across the county border. A by-product of this situation was the very real difficulty encountered in finding replacements for those men turned out of office in the spring of 1688, the new commissions issuing out of London notwithstanding.[34] Both among Catholics and other newly appointed officials—a mixed lot of ultra-royalists, Whigs, and Dissenters—there was considerable reluctance to take up the proffered reins of authority. Of the three Roman Catholics made deputies in the lieutenancy, only Sir

Henry Hunloke, the foremost adherent of that faith in the county, appears to have been really active in that position, and even he was constantly aware of the liability of his religion, refusing appointment both as sheriff and as a captain in the militia on the grounds of adverse public sentiment.[35]

Very little information survives about the other two Catholic deputies, Rowland Eyre of Hassop and William Fitzherbert of Norbury, but it would appear that Eyre at least accepted his commission while Fitzherbert attempted to avoid any active involvement in political matters.[36] Nor is there the slightest evidence to suggest that men such as Anchitell Grey or Sir John Gell, who had strong ties to the Nonconformist tradition, ever acted upon their commissions.[37] In fact, there were only two men who had qualified as deputy lieutenants, excluding Catholics, in the entire county by November, 1688. These were the ubiquitous George Vernon and the high Tory Thomas Gladwin, whose convenient illness at the time probably reflects an unwillingness to commit himself any further in the king's support.[38]

Somewhat the same condition evidently prevailed initially in the commission of the peace, with the records showing very few of those approved by London actually taking the oath of office. Consequently, additions to the original list had to be made, and this necessitated pressing pliable men from the lesser gentry into service, those lacking the land and connections to carry real influence, as well as the Tory lawyer Sir Simon Degge, whose legal expertise was desperately needed to keep the judicial-administrative machinery functioning. Perhaps if the Earl of Huntingdon had been in the county to do a bit of arm twisting things would have gone more smoothly, although the difficulties encountered in other shires of similar political make-up suggest that even with a resident lord lieutenant the problem was not an easy one with which to deal.[39]

Whatever the case, Derbyshire was left with a great many administrative-judicial posts either unfilled, staffed with men of limited influence, or, in the case of Degge, placed in the hands of a man unsympathetic to the royal cause. Basically, the business of government in the county seems to have devolved by default onto the shoulders of Hunloke, a Roman Catholic; George Vernon, a timeserver; and to a lesser extent John Spateman, a

Presbyterian; and Thomas Gladwin, a royalist who became increasingly disenchanted with the progress of events.[40] The attempted transformation of county administration in Derbyshire was quite obviously a failure from the start, for it lacked even the limited support provided by the more extreme Whigs in Nottingham as reinforced by the pressures exerted by the Duke of Newcastle. Something approaching the totality of the greater gentry, to say nothing of the majority of those of lesser consequence, stood aside, disaffected and unwilling to assist James in the face of threatened invasion unless there was real and convincing evidence of a total reversal of royal policy.[41]

Before leaving the question of the gentry in the two county area, some mention should be made of the militia, since it was from this class that the officers were drawn. Organized by counties, under the immediate command of the lord lieutenant and his deputies, the militia was a large, unwieldy, and inefficient organism of rather limited usefulness.[42] Doubtless part of the reason that James emphasized the development of a professional army was a reflection of this fact. Moreover, his policy of actually discouraging musters can be considered an indication that he wanted no rival to the military establishment which he controlled directly and that the army was the body to be relied upon in time of real emergency.[43]

The militia could not be entirely ignored, however, because it was a useful apparatus during the rough and ready of parliamentary and municipal elections for maintaining some semblance of order as well as for influencing a suitable outcome.[44] Consequently, the purge of militia officers, many of whom had also been deputy lieutenants or justices of the peace, was thorough, and it should be viewed basically in terms of the king's political objectives. With the realization in London in early September that invasion was imminent, the shortsightedness of royal policy in relation to the militia became immediately apparent. In the first place, it was totally lacking in any sort of effective training, which meant that at best it could be of only the most limited assistance in attempting to repel the forces of the Prince of Orange. More important, there was a universal lack of experienced officers, and attempts to recruit assistance from among those loyalists earlier displaced met with almost no success. The situation was not quite as desperate in Nottingham, largely due to the fact that Newcastle had managed to secure a reasonable complement of officers, but in Derby and elsewhere the militia was either virtually leaderless or totally unwilling to serve under those Catholics who had commissions.[45]

A two county sample does not provide adequate basis for sweeping generalizations. Yet some tentative conclusions of importance can be suggested, and it may be hoped that these will lead to further studies at the local level. Quite clearly James II consciously designed a dramatic curtailment of local liberties, the county community's independence from central control. Basically, this did not involve significant institutional change, although one can point to a much enlarged standing army and agencies such as the ecclesiastical commission and the commission of regulation. As historians have frequently noted, the policy was rooted in the hope of creating an alternative power elite, or rather power elites, to operate through existing forms. It depended upon the collaboration of ultra-royalists, the Catholic community, and the Dissenters, and it may have been partially grounded in the expectation that religious toleration would bring Anglican decline and a corresponding increase in the strength of Nonconformity.[46]

Examining the situation in the counties of Nottingham and Derby, James's program was unsuccessful for the short run and unrealistic even if he had continued in office much longer. Influence and power at the local level resulted from a compound of many factors, but a commission from the central government was only one element and not the most important. In a county like Nottingham where the Duke of Newcastle provided a combination of unwavering loyalty to the crown with paramount natural influence, some progress could be made. A coalition of ducal dependents, a few Catholics, and Whig collaborators was put together. Here it should be stressed again that the Whig collaborators represented the extremist wing of the old Country party, and that they were frequently men for whom religious toleration was a policy with personal meaning. However, their acceptance of office basically stemmed from a desire to dish the local loyalist establishment; local issues and local personalities were the key factor rather than any desire to cooperate fully with the king.

In the short term this coalition in Nottinghamshire was

enough to keep the wheels of government turning. Once the revolution began, defection became the byword, or at least careful neutrality as in the case of the strict Dissenters in control of the corporation at Nottingham. Other than Newcastle, however, those nobles with close ties to the county stood opposed to royal policy and unwilling to assist in local administration. The same is true for the bulk of the gentry whether one considers the Tory-Anglican squires and their response to the three questions or the moderate Whigs who refused to collaborate.

Derbyshire represents a different and perhaps in some ways more typical case. The absence of the lord lieutenant was an important element in the difficulties encountered in restructuring local government there. It was less significant, however, than the fact that the Earl of Huntingdon simply lacked the standing of the Duke of Newcastle in Nottingham or of a variety of other peers within the county who were hostile to James. Simply put he was the only choice available, but he faced insuperable problems in Derby and only to a slightly lesser extent in his home base of Leicestershire where the Earls of Rutland and Stamford were far more powerful figures. Compounding the situation, the Catholics in the area generally tried to avoid involvement, and there was virtually no Whig collaboration. Consequently, the situation was such that had a parliament been summoned in the autumn of 1688, Derbyshire and the borough of Derby were expected to return members hostile to James.[47]

VI

Nottingham and the Northern Risings

The conspiracy against James II was such a well kept secret that it was mid-September before the king became fully convinced that trouble was imminent, and then only because of repeated and increasingly detailed reports from abroad concerning the preparations of the Prince of Orange. Even at this relatively late date the central government apparently had little or no precise information as to which Englishmen were in league with William. When it was proposed that known sympathizers with the prince should be arrested, only two of those suspected were actually involved in the movement, while others, such as Halifax, had opted to remain on the sidelines. Had the king acted on this suggestion, however, it is quite possible that there would have been a failure of nerve among all but the prince's most ardent supporters.

Certainly a few well chosen arrests could easily have disrupted plans for the northern risings, with the flow of supporters to William upon his arrival reduced to a trickle of enthusiasts for the cause. Here the Earl of Sunderland's unwitting contribution to the revolution emerges, for it was upon his advice that the policy of widespread arrests was abandoned before it had really begun. Lord Delamer was later to characterize the government as supine in omitting to take such a basic precaution,[1] but rather it seems to have been one facet of the overall attempt to conciliate public opinion and to avoid pushing waverers into open opposition on the grounds that they had nothing to lose.[2]

The only direct action taken immediately against a peer suspected of complicity was the warrant sworn out for the arrest of Lord Lovelace. Lovelace had invited this unwanted attention by openly going to Holland in mid-September and then returning to England almost at once.[3] While this naturally led to a flurry of speculation concerning his association with William and the projected invasion, it is impossible to confirm the report that he brought back definite word as to when the prince would sail.[4] He could have been the means by which William notified his followers that the crossing to England would be delayed until mid-October, although his character was such that the journey may have been nothing more than a romantic gesture.

Not until early October was a warrant issued for the arrest of one of the men directly involved in the plans for the northern risings. Just what led the government to become suspicious of Lord Lumley is unclear, but apparently there was no realization of the extent of his commitment to the prince or his true role in the plans for the north. As in the case of Lovelace, attempts to secure his person resulted in little more than a comedy of errors, which at one point saw the Duke of Newcastle dispatching John D'Arcy in pursuit of his co-conspirator while Lumley moved back and forth between Durham and Yorkshire in comparative safety.[5]

Further indication that London had no clear idea as to the identity of the principal conspirators emerged when the prince's declaration began to circulate in England about the first of November. James was much perplexed by reference in William's manifesto to an invitation from spiritual and temporal peers, and this led to a series of interrogations of bishops and nobles in London to determine who his enemies were. Compton, of course, was the only bishop directly involved, and he managed to cover his tracks with minimal difficulty. Among the peers questioned were Halifax, the Earls of Peterborough, Bedford, Burlington, Abingdon, Nottingham, and Lord Weymouth. All of them could honestly deny involvement in any invitation and, with the exception of Abingdon, disclaim knowledge of plans relating to the invasion.[6]

There were others not in London, however, who came under suspicion with more justification. Danby, for instance, was regarded as something of a question mark, for despite offers of service he neatly sidestepped suggestions that he wait upon the king. An attempt was made to secure Devonshire's loyalty by returning the thirty thousand pound bond extracted the year before, but his refusal to submit to questioning about the invitation led James to conclude that he, as well as a number of others like Delamer, were in a class with Lovelace and Lumley. Generally, however, the king remained uncertain about the participants in the conspiracy until after William's arrival. Royal policy had created such hostility and opposition among the nobility as a class that it was difficult to know who could be trusted, and the problem was further exacerbated by the fact that many peers, whether involved in the plot or not, chose to remain in the country.[7]

The conspiracy against James II was also a well kept secret from the standpoint of the plans for the risings at Nottingham and York; there was, moreover, some uncertainty on the central government's part as to where William would land his invasionary force. The north was an obvious possibility on a number of counts: there were reports to the effect that horses were being concentrated at various points along the coast;[8] information from The Hague noted the presence of a number of Yorkshire gentlemen there;[9] and suspicions were generated by the conduct of Danby, Lumley, Sir Hugh Chomley, and others of influence in the area. Furthermore, there was the question of proximity to Holland, which was believed to figure importantly in William's thinking in terms of maintaining open lines of communication with the least interference from the English fleet.

Clearly a northern landing would have been no great surprise in official circles, and even after the descent at Torbay there was continuing concern about the possibility of a second beachhead in combination with internal disturbances.[10] Yet the directives issuing out of London for a coastal watch from Northumberland to Dorset indicate the court's uncertainty about where the prince would try to land.[11] Delamer later criticized the king's failure to deploy his forces efficiently on the assumption that the north and southwest were the only plausible sites,[12] but his analysis verges on the simplistic given the extensive coastline accessible to William and the off chance that a direct march on London might be attempted from a base established on the Kentish or East Anglian coast.

Inasmuch as James had an overall strategy for dealing with the situation, his plan was to concentrate the main body of the army in the home counties. Accordingly, the capital would be adequately protected in any contingency, and there would also be a large, mobile reserve that could readily be turned in whatever direction trouble threatened. In terms of the north, this meant that the king's military presence was spread rather thinly. Although Danby was afraid that large numbers of troops would be dispatched into the area in early October, those quartered nearby in the midlands and along the East Anglian coast had orders to join forces at Newark and move north only if the prince made a landing in that region.[13] Once William made his descent at Torbay, the regiments in question were withdrawn and dispatched to the west; this meant that the only experienced regular troops in the northern counties were those stationed at the garrisons in the area.

From the standpoint of sheer numbers, Hull was undoubtedly the most important, since Lord Montgomery's regiment and a Scottish battalion were quartered there. York, on the other hand, had been left with only a single company of foot, and the great fortress at Scarborough was entirely denuded of troops. In the far north there was a company of foot stationed at Tynemouth and an entire regiment at Berwick. Much like the three companies at Carlisle and the battalion of foot at Chester, the troops at Tynemouth and Berwick were too remote, as well as too few in number, to constitute any immediate threat to risings centered on Nottingham and York.[14] Nor was there much danger from the small detachments of regulars transferring from one garrison to another, or from the new regiments still in process of formation and generally lacking arms and experience. The regiments being raised and the garrisons in the north were apparently intended to function as adjuncts to the main body of the army if there were a Dutch landing there. Otherwise they had no clearly defined role.

The pattern is very clearly revealed in the history of the regiment of foot which the Duke of Newcastle was commissioned to raise in Northumberland at the end of September. Theoretically some eight hundred men strong, this unit was supposed to be armed from surplus military stores at Hull and quartered upon the city of Newcastle. In light of continuing speculation about the possibility of a Dutch descent at Bridlington Bay, James may have thought that the presence of royalist forces at Hull and Newcastle would divert the prince's energies long enough for the main body of the army to move north. Moreover, Newcastle itself was well worth protecting as a burgeoning center of population and commerce, although only the illusion of defense was given since the duke had orders to retreat if William actually approached the city.[15]

Whatever hopes James may have entertained about the usefulness of this regiment, its role in the annals of English military history was hardly distinguished. Recruitment proved particularly difficult, except among the Roman Catholics of the far north, and its total strength was never more than four hundred men.[16] Furthermore, Newcastle's appointment as lord lieutenant of Yorkshire in early October, in addition to his continuing responsibilities for the lieutenancies of Nottingham and Northumberland, ensured that proper attention was never given to the development of an effective fighting machine. The duke apparently felt that the very *raison d'être* of a regiment quartered at Newcastle had been eliminated with the landing at Torbay. Accordingly, only a single company was left there while the remaining men were ordered south to Hull, passing through York only shortly before Danby and his associates took control of the town. The regiment eventually quartered at Hull and remained there until disbanded shortly after the capitulation of the garrison was arranged by its Protestant officers.[17]

Basically, the accident of a southern landing left the conspirators in the north relatively secure from any threat to their activities by the main body of the standing army. Although there had been a regiment of horse quartered less than twenty-five miles from Nottingham, in the vicinity of Leicester, it was soon dispatched to Salisbury along with the bulk of the best trained and best equipped units in the home counties. There was, of course, always the danger that James had more troops on the way from

Scotland or Ireland which could be diverted into the north,[18] but the royal forces already there, with the possible exception of the garrison at Hull, were too widely dispersed and lacking in coordinated strategy to pose an insurmountable obstacle to plans for the risings.

Had there been anybody of real stature and ability on the king's side, it might have been possible to piece together a sizeable army from the various units in the region, perhaps in combination with elements of the militia. That there was no such figure is clearly indicated by the fact that the Duke of Newcastle was made virtual viceroy north of Trent because of his regiment and control of five separate lieutenancies: Nottingham, Northumberland, and the three ridings of York, which were normally administered as separate entities. Some assessment of the duke's character has already been made, and it should be readily apparent that, his loyalty aside, James was perforce relying on a broken reed.[19]

Newcastle was apparently even less aware than London of the sources of rebellious stirrings in the area for which he was responsible. The Earls of Devonshire and Danby were able to deceive him completely on the matter of their true intentions, and Danby went so far as to poke fun at the duke's efforts to prepare for the Dutch when he visited Welbeck in mid-October.[20] Nor was the duke's judgment much better when it came to filling vacancies in the lieutenancies of Yorkshire, for men like John D'Arcy and Sir Henry Goodricke were given commissions as deputies along with such reliable props of royal authority as Sir John Reresby.[21] Moreover, Newcastle so completely misjudged the situation in the north that he not only considered all danger to be past after Torbay but requested permission to join James when he went to Salisbury.[22] While this proposal was vetoed, events proved that it would have made little difference in view of the duke's lethargy and ineptitude at the moment of crisis.

Unfortunately for James, there was simply no one else in a position of authority who combined the leadership skills, influence, and commitment to the royalist cause necessary to fill the power vacuum in the north. The lieutenancies of Leicester and Derby and those of Cumberland and Westmorland were in the hands of the Earl of Huntingdon and Lord Preston respectively;

but their responsibilities in the south precluded taking effective, direct measures elsewhere. Those of Chester and Lancashire had been returned to the Earl of Derby, who had been a party to the conspiracy against James for well over a month before Torbay. The questions of age and calling aside, the Bishop of Durham stood totally discredited because of his cooperation with the king in matters considered detrimental to the church.

In Lincolnshire, the Earl of Lindsey raised the militia in obedience to royal command,[23] but his close connection with Danby, and the fact that his son numbered among the leaders in the rising at York, made it unlikely that he would attempt to fill the breach. Religion barred some from adopting prominent roles in support of James—men like Lord Langdale, governor of Hull and a man of some ability, Lord Widdrington, governor of the garrison at Berwick, or Viscount Molyneux, whose son had been commissioned to raise a regiment of horse in the northwest. As his diary clearly reveals, a royalist like Sir John Reresby simply lacked the influence, standing, and skills necessary to counteract successfully the craft of a Danby.

While the weakness of James's position in the north is obvious in retrospect, the conspirators themselves could hardly have assessed the situation in quite such a favorable light. Newsletters from London provided a fairly reliable guide as to the disposition of the main body of the army,[24] but there still were a great many unknown factors likely to give William's supporters pause. The possibility that regiments of professionals from Scotland or Ireland might be dispatched into the north and continuing uncertainty about the large garrison at Hull are but two obvious examples. Accordingly, they generally proceeded with a degree of caution and circumspection that was unnecessary.

News of the prince's landing at Torbay reached the north as early as November 7,[25] yet it was not until November 20 that the Earl of Devonshire entered Nottingham and two days later still that Danby and his associates secured control of York. This relatively long delay in taking up arms was essentially a by-product of the southern landing. Quite naturally there had already been a measure of near panic among the prince's friends when word filtered through that the first sailing of the expedition on October 19 had ended in failure. If the commentaries of Kennet and Echard are to be trusted on this point, both Danby and Devonshire were hard pressed to keep their associates from giving way to a completely defeatist attitude in the face of this reverse.[26] While the atmosphere of acute anxiety was dispelled by news of the second and successful attempt to reach England, the plans of the northern conspirators were thrown into confusion by the descent at Torbay. The situation was further complicated by the fact that they received neither communication from William nor the arms, officers, and money promised in the event a southern landing became necessary.

A few days may have been lost simply waiting for a task force from William to make a secondary landing along the northern coast. This presumably would have been taken as a signal to go into action much as if the prince had put down there. It is unlikely, however, that more than a week elapsed before new arrangements were concerted to deal with the change in circumstances. These included a determination to go ahead with the risings at Nottingham and York on November 21; to publish declarations in support of William's undertaking as agreed upon by those present in the two cities at the time; and to concentrate on raising horse rather than foot because of the lack of arms, experienced officers, and money.[27]

The mechanics of the decision making process are unknown, but apparently the question of when to act gave rise to some tensions, with Lord Delamer predictably favoring an immediate and open stand for the prince.[28] In the end the more cautious counsels of the Yorkshire contingent prevailed, and it is clear that the desire for delay stemmed largely from Danby's expectation that direction and assistance would be forthcoming shortly from William. Moreover, time was needed to execute the complicated maneuvers that Danby, Sir Henry Goodricke, John D'Arcy, and others had worked out for the seizure of York. These included gaining control of the militia units raised and stationed there, putting both Sir John Reresby and the Duke of Newcastle under house arrest, and then securing the support of an assemblage of gentry and freeholders brought together on the pretense of making a loyal address to the king.[29]

To an activist of Delamer's mold such complicated schemes and elaborate preparations seemed unnecessary. The essence of the matter was to raise as many horse as possible and join the prince at the earliest moment. Although it may have been a product of excessive enthusiasm, his estimation of the negligible danger from supporters of the king in the north corresponded more closely to reality than did that of the other leaders involved, and accordingly he chafed at delays resulting from needless cautionary tactics.[30] It is, however, quite wrong to accept the generally held notion that Delamer sparked the flame of northern revolt on his own by taking up arms and declaring for the prince on November 15.[31] To do so is to ignore the overwhelming weight of evidence conclusively demonstrating that his actions were part of the generally agreed plan for the northern risings, which called for him to join the Earl of Devonshire and a half dozen other peers at Nottingham on November 21.[32]

That Delamer took up arms as early as he did was a compound of the distance between his country seat (located just outside Altrincham) and Nottingham and the time needed to raise and organize troops. Obviously the other leading participants in the northern risings were in motion some time before the twenty-first, but in general they were more circumspect in their conduct so as not to give alarm or to commit themselves too fully in case of unexpected complications. But Delamer's political proclivities were such that it would have been difficult in the best of circumstances to disguise the purport of his activities. In the eyes of one critic he was "The King of Hearts."

> I sing the man that rais'd a Shirtless Band
> Of *Northern* Rabble, when the Prince did land;
> A Sniveling Heroe with a Weasel Face,
> And Features which an Eunuch would disgrace;
> Of a dark Spirit, turbulent and proud,
> Rude to Superiors, fawning to the Crowd;
> Prompt to Revenge, and treacherously base,
> Plotting when private, blustring when in place;
> Too weak to hurt, yet ever working ill,
> Harmless in Action, Mischievous in Will:
> Stiff for Religion, which he ne're profest,
> A Modish Zealot, with bad Morals blest,
> Lewdly profane, and wicked like the rest;
> Sainted i'th Womb, and born with mortal hate
> To the Establish'd Forms in Church and State.[33]

Delamer's conscious avoidance of subterfuge is clearly reflected in the vigorously phrased declaration he issued, which circulated among his tenantry and dependents in Warrington, Ashton, Manchester, and the lesser villages around his country seat at Dunham Massey.[34] Unlike many position papers later to appear in the north, his statement shows no evidence of an attempt to stay within the letter of the law by couching demands in the form of a petition for a free parliament and redress of grievances. Rather, the case for supporting the Prince of Orange is put in simple terms of making a choice between acceptance of Catholicism and slavery or striking a blow for Protestantism and traditional English liberties. The general tenor of the document is such that Delamer's total commitment to removing James II from power cannot be mistaken.

Although their numbers were not large, other prominent men were associated with the movement in Cheshire at this juncture. Perhaps most important was the Earl of Derby who, as a result of advice received from the Cockpit circle, had initiated correspondence with Delamer in late October. The result was a meeting on November 1 at the village of Bold, located halfway between Dunham Massey and Knowsley, where arrangements were concerted for the role each would play in the northern risings. Derby, for his part, was initially to conceal his support for the prince in order to avoid having his commission as lord lieutenant of Cheshire and Lancashire revoked. Instead, he was to ignore Delamer's activities until the latter was safely clear of the area, and then call out the militia and quarter a troop of horse at Warrington to protect Delamer's family and property from possible Catholic reprisals. By this plan control of the two counties for the prince would be secured with minimal difficulty. Moreover, the militia could be used to deal with any Catholic countermovement—the proportion of Romanists being high[35]—and also to block troop movements from Ireland.

While Derby technically fulfilled his part of the bargain, he moved so cautiously that at worst the king could have accused him of being dilatory. On the one hand, he promptly dispatched a copy of Delamer's declaration to Lord Preston and took no action against Colonel Henry Gage's new regiment of foot—raised in Lancashire and composed largely of Roman Catholics—as it marched from that county to take up quarters at Chester castle. On the other hand, early reports about Delamer's activities were ignored so that it was too late to do anything by the time orders were received from the privy council to suppress the movement. It would also appear that Derby had come to an understanding with the governor of Chester, Peter Shakerley, about securing the surrender of that garrison if the circumstances warranted such a move. Despite his seeming ambivalence, however, not a few people felt that Derby was acting "as coning as his predesessor was in Crookback Richards time."[36]

The only other peer directly associated with Delamer at this time was Viscount Cholmondeley, a moderate Whig with considerable estates centering on Malpas in southern Cheshire. When or by whom he was brought into the conspiracy is difficult to determine, although there is evidence to suggest advance preparation for the northern risings.[37] Accounts vary considerably about which members of the gentry took up arms with Delamer and Cholmondeley, but apparently a dozen or more Cheshire squires—eldest sons in a number of instances—were party to the movement. Very little is known about most of these men and even less about their activities and attitudes just prior to the revolution. If there is a common denominator, it exists in the form of family connection or previous political association with Delamer. Taking up arms under the leadership of a man so totally committed to the prince's cause was a risky business, and men of substance could hardly be expected to take the gamble unless there was an established element of trust and similarity of outlook.[38]

While one might suppose that Delamer's reputation discouraged others from joining the movement, it does not seem to be the most significant factor. Rather, the pattern established in Cheshire and elsewhere in the north was one which saw only those members of the gentry initially making an appearance who were either connected with or in some sense dependents of the nobles involved. There was, as Kenyon has noted, something almost feudal in the fact that those who acted did so in the train of one or another member of the peerage. Clearly the marked decline in the influence and power of the titled aristocracy in the earlier seventeenth century was largely a thing of the past by 1688. The role and function of the nobility obviously had changed considerably in the intervening years, but as a class it was well on the way toward re-establishing a predominance in English society that was to be a hallmark of the eighteenth century.[39]

After Delamer gave the signal to take up arms on November 15, he and his associates spent the next few days raising horse, organizing the new levies, and trying to secure arms. The majority of the recruits assembled on Bowden Downs were drawn from among the tenantry of the leading participants, and in this connection it should be noted that the declaration issued was less a position paper than an attempt to sway men of this background. Delamer himself appeared in many villages and towns in which he had tenants, openly declaring for the Prince of Orange and seeking followers. At Manchester he also managed to recruit a number of supporters from the company of foot temporarily quartered there.[40] Had considerations of mobility not precluded raising foot, it is clear that a very substantial body of men could have been raised. As it was, a party of about three hundred horse—ill trained and poorly armed for the most part—had been readied to begin the march to Nottingham on the morning of November 18.

Delamer's line of march brought his troops to Newcastle-under-Lyme the first night out. Near that point a wagon of arms intended for the company of foot at Manchester was seized, and the following morning all moneys in the hands of hearth and excise collectors were taken up after Delamer again declared himself in arms for the defense of Protestantism and the Prince of Orange at a mass meeting in the market square. There, as elsewhere along the route to Nottingham, the response of the populace was overwhelmingly favorable to an undertaking whose objectives were depicted in these terms. At no point was the support of the "rabble" effectively countered by royalist partisans or local officials. The Earl of Derby had, of course, done nothing to hinder passage through Cheshire. Lord Aston, the Catholic lord lieutenant of Staffordshire, was apparently well-intentioned, but the militia was in such a state of total disorganization that his efforts were hopeless from the start. When he finally summoned the militia horse to meet at the county town, so few appeared and their reliability seemed so questionable that they were dismissed almost immediately. Meanwhile, Delamer and his Cheshire supporters marched from Newcastle to Uttoxeter and then to Derby. Sometime in the afternoon of November 21 this contingent, swelled by new recruits to perhaps four hundred in number, rode into Nottingham where the Earl of Devonshire had already taken up quarters.[41]

A colorful figure in the revolutionary panorama, Lord Delamer was considered particularly newsworthy, and as reports of his activities were passed along they lost nothing in the telling. The first estimates in general circulation put the number of horse under his command as high as two thousand; there were continuing accounts of depredations visited upon Catholics and their houses of worship, and at Oxford Anthony Wood found no difficulty in giving credit to a report that Delamer had taken up arms with the cry "No Bishops."[42] Delamer himself was not unaware of the psychological advantage to be gained from publicity that inflated the strength of the movement against the king.[43] In fact, his penchant for public pronouncement on matters of personal principle and policy may well have been intended to focus attention on his actions from the very first. Whatever the case, the central government assisted in putting Delamer in the limelight by requesting intelligence concerning his actions and the size of his following from postmasters and other likely informants along the probable line of march to Nottingham.

Meanwhile, the Earl of Devonshire and his immediate associates were involved in preparing for their part in the rising. The first stages of their effort were accomplished with minimal fanfare, and as a result there are some serious gaps in the evidence pertaining to their activity. It is clear, however, that the earl cannot have taken up arms much later than Delamer, for he entered the town of Derby on November 17 accompanied by a sizeable retinue of horse drawn from among his tenantry and household, and even including men then employed in the reconstruction of Chatsworth.[44]

Derby apparently served as something akin to a staging area, and there the Earl of Devonshire was joined by a number of the gentry from his own and surrounding counties. Unfortunately, no detailed record of the identity of these men has survived; the only two who can be named specifically are Sir Scrope Howe and Sir William Russell, both of whom came in accompanied by a party of some fifteen fully armed men the same day as the earl.[45] While intelligence reaching the central government referred to a "great concourse" of men assembling at the county seat, the numbers involved were quite probably less than two hundred.[46] Additional support was needed, but general recruitment required a declaration of objectives in both the immediate and broader sense, which in turn would have made a mockery of the plans and precautions adopted for securing Nottingham and York without untoward incident.

Certainly those at Derby could not have known that the entire project would be carried out with relative ease, and presumably they still believed that their objectives were a well kept secret. Doubtless this partially accounts for Devonshire's delay in issuing any sort of position paper explaining his activities until just before leaving for Nottingham. Even then the statement he made, apparently delivered to an open assemblage of townspeople and corporation officials, was indeed a cautious one compared to Delamer's publication. The grievances mentioned are much the same—the present danger to the laws, liberties, and religion of the English people—but the essence of the content is an appeal for the meeting of a free parliament.

By tradition, the Prince of Orange's declaration is also supposed to have been read, yet it is interesting to note that Devonshire himself made no outright commitment to William's cause and studiously avoided any implication of acting in concert with him against the king.[47] While some apparently assumed that nothing less than rebellion was intended no matter what the tenor of the earl's remarks, a few members of the gentry in the vicinity were evidently ready to throw in their lot with him in any event. However, the vast majority of this class, including men of such substance and influence on the local scene as John Coke and Sir Henry Every, seem to have remained aloof and unsure of what interpretation to put on this turn of events.[48]

What with the absence of the lord lieutenant and the total disorganization of the militia, Devonshire had stood in no danger of organized opposition in Derbyshire, and there was little immediate prospect of interruption when his followers moved into Nottingham on the afternoon of November 20. At this juncture the Duke of Newcastle had just left York, moving without hindrance because the conspirators there had made a last minute change of plans. But he was not to receive notice of the impending danger to Nottingham until the following day, which saw him vainly waiting at Tadcaster for the Yorkshire militia horse to respond to his summons.[49]

Meanwhile, Devonshire found the Earl of Stamford waiting for him at Nottingham with wagons and arms. He was also met there with a message from the Earl of Danby containing news of the final resolutions of the earl's associates. To this a reply was made indicating that Lord Delamer was expected the following day, that a messenger had been dispatched to the prince, and that word had been sent south to the Earl of Manchester and others urging them to come to Nottingham immediately.[50] Just as in the case of Derby, however, Devonshire made no declaration of objectives upon his arrival in town. Even after Delamer joined the earl on November 21, the matter of a public pronouncement was delayed some four days, although the appearance of the peers in question was generally associated with the Prince of Orange's invasion and the summoning of a free parliament.

There is no direct evidence to explain this delay in taking a stand, but it may be reflective of the tensions that developed among the leaders of the movement then at Nottingham. Delamer, in particular, was anxious to set out to join William as soon as possible. He seems to have felt that Devonshire had been remiss in failing to bring more men into the project in advance and in his reluctance to make an open and clearcut commitment to the prince's cause once he had taken up arms. If Morrice is to be credited on this point,[51] the antagonisms that developed between these two peers over questions of policy and strategy led directly to Delamer's decision to strike out for the southwest just three days after his arrival. Devonshire, on the other hand, chose to remain at Nottingham with his supporters in order to recruit additional horse and to await specific direction from the prince before making a move.

As already noted, the earl's contingent was not particularly strong in numbers, which gave rise to the possibility that Delamer's withdrawal would leave him exposed if a royalist force should make an appearance. Since the temper of the city was still only a matter of speculation, an experiment was devised to test the sentiment of the populace.[52] Accordingly, a false alarm was given to the effect that a segment of the royal army was approaching from the south, and an appeal was made to the citizenry to join the men already in arms to prevent the town from being occupied. The response was immediate and positive. Under the direction of Delamer's lieutenants the Trent bridge was barricaded, boats in the area were drawn up on the north bank and secured, and hastily improvised fortifications appeared within a matter of hours. Although a public declaration had yet to be issued, a considerable element among the inhabitants of the borough had drawn their own conclusions as to the issues at stake.

As far as can be determined, there was no significant pro-royalist opposition. Certainly the officials of the corporation did nothing, despite the fact that London had urged the magistracy to prevent any concurrence between the populace—particularly the Dissenters in the city—and the insurgents. Given Delamer's reputation as a sympathizer with Nonconformity, the central government apparently feared that its efforts to attract the support of this group would be effectively counteracted. In all probability this is precisely what happened, and it is doubtful that the corporation could have stemmed the tide even if it had attempted to do so. The local officials were in an isolated and insecure position at best, and their policy throughout the period of the rising was an attempt to maintain their neutrality so as to avoid trouble whichever way events turned.[53]

The ruse devised to test the sentiment of the citizenry having produced such a positive response, Delamer directed his followers to leave for Derby that evening as a first step on the route to join forces with the Prince of Orange. He himself remained at Nottingham until the following morning, November 24, when the principals involved in the rising issued a joint declaration at the Saturday market.[54]

The content of this statement indicates that it was a composite work—a compromise between the more cautious petition for a free parliament put out by Devonshire at Derby and the trenchantly phrased appeal for support produced by Delamer in Cheshire. Defense of the traditional laws, liberties, and religion of the English is the statement's justification for taking up arms, with substantive redress of grievances by a freely elected parliament the declared objective. There is an extensive listing of acts reflective of the "Arbitrary and Tyrannical Government" resulting from the "Influence of Jesuitical Councels," acts which range from maintenance of a standing army to attacks upon the established church. All told, there is nothing unexpected in the content of this document, yet at the same time it represents a powerfully phrased catalogue of the immediate issues leading to revolt. Furthermore, in distinct contrast to the declaration circulating simultaneously at York,[55] there is open expression of support for the Prince of Orange and a general appeal for assistance in the movement against James II.

Delamer's departure was marked by a switch in partners, with the Earl of Stamford accompanying his cousin and Viscount Cholmondeley remaining behind with Devonshire and Sir Scrope Howe. Although reports vary concerning the size of the contingent Delamer and Stamford took with them, there were perhaps four hundred horse consisting primarily of men who had originally come from Cheshire. Presumably news of the king's retreat from Salisbury had not yet reached the north, and the line of march was accordingly selected with an eye to avoiding contact with the royal army. Hence Delamer's party first moved west to Lichfield and then turned more directly south, passing through Birmingham and Worcester before arriving at Gloucester on the last day of the month. There a message was dispatched to William, who by this time was about fifteen miles from Salisbury, requesting orders and indicating intent to quarter at Bristol until direction was received.[56]

Not the slightest opposition was encountered during the entire march south, although a determined effort by the militia of even one county could have disrupted the progress of the Cheshire contingent. The only lord lieutenant along Delamer's path who made any stand for the king was the Duke of Beaufort, who had managed to capture Lord Lovelace as he tried to make his way to the prince with a small group of retainers. Before the end of November, however, Beaufort had lost his nerve as the prince's army advanced and as promised reinforcements from the king failed to appear. Ultimately, the duke's solution to this dilemma was to drop out of sight. Delamer and his followers accordingly encountered no difficulty in freeing Lord Lovelace from the Gloucester jail, and when they arrived at Bristol on December 2 a task force from William was already in control of the city.[57]

Two days later the prince finally directed Delamer and Stamford to join their men with the main body of his army at Hungerford on December 7.[58] By the time this was accomplished, events in the south were already nearing a stage that rendered this small accretion of strength relatively unimportant. However, Delamer and Stamford had performed signal service by marching rapidly south to link up with William, for rumor generated by their movement had contributed to the general confusion and disorganization of the royalist side. Moreover, the reports relating to Delamer and Cholmondeley which earlier reached the king at Salisbury may well have been a factor in his decision to return to London rather than test his army against that of William.[59]

The Cheshire contingent carried messages south that the parties of cavalry assembling at Nottingham and York intended to follow suit shortly. At least initially, Devonshire and his followers planned to leave Nottingham by November 28 at the latest; whether the Earl of Danby and his Yorkshire associates were prepared to move out at the same time is more difficult to determine.[60] However, Devonshire's need to raise additional horse and funds caused the projected date of departure to be advanced almost immediately. The last week in November found the earl and his associates moving along the four sides of a trapezoid formed by the towns of Nottingham, Derby, Chesterfield, and Mansfield recruiting followers and seizing excise and hearth moneys in the hands of local collectors. Simultaneously, Sir Scrope Howe sent a representative into Leicestershire to seek men willing to take up arms there, although this was apparently an isolated instance of active recruitment outside the general geographical limits of the two county area.[61]

By the end of November, Devonshire had approximately doubled the size of his following, which was organized into a regiment of horse consisting of eight or nine troops of about fifty men each.[62] He himself assumed command with the rank of colonel, and his immediate subordinate was John Coke of Melbourne. While Coke was fitted for the position by virtue of previous military experience, his appointment as lieutenant colonel was at least partly political in motivation. Excepting Sir Scrope Howe, he was the only member of the greater gentry from the two counties actually in arms and, even more important, he was the sole Tory of prominence associated with the rising at Nottingham.

Just when Coke was first approached is difficult to determine, but as late as November 24 he was disclaiming knowledge of or association with the rising at Nottingham.[63] However, he may have been contacted by Devonshire when the latter returned to Derby a second time on November 26, since a day later Coke appeared there with nine followers and thirty horses. A man given to action by impulse and a dedicated, longstanding opponent of James II's policies, his willingness to take up arms is not overly surprising. In the end, events were to lead a good deal further than Coke's principles would allow him to go. Yet initially he seems to have been inspired by a flexibility of Tory conscience similar to that of Bishop Compton, which made resistance to the throne a necessity if not a virtue.[64]

Coke and Howe were the only two members of the greater gentry, those men whose wealth and standing made them leading figures on the local scene, who can be identified as appearing in Devonshire's train. Others of similar status—Anchitell Grey and Sir Thomas Gresley from Derbyshire and Charles Hutchinson from Nottinghamshire—contributed money and horses and, in Hutchinson's case, joined in issuing the declaration.[65] These men were a part of the same Whig tradition as the earl, but there were as many and more of similar background who did little or nothing. In Derbyshire, for instance, both Sir Philip Gell and Sir John Curzon ignored direct appeals for assistance. And in Nottinghamshire Sir Thomas Parkyns, who had been in the forefront of the Whig opposition to surrender of the county town's charter in 1682, apparently sat out events at home, while William Sacheverell limited his role to providing some wagons and ammunition.[66]

Rather, it was men like Francis Palmes of Stapleford, John Charleton of Breason, Philip Prime of South Normanton, and James Wright of Shirland who actively assisted in recruitment and served as officers in the regiment. In general they were drawn from the ranks of the lesser gentry of the two counties, and insofar as can be determined they were Whigs and at least sympathetic to the Nonconformists.[67] Presumably the social status and political outlook of these men made them amenable to the influence of the Earl of Devonshire. In fact, the support of some may have been secured before the start of the rising. While it is often assumed that the dependence of the gentry on the nobility was a thing of the past by the later seventeenth century, clientage among the lesser gentry is a phenomenon which clearly needs further investigation.

The number of men in arms at Nottingham was more than doubled on November 29 with the arrival of the Earls of Manchester, Northampton, and Scarsdale, and Lord Grey de Ruthin at the head of almost five hundred horse. Although these peers had originally agreed to come in whenever William landed in the north, the descent at Torbay had put a very different complexion on matters. A lengthy period of indecision followed, for the king's army stood between this group—whose collective base of power (with the exception of Scarsdale) centered in the southern midlands—and the forces of the prince in the west.[68] But eventually they responded to Devonshire's strong recommendation that they come north as previously arranged so that new plans could be concerted jointly.[69]

Included in this contingent from the southern midlands were two troops of horse from the Buckinghamshire militia—an area known for the strength of both Whig and dissenting elements— which apparently were raised under pretense of an order from the privy council by two officers party to the conspiracy. Otherwise this force was composed of smaller groups of men recruited by the leading figures involved. Captain Henry Bertie, younger brother of the Earl of Abingdon, brought in fifty horse from Oxfordshire.[70] The Earl of Manchester and Lord Grey de Ruthin each headed up a party of about twenty men when they joined the Earls of Northampton and Scarsdale at Castle Ashby before moving on to a general rendezvous at the county seat. Among prominent members of the gentry making an appearance were the Montagus of Horton, connections of the Earl of Manchester and a family of considerable political weight,[71] and Sir Justinian Isham, a leading figure among the Tory squirearchy of Northamptonshire.

The constituent elements of this contingent had converged upon the town of Northampton on November 26, with the intention of remaining there for several days to allow further recruitment. There is no evidence of a declaration being issued, but it was perfectly clear that the men involved had taken up arms against the king. Plans to raise additional horse were disrupted, however, by a rumor that a regiment of dragoons, on the march from Salisbury, expected to quarter at Banbury the night of November 27. While the report had no basis in fact, the spectre of actual combat led to the decision to set out for Nottingham immediately via Market Harborough and Leicester.[72]

With the addition of this force from the southern midlands, the total number of insurgents at Nottingham was still something less than one thousand. Efforts were made to secure sufficient arms and to impose effective military discipline, but not much could be expected considering the lack of experienced officers.[73] Unquestionably, any confrontation with regular units from the army would have ended in disaster. Even the Duke of Newcastle, had he possessed a modicum of talent, should have been able to put together some combination of royalists and militia units sufficient to make things difficult. Shortly after his departure from York on November 21, however, the duke saw fit to retire to Welbeck Abbey. There he remained for the duration, less than twenty-five miles from Nottingham.

While one newsletter indicates that Newcastle embarked on a futile attempt to raise the Nottinghamshire militia,[74] he was clearly regarded as too ineffectual to pose any serious threat to those in arms. The Earl of Devonshire actually tried to enlist his support toward the end of November, but apparently he was more interested in the arms for the militia stored at Welbeck than Newcastle's physical presence. Eventually two troops of horse, one from York and the other from Nottingham, relieved him of all weapons and horses in his possession. The response to this affront to ducal dignity was a letter demanding the return of both and a plaintive missive to London protesting that his wife and servants had betrayed him at this critical juncture. With the disarming of Newcastle, any possibility of effective royalist opposition within the area seemed at an end.[75]

Meanwhile, the Earl of Devonshire was still thinking in terms of marching south to join the prince at the earliest possible moment.[76] Difficulties in recruitment and organization, compounded by the relative slowness of the southern midlands contingent in making an appearance, had delayed matters considerably. But it is apparent that Devonshire had no strategy or plan of action based on a continuing independent movement in the north. Presumably the other peers associated with him—the Earls of Manchester, Northampton, and Scarsdale, Viscount Cholmondeley, and Lord Grey de Ruthin—were in basic agreement. Differences would surely have emerged had there been any effort to define ultimate objectives in joining William, but as yet the momentum of events sustained a basic unanimity.

There was, accordingly, no attempt to establish a power base in Nottinghamshire such as Danby was putting together at York. The possibility of playing kingmaker or arbiter between princes seems to have been the exclusive preserve of the former lord treasurer. Furthermore, reports to the effect that the northern lords, including both those at Nottingham and York, intended to march upon London directly to demand a free parliament were entirely without foundation.[77] Nottingham was basically regarded as a convenient and reasonably safe rallying point for one group of royal opponents once the prospect of a northern landing ended. Activity there was merely a preliminary to joining forces with William. Any expectation of moving south in the first week of December ended, however, with the news that Princess Anne was making her way north and could be expected at Nottingham momentarily. Her presence was to alter profoundly the scope, character, and orientation of the rising.

VII

PRINCESS ANNE AND THE NORTH

PRINCESS Anne has generally received an unfavorable press from historians, but it is unfortunate that the significance of her role in the revolution has elicited so little attention. Her attitudes and activities in the autumn of 1688 were of importance to both James II and William of Orange, to say nothing of the English supporters of the prince. As the only Protestant member of the immediate royal family in the country, a favorable stance on her part would have assisted either side. Furthermore, when Anne openly cast her lot with those in rebellion, many then found it possible to differentiate between taking up arms in opposition to James II and challenging the established social order. This was an important distinction in an age when the political power exercised by a monarch was still generally regarded as a property right.[1] With Anne, Mary, and William united against the king, the revolution could be viewed as an attempt by the immediate heirs to prevent the wasting of the family estate.

Initially, James had little reason to suspect that Anne was in any way connected with William's supporters, and he certainly was unaware of the secret correspondence passing between the princess and The Hague. In this respect William had carefully prepared the ground before his coming. Anne's basic Protestant prejudice had been cultivated to the extent that she clearly favored the project, at least in terms of the limited objectives outlined in her brother-in-law's declaration. For a person of Anne's upbringing and station the choice between two loyalties was particularly difficult, but her decision was reflective of the sense of urgency that dominated the thoughts of many. Direct action was necessary to prevent her father from recatholicizing England.[2]

After William landed, Anne seems to have wavered between remaining at the Cockpit and withdrawing into the city of London to stay with Bishop Compton.[3] The former alternative was plausible so long as the principal theater of action was centered in the west. Prince George and Lord Churchill would actually cross the lines to join William at the appropriate moment, but the princess herself could sit out events without having to make a move. On the other hand, complications might arise that would leave her in an exposed position if no line of retreat were open. This contingency accounts for the fact that Compton remained in London rather than joining William or those in arms at Nottingham and York.

As circumstances proved, the precaution was a wise one, for word was received at Whitehall on November 24 that James expected to return to the capital two days later.[4] This information placed Anne in a difficult situation. A confrontation with the king was inevitable given the suspicions aroused by the desertion of Prince George and other intimates of the Cockpit. Accordingly, the princess dispatched Lady Churchill to meet with the Bishop of London, and they arranged for Anne to withdraw secretly from the palace on the night of November 25.

Unfortunately, the timing involved leaves open the question as to whether the princess waited to receive definite news of her husband's departure from the royal camp before acting. The official express bringing word of the defections apparently arrived in London several hours after the plans for leaving the Cockpit had already been laid.[5] While a number of retrospective accounts by contemporaries suggest that a private messenger bearing the same information reached Anne in advance,[6] the point may be considered of relatively minor importance. Given the definite commitment of Prince George and the others to join

William, news of the king's impending return left the princess with little choice but flight. The alternative was to allow herself to be subjected to James's will, and she was sufficiently in tune with the spirit that had given rise to the invasion—as well as genuinely fearful of her father's wrath—to rule out that possibility.[7]

The rescue mission engineered by the Bishop of London has something of the flavor of a twentieth-century spy thriller. Compton and his nephew, the Earl of Dorset, arrived by prearrangement in the vicinity of the Cockpit about one o'clock on the morning of November 26. Meanwhile, Anne had retired at her usual time that evening to avoid suspicion, but at the appointed hour she slipped out a street door accompanied only by Lady Churchill and the wife of Colonel John Berkley, another of those deserting the king at Andover. Juncture with their rescuers was effected without difficulty, and the entire party then proceeded to the house in London that Compton had been using as a retreat. Although one of the sentries at the Cockpit witnessed a coach picking up passengers, he did not recognize the individuals involved.

An hour's delay and the situation would have been quite different, for by then the queen had posted a guard to ensure that the princess and the two ladies in question did not leave their lodgings. However, Anne's absence was not detected until the following morning, since the guard was under strict orders not to disturb her. By that time not the slightest clue could be found to indicate what had happened to the princess. So effectively were her whereabouts concealed that several days passed before reports told of her passage through the town of Hitchin in the company of the Bishop of London and a small party of horse.[8]

Anne's sole desire was to rejoin her husband. But with the roads to the west choked with royal troops, a roundabout route through the north was indicated. Presumably such a plan was attractive to Compton, since he was so closely linked with the northern risings and would be on home ground in terms of family connections and influence in the Northamptonshire area. In any event, the journey actually began on the morning of November 26 when Anne, the bishop, and perhaps a dozen others left London for Copt Hall in Essex, the country seat of the Earl of Dorset. The following day this group, now accompanied by a small party of horse recruited among the local gentry, moved on to Hawnes, Bedfordshire. With Lord Carteret and others joining the cavalcade en route, the princess arrived at the Earl of Northampton's seat at Castle Ashby on November 28. In view of the fact that Northampton and his associates had set out for Nottingham on the preceding afternoon, it is clear that the decision to take Anne into the north had been made on the spur of the moment and without establishing contact with those in arms.[9]

For reasons of security the movement of Anne's party was cloaked in secrecy during the first stages of the journey to Nottingham. By the time the princess arrived at Market Harborough, however, it was considered safe to make open appeals for support and protection. News of her presence in Leicestershire spread rapidly, and her escort was considerably enlarged by the addition of several parties of horse brought in by local men of substance such as Lord Cullen and Sir Charles Shuckburgh. Almost immediately Anne's flight began to assume the proportions of a royal progress, which culminated in an official celebration upon arrival in the county town. There Anne spent two nights before finally moving on to Nottingham on December 2.[10]

From the standpoint of the general atmosphere among governmental circles in London, Anne's flight into the north contributed substantially to a feeling of being caught in an ineluctable train of events. News of desertions, defections, and disloyalty in the form of risings and petitions for a free parliament flowed in from many directions, and to this confusion was now added the psychological impact of the mysterious departure of a leading Protestant member of the royal family from the Cockpit.[11] Rumors that Anne had been spirited away by the papists were bad enough, but the realization that she had willingly put herself in the hands of William's supporters indicated an inexorable trend that was to leave the king and his Catholic advisors completely isolated.

Anne's arrival at Nottingham was not, however, an unmixed blessing for the Earl of Devonshire and his associates. On the one hand, her presence seemed to put something akin to a stamp of approval on the proceedings there, with the consequence that many men who had held aloof by reason of conscience or circumspection now saw their way clear to coming into the city. On the other hand, the focus of the movement became somewhat obscured, since the assembled forces came to include peers and members of the gentry committed only to providing for the protection and safety of the princess. Not surprisingly, disputes and tensions between these men and the original participants in the rising quickly surfaced. Leadership was difficult in such a fluid situation, but the Earl of Devonshire and Bishop Compton emerge as the primary figures, with Anne's wishes clearly regarded as of paramount importance.[12]

No basic change of objectives was necessary, but it was essential to await specific instructions from William before attempting to bring the princess south.[13] Anne was too important a personage in the game to venture forth without permission from the top—especially since no one at Nottingham had specific knowledge as to the prince's whereabouts, his immediate plans, or what the king and his army might be doing.[14] Furthermore, the force assembled in the city suddenly seemed very inadequate for the task of providing escort, for despite a numerical strength of a thousand horse, it was still sadly lacking in training, discipline, and experienced officers. In retrospect this amateur army was more than sufficient for the job. But Anne's arrival was immediately preceded by reports that James had dispatched troops to take her prisoner,[15] and there were also rumors concerning the activities of a regiment of Lancashire Catholics supposedly raised by Viscount Molyneux.

Unlike many of the rumors current during the revolution, those relating to the Lancashire regiment had some factual basis, although the truth of the matter was considerably distorted as it passed from mouth to mouth. Actually, command of this unit was vested in Colonel Henry Gage rather than Viscount Molyneux; confusion on this score among contemporaries seems to have arisen because the latter's son served as lieutenant colonel.[16] Gage was commissioned about the first of October, and it is clear that the king expected him to recruit men among the Catholics of Lancashire just as the Duke of Newcastle was supposed to do in Northumberland. The regiment was still in process of formation, with component elements quartered in a number of Lancashire towns, when Delamer first took up arms in Cheshire. By the end of November, however, Gage had succeeded in raising eight or nine companies composed largely of papists.

Gage apparently had orders to march his men to Chester to reinforce the small garrison charged with the defense of that city. Their arrival on the evening of November 27 very nearly precipitated a riot, for the populace was clearly anti-Catholic in sentiment and very much in sympathy with the Prince of Orange's cause. The governor of Chester castle, Peter Shakerley, had already experienced difficulty in maintaining control over the town, and for a while it appeared likely that the citizenry, in combination with two troops of the Cheshire militia stationed there, might offer open resistance to the entry of the Lancashire unit. The local magistrates finally managed to defuse the situation, but tensions ran high between Gage's men and the inhabitants of Chester during the next few weeks.[17]

Meanwhile, the Earl of Derby continued to play a balancing game. He delayed raising the militia in Cheshire and Lancashire until Delamer was safely clear of the area and then stationed units at Chester as well as at Warrington and Manchester to protect Delamer's family. He also concluded a secret agreement with Peter Shakerley for surrender of Chester castle. However, neither Derby nor Shakerley moved decisively to take control of the city for the prince until word had been received of the king's flight. Even then it was Shakerley who actually engineered the militia's admission into the castle and the disarming of Gage's regiment on December 13.[18] Despite an urgent request that Derby bring in units of the Lancashire militia to help maintain order, almost another week elapsed before the earl appeared and began to circulate a moderate declaration in support of William.[19]

It could be argued that Derby moved so cautiously between mid-November and mid-December to avoid being dismissed as lord lieutenant. Otherwise the advantage of his holding office would have been lost to the Orangist cause, particularly the ability to commission officers and to raise the Cheshire and Lancashire militias. This would have left the door open for a Catholic rising in Lancashire in support of the king. It would also have meant discarding plans for taking control of Chester, and would have prevented the earl from doing anything if Irish troops were landed in the northwest. Furthermore, there were dangers in taking an open stand because of the proximity of Colonel Gage's regiment, especially in view of the rumor that Derby's arrest had been discussed.[20]

The fact remains, however, that the necessity of decisive action in any of the above circumstances would have resulted in what was tantamount to an anti-royalist declaration. If the militia could not be depended upon then, there was little advantage in having raised it at all. The time would have been much better spent putting together a volunteer force composed of tenants, dependants, and political associates. Moreover, all companies but one of Gage's regiment were totally lacking in arms until the last week in November, a fact known to the earl and one which makes his fear of capture seem a bit exaggerated. At the very least, Derby could have adopted the Earl of Danby's strategy at York by rallying support for a free parliament without making a specific commitment to William. But Derby was very much a reluctant revolutionary. Personally he seems to have been convinced of the necessity of constraining the king, yet the risks involved made him reluctant to act decisively.

At Chester the earl's lack of nerve resulted in acute tensions between the citizenry and himself, with accusation and recrimination the order of the day. While Derby busily justified his actions in terms of the necessities of the situation, the local magistrates maintained that too little had been done too late.[21] That such was the case is not surprising, for Cheshire in general and the county town in particular were notable for a fairly extreme Whig-Nonconformist element.[22] The Earl of Derby's tepid leadership caused many to wonder where his true sympathies lay. In fact, some of the difficulties he encountered in reorganizing and raising the Cheshire militia may well have been a consequence of his lack of forwardness rather than the reverse, especially in light of the role that body played in securing control of the castle garrison.

Perhaps in this instance more clearly than any other, the problems of Whig and Tory joining together in common cause becomes apparent. The atmosphere at Chester was charged with suspicion and mistrust exacerbated by the lack of a Whig leader of sufficient stature to smooth matters over in combination with Derby. At least in the county town, Lord Delamer was a considerably more influential figure than the lord lieutenant, and to the inhabitants the Tory earl seemed to have done nothing whatever to assist Delamer or to render aid to the city itself. Derby's indecisiveness was the basis of much of the trouble, but the political tradition he represented was also considered suspect by many among the populace.

The Earl of Derby's dilatory pace, and in particular his failure to deal promptly and effectively with Colonel Gage's regiment, had an impact that went beyond the local setting. Wildly exaggerated reports circulated to the effect that Gage's Lancashire Catholics had burned Lord Delamer's house, seized Chester by force, and generally posed an unchecked menace to the population. From the south of England, Delamer reacted by dispatching a savage letter to Derby, accusing him of betraying the prince's cause as well as the agreement they had concluded in early November.[23] These same rumors largely account for the willingness of the Nottingham leadership to accept the qualified support of men basically hostile to the overall objectives of the rising.

Perhaps the most notable figure in this category was the Earl of Chesterfield, who appeared in the city with Lord Ferrers shortly after Anne's arrival.[24] Neither of these peers had been connected with the first stage of the rising, although Chesterfield had been forewarned in a general way about what would happen when the Earl of Danby had tried to enlist his support in October. While Chesterfield disapproved entirely of the princess's flight from the Cockpit, at her request he did raise about a hundred horse among his dependents and the gentry of southern Derbyshire. He refused, however, to take part in a council to coordinate the component elements of the army at Nottingham, and insisted on making a public declaration that he was taking up arms only to provide for Anne's safety.[25]

The tensions created by Chesterfield's stand were subsequently increased as the result of a none too subtle ploy used by Compton and Devonshire in an attempt to secure the earl's support for the association. Originating in the south, the association pledged those signing it to remain in arms until a free parliament met and avenge the death of the Prince of Orange should he be assassinated by Catholics.[26] Some time elapsed before word of it reached the northern insurgents, but thereafter every effort was made to secure the adherence of the peers and gentry then in process of conducting Anne toward Oxford. Chesterfield was confronted with the matter publicly, evidently in the hope that he would feel constrained to sign rather than incur general obloquy. But the earl was a man of too rigid Tory principle to be swayed in this fashion, and his refusal to engage set an example followed by several peers, including Lords Ferrers, Cullen, Brook, Leigh, and Digby, and perhaps a hundred or more of the gentlemen present.[27]

It is impossible to determine which of the gentry declined to sign the association, but in all probability the majority numbered among the party of horse Chesterfield brought in. Included in this group were men such as Sir Henry Every, his son Captain John Every, Robert Burdett of Foremark, Gilbert Thacker of Repton, John Dalton of Derby, Sir Gilbert Clarke, and apparently most of the other leading south Derbyshire gentlemen who had been sitting out events at home until Anne arrived.[28] While fewer than a dozen individuals can be specifically identified, it is clear that this group consisted primarily of the loyalist gentry dominant in local government and politics from the end of the exclusion crisis until the purges of 1687. Generally, these were the men who had been turned out of office as justices of the peace, officers in the militia, and deputy lieutenants as a consequence of their refusal to respond affirmatively to the three questions.[29] From political, religious, and personal standpoints their grievances were sufficient to ensure that they would not rally to the side of the king; but as a group they were equally unprepared to participate in a movement seemingly directed against the monarchy and headed by the Earl of Devonshire.

The arrival at Nottingham of Princess Anne, accompanied by the Bishop of London, seemed to ease the dilemma of this important sector of the gentry, who could then make a stand against the trend of royal policy without the stigma of rebellion necessarily attaching. Yet those gentlemen making an appearance could not in good conscience sign the association. To have done so would have meant obliterating the subtle but important distinction between coming to the assistance of a member of the royal family and outright support of the rising. So long as the Nottingham insurgents were not confronted by the royal army, this distinction worked to the advantage of the Williamite side, giving the illusion of an even broader base of support than was actually the case. The price to be paid for such support was acceptance of this quasi-participation and the difficulties it engendered.

In all this, the predominance of the nobility and the importance of political ties becomes apparent, for it was the Earl of Chesterfield, and to a lesser extent men like Lord Ferrers, who initiated and established the limits of semi-insurgency. Apparently, there was no corresponding success in drawing out the Tory gentry of substance in Nottinghamshire. The same general background circumstances pertain as in Derbyshire, and again these were sufficient to ensure a neutrality that worked to the detriment of James. But the two peers whose political orientation, associations, and influence put them on a par with Chesterfield—the Marquess of Halifax and the Duke of Newcastle—could not and would not do anything to bring this group into even a limited participation in the rising. Halifax, of course, was preoccupied with his role in the politicking and diplomatic maneuvering in the south, while Newcastle remained consistently obdurate throughout. Moreover, the latter's influence was still sufficient to prevent the raising of the Nottinghamshire militia to supplement the force already in arms. While some individuals may have responded to the call made by the peers at Nottingham, most seem to have given heed to Newcastle's countermanding direction and to have remained at home.[30]

In rather striking contrast, however, the Earl of Devonshire's attempt to raise the Derbyshire militia after the arrival of the princess was successful.[31] The absence from the county of the lord lieutenant, who otherwise might have been in a position to create difficulties (by this time the Earl of Huntingdon had been imprisoned following the capitulation of the garrison at Plymouth); the influence of Devonshire himself, whose family had traditionally held the post; the presence among the insurgents of the Earl of Scarsdale, who had been ousted from the lieutenancy in the purges of 1687; and the appearance at Nottingham of Chesterfield with a substantial contingent of the Tory gentry who had formerly served as deputy lieutenants and officers constitute the prime factors which in combination produced a good response to the issuance of warrants for the county horse and some companies of foot.

The Earl of Huntingdon's absence from the scene was also a factor in the subsequent success in turning out a substantial proportion of the Leicestershire militia to meet Anne as she moved south. Warrants were sent out from Nottingham over the signatures of a group of the principal gentry of the county, including men who had come in both before and after the arrival of the princess. Prominent among these were John Coke, a figure of considerable standing in Leicestershire as well as in Derbyshire, and Lord Sherard, an aging roundhead of Whig connection.[32] The efforts of this group were doubtless assisted by the presence of Lord Ferrers at Nottingham and also by the fact that the Earl of Rutland, whose family traditionally held the lieutenancy, adopted a stance of benevolent neutrality. While reluctant to commit himself to the extent of actually taking up arms, it was generally known that Rutland contributed heavily toward meeting expenses incurred by Sir Scrope Howe in connection with recruitment of horse in Leicestershire.[33]

Within a short time after warrants went out in Leicestershire, orders of a similar nature were dispatched to raise the militia in both Northampton and Warwick, counties whose shared lord lieutenant, the Earl of Sunderland, had already departed England for safer climes. In the former instance the necessary documents were sent out over the signatures of Sir Justinian Isham, John Andrews, and Christopher Montagu, three influential former deputy lieutenants who had come in with the Earl of Northampton. In the latter case the necessary directives were issued by Northampton himself, whose standing in Warwickshire had been enhanced by his removal from the lord lieutenancy in the preceding year. The response of the militia in both counties to this irregular summons was good, but the decision to act was doubtless facilitated by precedents set in the north and by the commitment of so many of the natural leaders from the area. There were men of stature and influence opposed to the proceeding, such as Viscount Hatton and the Earl of Westmorland, yet they were sufficiently attuned to the general trend of events to realize the futility of openly trying to rally support for the king.[34]

At best the county militias were inefficient, and the infrequency of musters in the reign of James II had rendered them even more disorganized than usual. While there could be serious question as to their value in any sort of military confrontation, nevertheless their response to summons doubtless had a positive psychological impact in terms of the substantial increase in the sheer number of men in arms joined in common cause. Furthermore, the very circumstances surrounding their appearance gave clear indication of the chaotic and confused condition of local government as well as the virtual collapse of royal authority. The success in raising the militia of these four counties cannot, however, be interpreted as a manifestation of widening popular sentiment favorable to the original revolutionary cadres. But for Anne's presence in the north, it is extremely doubtful that any effort would have been made to call out the militia, or that the summons would have been met with good response in the event the attempt had been made. It should be recognized that in each instance the warrants dispatched justified the action solely in terms of providing a protective escort for the princess.[35]

In the final analysis, three factors were crucial in determining which counties would supply units of horse and foot: the proposed route of the princess's southward journey, the absence or inactivity of the lord lieutenant, and the presence at Nottingham of one or more natural leaders from a given shire. With minor variations Derby, Leicester, Warwick, and Northampton all fit into the same pattern. Because of the obstruction of the Duke of Newcastle, Nottingham did not. Proximity might also have made Lincolnshire a possibility, but no substantial contingent came in from that area, and the lord lieutenant, the Earl of Lindsey, apparently through it politic to play a waiting game.

Personally, Lindsey was at least favorably disposed toward the basic objective of securing a free parliament. His son and brother, as well as other connections were in arms both at York and in the south with William, and he was also in close touch with the proceedings at York by means of correspondence with his sister and her husband, the Earl of Danby. It was not until the second week in December that Lindsey moved to arrange a meeting of the gentry, however, and several more days elapsed before an address to the prince was forthcoming, presumably in response to the news of the king's first flight.[36] Perhaps Lindsey would have moved faster if William had landed in the north.

Certainly control of Lincolnshire would have been desirable in that event, and one can probably assume that Lindsey had been brought into the conspiracy sometime in the early autumn.

Whatever the case, his departure from a public position of neutrality came much too late to be of assistance to those concerned with Anne's safety. The circumstances predicated the lord lieutenant's open cooperation if the Lincolnshire militia were to be raised, and by the time Lindsey was ready the princess was well on her way south. Further to the west, considerations of distance and the proposed route of march seem to have ruled out summoning the Staffordshire militia, although there was reason to expect a good response. Lord Aston, the Catholic lord lieutenant, had virtually abdicated his responsibilities after his ill-fated attempt to halt Lord Delamer's progress through the area. Furthermore, an assemblage of Protestant gentry had joined in declaring for a free parliament in the first week in December, and a number of prominent gentlemen—most notably the Tory John Leveson Gower—subsequently brought in parties of volunteers to Nottingham.[37]

Quite possibly the quest for reinforcements at Nottingham would have loomed less large had the Earl of Danby responded positively to suggestions that troops be sent from York.[38] The earl made no outright refusal, but instead proposed that the princess withdraw further north. He argued that Anne would be safer in Yorkshire, proposing that she take up residence at Scarborough castle from which an escape could be made by sea if the need arose. Moreover, the earl noted that her presence would be of incalculable assistance in terms of drawing waverers into the movement and securing control of the entire north.

A consideration of even greater immediacy concerned plans to secure the capitulation of the garrison at Hull, the only remaining royalist stronghold in Yorkshire. This was a project Danby had embarked upon several days earlier, and it was an undertaking expected to require a very considerable body of men. Although there are no particularly reliable estimates as to the size of the army at the earl's disposal,[39] he apparently felt that the project would have to be abandoned if any significant number of troops was diverted to Nottingham. Matters were complicated in this respect by virtue of the fact that Lord Lumley had just left York with a sizeable party of horse to engage in a recruiting expedition in Durham.[40] As events soon proved, however, force was not needed to take Hull. Sir John Hanmer, the Protestant lieutenant colonel of the regiment quartered there, engineered a bloodless coup that virtually placed the fortress at the earl's disposal.[41]

Yet even after the fall of Hull Danby demonstrated no strong inclination to send any of his troops to Nottingham.[42] Taking into account something of his personality and ambitions, it is apparent that he felt that such a step would diminish his voice in the whole affair.[43] From the very first Danby had worked to establish a solid base of power in Yorkshire and further north,[44] which clearly differentiated his efforts from those of the insurgents at Nottingham. Quite possibly he hoped that William would think conditions too unsettled to order Anne's immediate departure, and in that circumstance his offer of asylum in Yorkshire might well be accepted. Such an arrangement could have put Danby in a position to dictate the terms for settlement of the revolution. Certainly if a stalemate developed in the south he would have been left holding the balance of power by virtue of the area he controlled and his influence with one of the immediate heirs to the throne.

That Danby's calculations were actually running along these lines is further substantiated by two additional pieces of evidence. First, he asked William for a commission as lieutenant general of the five northern counties of York, Durham, Northumberland, Cumberland, and Westmorland, and at the same time he sought wide powers to raise additional troops and to collect public moneys for their support. At least as far as the supporters of the prince were concerned, the earl would have emerged as virtual viceroy of the north, with his authority further enhanced by the presence of Princess Anne.[45] Second, there is a suggestion in some sources that Danby was not totally averse to the prospect of entering into direct negotiation with James during the second week of December. It is impossible to determine how far this affair had proceeded before the king's decision to flee cut short any thought of making an appeal for the support of the assemblage at York. But the evidence is sufficient to lend additional credence to the suspicion that the earl viewed himself as something of a kingmaker.[46]

Had the wishes of the Bishop of London prevailed, it is likely that the princess and her immediate entourage would have accepted Danby's offer of protection.[47] Compton was never entirely comfortable working in tandem with Devonshire, and it was only natural that both he and Anne were inclined to gravitate toward Danby by reason of longstanding association and generally similar political outlook. Furthermore, the bishop continued to be distressed by the condition of the army at Nottingham and was disappointed that the arrival of the princess had generated no movement to issue a new declaration. That such a document was not forthcoming is hardly surprising given the divergent viewpoints of the principal figures in arms, which ran the gamut from committed Williamites like Devonshire and Howe to somewhat compromised royalists of Chesterfield's ilk. Even the most skilled of politicians would have found it next to impossible to smooth over the tensions generated among the various groups, and agreement on a common statement of purpose was obviously out of the question.

In any event, there is little likelihood that the Earl of Devonshire shared Compton's inclination to move into Yorkshire, since he had remained committed throughout the proceeding to joining William as soon as possible. However, he regarded Anne's opinion in the matter as decisive, and she was unwilling to make a decision until a reply was received to the messages dispatched to the prince on December 3.[48] The question was finally resolved a week later with the arrival of instructions directing that Anne be brought south immediately and designating the city of Oxford as the place of rendezvous.[49] Preparations for departure were immediately set in motion, and by the afternoon of December 9 the total assemblage of horse and foot at Nottingham had left the city on the first leg of the journey.

According to the Earl of Devonshire's estimate, the army accompanying Anne comprised some fifteen hundred horse and two well-armed companies of foot, which were presumably drawn from the Derbyshire militia.[50] These figures do not, of course, include the contingents of militia horse from Leicester, Northampton, and Warwick which subsequently joined the main body of troops. No precise count of the reinforcements picked up along the way to Oxford is possible, but apparently the army from Nottingham had swelled in number to well over twenty-five hundred men by the time its destination was reached.[51]

Nor is it possible to describe satisfactorily the organization of this force. The major component elements seem to have been the regiment of horse raised by Devonshire with the assistance of John Coke, a second regiment of horse recruited by Sir Scrope Howe, the considerable number of independent troops of horse brought in by other leading figures in the movement, the gentry and dependents grouped around the Earl of Chesterfield and other semi-insurgents, and the various units of militia horse and foot already mentioned. There was also a select troop of about seventy wealthy gentlemen, for the most part from the North-amptonshire area, forming a personal guard for Princess Anne. Riding under a banner inscribed "Nolumus Leges Angliae Mutari," this unit was commanded by Bishop Compton whose willingness to exchange Bible for sword elicited a great deal of comment from the Oxford dons upon his arrival there.[52]

Efforts to coordinate the various segments of this amateur army through development of an effective council of war had, of course, been frustrated in part by the Earl of Chesterfield. Even without this divisive element, however, it is doubtful that the leadership of the movement possessed either the talent or time to weld the constituent units into a tightly knit and well structured organization. Had an external threat actually materialized, necessity might have prompted selection of an overall com-mander-in-chief. Without that impetus no formal chain of com-mand developed, and decisions evidently evolved from discus-sions and consultation among the leading peers who had brought in substantial contingents.

In the circumstances, it was probably fortunate that the march to Oxford took on the character of a triumphal progress, with friendly crowds lining the route in village and town.[53] The first stage of the journey brought the total company to Leicester where the ranks were considerably swelled by the arrival of al-most all the militia horse and foot for the county. Two days later the army was again set in motion, but at this point the troops were divided into two segments. The larger contingent, includ-ing Princess Anne and most of the peers, moved on to Coventry and then more directly south through Warwick and Banbury. News of James's first attempt to leave England and of the virtual dissolution of the royal army reached this party at War-wick on December 12. With elements of the Warwickshire militia streaming in, Anne suggested to the Earl of Chester-field that his presence was no longer necessary to ensure her safety. The earl's general uncooperativeness and frequently voiced promptings of royalist conscience had made his assis-tance of limited value from the start. His departure with Lord Ferrers and a number of Derbyshire gentlemen was not a matter of consequence. Chesterfield himself was evidently quite content to withdraw, since he felt he had fulfilled his obligation to assist Anne and that further participation in the movement would require compromise of principle.[54]

Meanwhile, the smaller contingent leaving Leicester, which included John Coke's troop of horse and possibly others, fol-lowed a route taking them through Market Harborough, North-ampton, Towcester, and then west to Banbury.[55] Why this group did not accompany the main body of troops is difficult to determine. Possibly the raising of the Northamptonshire militia has some bearing on the matter, although apparently that body assembled by order at Daventry on December 12 and then marched directly south to join the main contingent at Banbury.[56] It is much more likely, however, that Coke and his followers were sent to take up hearth and excise moneys in the hands of local collectors. The various militia units raised each brought in a month's pay as stipulated in the warrants issued, but the larger problem remained of providing for the subsistence of the rest of the troops to say nothing of meeting expenses incurred for ad-ditional arms, ammunition, transport, messengers, and the like.

In large part funds for the rising at Nottingham had been sup-plied initially by the leaders of the movement.[57] Especially after Anne's arrival in the north, contributions were also forthcom-ing from a number of individuals sympathetic to the general trend of events but unwilling or unable to appear in person. As already noted, the Earl of Rutland sent a thousand pounds to Sir Scrope Howe, and others such as Sir John Gell and Anchitell Grey gave substantial support to the Earl of Devon-shire in the form of money and supplies. John Coke received well over four hundred pounds from associates and connections among the Derbyshire and Leicestershire gentry, and in Derby, Nottingham, and perhaps other towns as well, purses were circulated with varying success.[58] Even so the combined resources available were inadequate, with the result that the Earl of Devonshire issued warrants authorizing collection and expenditure of public funds. The sums impounded in the counties of Nottingham and Leicester were far from small,[59] and this may well have led to a decision to spread the nets more widely.

Coke's contingent rejoined the main body of the army at Banbury on December 13. From there the entire force moved south through Woodstock and finally reached Oxford two days later where it was met by Prince George, the Duke of Ormonde, the Earl of Abingdon, and perhaps a half dozen other peers and associates of the Cockpit circle. William himself had originally intended to be present, but had abandoned the plan because of the king's flight and the need to push on rapidly toward London.[60] Although the prince had little choice in the matter, a meeting at Oxford might have provided the basis for a working relationship with Anne. However, the importance of winning her full support and confidence had diminished substantially in comparison with the need to seize the opportunity provided by the breakdown of all royalist resistance. Matters were temporarily complicated when James returned to London briefly, but the fact still remained that the princess's immediate usefulness had become a relatively minor consideration now that she had reached an area under William's direct control.

Accordingly, the arrival of the insurgents at Oxford proved to be something less than climactic, and the immediate concern of the leading personages involved was to move on to the main arena. Since the Prince of Orange was unwilling to have the army from Nottingham brought nearer to the capital, some time was inevitably lost in making provision for the main body of troops . The militia units were simply sent home. The remaining horse and foot were quartered in and around Oxford where they remained until either disbanded or reconstituted as part of regular regiments.[61] In any event, Anne and her entourage finally reached the Cockpit again on the evening of December 19, the day after James left London the second time prior to his successful escape to France. With the exception of the Earl of Devonshire and a few close associates who joined William a day or two earlier, she was accompanied by all the nobles and more prominent gentlemen coming south from Nottingham.[62]

In a very real sense the revolution in the north ended as a separate and semi-independent movement with Anne's departure from Nottingham. It is true that the Earl of Danby and his associates remained at the head of an army at York for well over a week thereafter, but for lack of a better alternative the earl was involved in planning and preparing to take his troops south as late as December 11.[63] There was still unfinished business in terms of securing total control over the far north, for the garrisons at Carlisle, Berwick, and Tynemouth held firm until word of the king's flight was received. Yet once the princess had left for Oxford, Danby evidently concluded that he stood little chance of influencing the outcome of events unless he also moved to join William.

The coincidence of a complex series of factors temporarily diverted him, however, and of these it was the turmoil caused by the Irish scare that delayed him the longest. Spreading northward from London, rumors that the Irish Catholic soldiery disbanded by James was running amuck generated a massive panic, which was particularly severe in the midlands and further north.[64] With reports of burning, massacres, and unchecked pillaging coming in from several directions and seemingly providing collective corroboration, the earl dropped any thought of leaving Yorkshire and began to organize his forces to meet the Irish menace. Not until December 19, some five days after the first alarm had been received, were these false harbingers sufficiently discredited to allow disbandment of the army there as ordered by William. Thereupon Danby set out for London in the company of some eighty gentlemen involved in the rising, finally arriving in the capital on Christmas day.[65]

The events that followed were a part of the revolutionary settlement rather than the revolution itself, which was basically an accomplished fact by the last week in December. While this was not immediately apparent to contemporaries, much of the ensuing debate and discussion represented little more than the slow process of adjusting to the new reality. The question of James's religion aside, too many peers and commoners sitting in the Convention had worked closely enough with William or his more ardent supporters to risk the consequences of the king's return to power.

This was a political fact of life accepted by all the participants

118

in the rising at Nottingham who subsequently sat in the Convention. Even the nine men among this group who stood opposed to declaring the throne vacant fit into the pattern.[66] Had the goals of the movement against the king been defined in this context initially, or had the final outcome of the prince's expedition been apparent, it is doubtful that any of the nine would have given even limited assistance in the north. Yet once the course of events had moved to its logical conclusion, they recognized that there could be no turning back. Their alternative to dethroning James was the establishment of a regency. Such a plan would have salved the less flexible Tory consciences and also have avoided the tensions generated by the question of Anne's place in the succession.[67] It was not a totally implausible solution until William put an end to the idea by setting his price.

In the House of Commons there was a sufficient majority prepared to offer the crown to William and Mary to allow men such as John Coke and Sir Justinian Isham to continue their protest in principle without significant adverse effect. The situation was much tighter in the Lords, however, and it should be noted that the Earl of Chesterfield and Lord Ferrers as well as other peers not connected with the rising at Nottingham—men who had pressed strongly against declaring the throne vacant—simply abstained from the final crucial vote on February 6.[68] By this tactic they permitted a final resolution and settlement of the immediate crisis of government. Clearly the power elites represented in the Convention were agreed not to let the revolution proceed further, but beyond that there was no general consensus.

VIII

Some General Conclusions

Renewed interest in the revolution of 1688 has resulted in a better understanding of the complexity of the event, while at the same time pointing up the need for further investigation and research. Until studies of the revolution in Scotland and Ireland and additional work in regional and local history are undertaken, there is simply no basis for sweeping generalizations about the deposition of James II and its consequences. Yet the evidence clearly indicates that what happened in England during this period was not a revolution, except perhaps in the narrowest sense of the word. If the term is to be used at all, it can be applied much more aptly to the policies and objectives of the king than to the activities of his opponents. In their view James had embarked upon a program designed to alter the traditional power structure, social order, and religious complexion of the country. And to no small extent this was what the king intended when it became impossible to work through the traditional power elites.

Essentially, the revolution was a successful *coup d'état* engineered by forward elements among the political nation in combination with the Prince of Orange. It was of relatively limited immediate consequence in terms of the two principal institutions of central government—monarchy and parliament. While subsequent political, social, and economic developments may have brought about significant constitutional alterations over a period of time, these changes cannot be traced directly to the movement against the king. It is, of course, highly unlikely that the term revolution will cease to be used in reference to the events of 1688, especially since contemporaries referred to it in that manner. But at least historians might more properly adopt the designation of "conservative" rather than "glorious" revolution.

Institutions of government on the local and national level, the church, the law, and almost every other important aspect of social and political organization were operated by and for the benefit of the upper classes in later seventeenth century England. The administration of James II posed a threat to this arrangement, and accordingly the political elites united in opposition to the king. Fear of Roman Catholicism provided an immediate and real issue, but the stress contemporaries placed on this should not be allowed to obscure the larger challenge to property, prestige, privilege, and power that was inherent in royal policy. Fear of Catholicism also provided a convenient handle for rallying mass support behind the opponents of the king. However, the revolution did not in any significant sense represent a popular uprising against James. It was an upper class movement initiated and dominated by members of the nobility and scions of aristocratic houses. Considered from this angle, the revolution can be interpreted as yet another manifestation of the centuries old struggle between baronage and crown.

Obviously the composition and function of the titled aristocracy was far different from what it had been in the middle ages. But the increasing wealth and prestige of the later seventeenth century nobility cast it in a role of leadership not totally dissimilar to that of its medieval counterpart when monarchy became too insensitive to the upper class viewpoint. As the greatest beneficiaries of the political and social system in Restoration England, the peerage also stood to be the greatest losers as the result of James's policies. Opposition in principle thus merged with opposition to the implied threat to the position of the peerage, and the resultant fusion provided both the impetus and rationale for action. However, the objectives were strictly limited, for as the first Duke of Newcastle had pointed out to Charles II, "the worste In the Nobiliteye Is butt to pull downe one kinge & sett upp an other, So that theye are alwayes for monarkeye. . . ."[1]

In this connection something must be said about the role of the Prince of Orange. Recent scholarship has provided a much needed corrective to earlier interpretations of the revolution which ignored William's contribution, to say nothing of his objectives. Clearly the prince had his eyes fixed on the English crown from the outset, and it is apparent that he played a crucial role in initiating the train of events leading to open rebellion. It should be obvious as well, however, that William was very much dependent from the beginning upon the active support of a considerable segment of the political nation and the neutrality of a significant percentage of those not directly involved in the affair. James had ensured that these prerequisites would be met by attempting to drive England toward acceptance of Roman Catholicism. The concomitants of this policy had not only alienated the generality of the upper classes, but had also undermined the dependability and strength of those institutions on which the king's power was ultimately based.

William of Orange stood as the prime beneficiary of this situation, and he was committed from the first to reaping the fullest possible advantage. Had his English supporters been fully aware of his goals, or had they even attempted a collective definition of their own objectives, the movement against James might well have collapsed before it started. Yet recognition of this fact in no sense detracts from the essential nature of their contribution to the success of the revolution. This contribution must be viewed largely in psychological terms, however, since the northern strategy was indisputably a failure in the technical sense. The prince's descent at Torbay shifted the central arena to the south, while the confusion and delay resulting from this change in circumstances reduced the overall impact of the actions of those involved in the plans for the north. But the fact remains that the risings at Nottingham and York, to say nothing of related activity in areas as distant as Northamptonshire and Cheshire, greatly affected the final outcome of events.

In the first place, the northern risings provided striking confirmation of the assertion in William's first declaration that he came in response to English invitation and clearly established the fact that the prince's invasion was part of a larger movement directed against the policies of James II. Furthermore, these risings graphically illustrated the extent to which the country was alienated from the king and particularly the depth of opposition among a considerable segment of the upper classes, regardless of previous political orientation. This was revealed not only by the number of peers taking up arms in the north and the generally favorable reception given them by the populace at large, but more significantly by the failure of the movement to generate any substantial activity in support of James. Especially among the gentry many stood aloof and uncommitted, but their very neutrality rendered effective judgment against the regime. Moreover, it virtually ensured that the organs of local government, particularly the militia, would provide no assistance for the royal cause and might in some instances be turned against it.

The risings at Nottingham and York and related manifestations of Williamite support doubtless played a part in James's decisions both to avoid a direct confrontation with the prince at Salisbury and later to flee the country. While it cannot be argued that they were crucial determinants, clearly they contributed substantially to the defeatist attitude that settled over the king, the central government, and the remaining royalist supporters. The accident of Anne's flight to the north reinforced the feeling in the royal camp of being caught in an ineluctable chain of events from which there was no escape. Further, the rumors and reports concerning the northern risings exacerbated the tensions of the situation, for the objectives of the leading participants were not at all clear. Their forces might be ill-trained and ill-equipped, but by default they stood in unchallenged control of the northern third of the country, and there was always the possibility that they might be tempted to march on London as the prince advanced toward the capital from the west.

The rising at Nottingham is itself of particular interest not only in terms of analyzing the impact of the north on the final outcome of events, but also as a microcosm of the English side of the revolution. It clearly reflects the forward position of a considerable sector of the peerage in the movement against James, while at the same time it reveals the difficulties and tensions which arise when men of divergent political orientation attempt to work together in a fluid situation lacking well defined ends. The curiously feudal aspect of the rebellion also emerges, for in direct contrast to the earlier part of the century, the gentry as a class plays a distinctly secondary role, either appearing in the train of one or another of the nobles or remaining uncommitted altogether. Moreover, the very events leading up to the rising indicate something of the extent of the conspiracy against James, the process by which it was enlarged in the month or two before William landed, and the elaboration of a plan of action that involved men in widely scattered locations throughout the north and midlands.

Analysis of local background in connection with the Nottingham rising reveals the near total collapse of government on the municipal and county level at least in terms of providing an effective extension of royal authority. The attempts by both Charles and James to tighten control over municipal corporations by extensive regulation failed ultimately because James could not find collaborators with sufficient standing in the community to provide a workable alternative to the local Tory-Anglican establishment. The lieutenancies and militia were in a state of disorganization that approached chaos for lack of a committed royalist element among the upper class groups that normally held the reins of power. While Nottinghamshire was something of an exception because of the influence and efforts of the Duke of Newcastle, even there no effective support was generated for the king at the moment of crisis.

The rising at Nottingham is also of especial interest because of the widely divergent political viewpoints represented by the leading participants. Temporarily united in opposition to James, peers of almost every shade in the political spectrum made an appearance. The real strength of the movement, however, came from the center—a coalition of moderate Whigs and Tories—rather than from the extremes, as represented by Lord Delamer and the Earl of Chesterfield. The coalescence of men of such widely differing outlooks could not last, and indeed the pressure of events caused tensions to build almost from the very first. But while difficulties emerged, belief that the king had to be constrained provided a sufficient binding force to hold the movement together until after the final outcome had been decided. Dissent, recrimination, and even bitterness were later expressed by some who had taken up arms at Nottingham and elsewhere, yet by then the realities of the situation permitted no turning back.

NOTES

Notes to Chapter I

1. Several recent books provide useful correctives to the traditional Whig view of the revolution as summarized by Trevelyan. Professor J. R. Jones's study represents a particularly valuable rethinking of the whole problem of 1688, and it contains many suggestions for new lines of investigation. See Maurice Ashley, *The Glorious Revolution of 1688* (London, 1966); John Carswell, *The Descent on England* (New York, 1969); James R. Jones, *The Revolution of 1688 in England* (London, 1972); Stuart E. Prall, *The Bloodless Revolution in England* (New York, 1972); G. M. Trevelyan, *The English Revolution, 1688-1689* (Oxford, 1965).

2. For the clearest statement of opposing views on this point, see Lucile Pinkham, *William III and the Respectable Revolution* (Cambridge, Mass., 1954), pp. 37-38, and Stephen Baxter, *William III and the Defense of European Liberty, 1650-1702* (New York, 1966), pp. 242-43.

3. In slightly different terms this question is posed in Gerald M. Straka, ed., *The Revolution of 1688: Whig Triumph or Palace Revolution?* (Boston, 1963), p. xi.

4. See John R. Western, *Monarchy and Revolution: The English State in the 1680's* (London, 1972), p. 3.

5. See, for instance, Macaulay's abbreviated treatment of events in the northern counties during the revolution. [Thomas Babington], Lord

Macaulay, *The History of England*, ed. Charles Harding Firth, 6 vols. (London, 1914), III:1157-58.
6. Alfred C. Wood, "The Revolution of 1688 in the North of England," *Transactions of the Thoroton Society of Nottinghamshire* XLIV (1940):72-104.
7. Andrew Browning, *Thomas Osborne, Earl of Danby and Duke of Leeds, 1632-1712.* 3 vols. (Glasgow, 1944) I:396-418 *passim.*
8. Memorandum in the hand of Admiral Arthur Herbert, c. October 1688, Portland MSS, Pw A 2202, University of Nottingham, Nottingham, England (Nicholaas Japikse, ed., *Correspondentie van Willem III en Hans Willem Bentinck, eersten graaf van Portland,* 5 vols. [The Hague, 1927-37], pt. I, vol. II (24):612-13).
9. Macaulay, *History of England,* II:1037.
10. See Andrew Browning, ed., *English Historical Documents, 1660-1714* (London, 1953), p. 19; John P. Kenyon, *The Nobility in the Revolution of 1688* (Hull, 1963), pp. 18-19. Miss Pinkham is perhaps most charitable, but she is interested in the northern risings primarily as they illustrate factional quarrels leading to dissention among the victors after the revolution. Pinkham, *Respectable Revolution,* pp. 162-68.
11. Philippe Johann Hoffmann to Emperor Leopold I, 3 December 1688, Emilia, Marquise Campana de Cavelli, *Les Derniers Stuarts à Saint-Germain en Laye: Documents Inédits et Authentiques,* 2 vols. (Paris, 1871), II:338-39.

Notes to Chapter II

1. Francis C. Turner, *James II* (London, 1948), pp. 233, 238. For a different view see Western, *Monarchy and Revolution,* p. 190.
2. John P. Kenyon, "The Reign of Charles II," *Cambridge Historical Journal* XIII (1957):85; Kenyon, *Nobility in the Revolution,* p. 6.
3. Keith Feiling, *A History of the Tory Party, 1640-1714* (Oxford, 1939), pp. 208-09; Helen C. Foxcroft, *The Life and Letters of Sir George Savile, Bart., First Marquis of Halifax,* 2 vols. (London, 1898), I:448-56; David Ogg, *England in the Reigns of James II and William III* (Oxford, 1955), pp. 160, 162.
4. *Journals of the House of Lords,* XIV:73-74.
5. Leopold von Ranke, *A History of England Principally in the Seventeenth Century,* 6 vols. (Oxford, 1875), IV:276. See also Barrillon to Louis XIV, 2 June 1685, Charles James Fox, *A History of the Early Part of the Reign of James the Second* (Philadelphia, 1808), app. I:

cxvi. Macaulay refers to Devonshire as chief among the Whigs at the time of the revolution, and the earl may well have had a hand in Thomas Wharton's abortive attempt to raise the question of the king's conduct in the House of Commons.

6. Edward Carpenter, *The Protestant Bishop, Being the Life of Henry Compton, 1632-1713, Bishop of London* (London, 1956), pp. 83-84; see also p. 29.

7. N. Johnston to Dr. Johnston, 21 November 1685, HMC 5, 6th Rep., pt. I, *Frank*, p. 463; *Journals of the House of Lords*, XIV:88. For the best accounts of the proceedings in the Lords and sources bearing on the subject, see Foxcroft, *Halifax*, I:458-59; Ranke, *History of England*, IV:276; Feiling, *Tory Party*, pp. 211-12.

8. Carpenter, *Protestant Bishop*, p. 33.

9. Feiling, *Tory Party*, pp. 212-13; Jones, *Revolution*, pp. 51-52.

10. Charles Bertie to Countess of Rutland, 17 December 1685, HMC 24, *Rutland*, II:97. See also Dr. O[wen] Wynne to Sir William Trumbull, 21 December 1685, HMC 75, *Downshire*, I, pt. I:75; John Reresby, *Memoirs of Sir John Reresby*, ed. Andrew Browning (Glasgow, 1936), p. 399.

11. Foxcroft, *Halifax*, I:460-61.

12. Marquess of Halifax to Earl of Chesterfield, 20 July 1686, *Ibid.*, p. 467.

13. Carpenter, *Protestant Bishop*, pp. 97-100. See also John Evelyn, *The Diary of John Evelyn*, ed. Esmond S. De Beer, 6 vols. (Oxford, 1955), IV:524; John Sheffield, Duke of Buckingham, *Works of John Sheffield, Earl of Mulgrave, Marquis of Normanby, and Duke of Buckingham*, 2 vols. (London, 1729), II, app., p. 5.

14. Turner, *James II*, p. 322. For the most comprehensive contemporary view of this process, see Reresby, *Memoirs*, pp. 442-50 *passim*.

15. William Blathwayt to Sir Robert Southwell, 3 December 1686, and 25 January and 1 February 1687, Portland MSS, Pw 53; Arnout van Citters to the States General, 4 February 1687, BM, Add. MSS 34,510, fol. 12; Helen C. Foxcroft, ed., *A Supplement to Burnet's History of My Own Time* (Oxford, 1902), p. 220.

16. Feiling, *Tory Party*, p. 217; Narcissus Luttrell, *A Brief Historical Relation of State Affairs*, 6 vols. (Oxford, 1857), I:396; Reresby, *Memoirs*, p. 449.

17. Reresby, *Memoirs*, p. 450.

18. *Ibid.*, p. 449; Feiling, *Tory Party*, p. 213; Foxcroft, *Halifax*, I:479.

19. Although primarily concerned with the negotiations with James II, the most extensive account of this embassy is to be found in James Muilenburg, "The Embassy of Everaard van Weede, Lord of Dykvelt, to England in 1687," *The University Studies of the University of Nebraska* XX (1920):85-161.

20. Baxter, *William III*, pp. 217-18.

21. George Hilton Jones, *Charles Middleton: The Life and Times of a Restoration Politician* (Chicago, 1967), p. 204.

22. Gilbert Burnet, *Bishop Burnet's History of His Own Time*, 6 vols. (Oxford, 1833), III:180-81.

23. *Ibid.*, p. 181.

24. James II to Prince of Orange, 23 May 1687; Prince of Orange to James II, 17 June 1687, John Dalrymple, *Memoirs of Great Britain and Ireland*, 3 vols. (London, 1771), II, app. II:193-94. 1661-1689 (New Brunswick, N.J., 1969), pp. 185, 190.

25. Douglas R. Lacey, *Dissent and Parliamentary Politics in England, 1661-1689* (New Brunswick, N.J., 1969), p. 185, 190.

26. Macaulay, *History*, II:965; James Mackintosh, *History of the Revolution in England in 1688* (London, 1834), p. 197.

27. Kenneth H. D. Haley, "A List of the English Peers, c. May, 1687," *English Historical Review* LXIX (1954):302-06. See also David H. Hosford, "The Peerage and the Test Act: a List, c. November 1687," *Bulletin of the Institute of Historical Research* XLII (1969):118-20.

28. [Bonrepaux to M. de Seignelay], 4 December 1687, Archives du Ministère des Affairs Étrangères, Correspondance Politique Angleterre, vol. 163, fols. 215-17. Comments to this effect are also to be found in two unsigned, undated letters dispatched to The Hague by informants in England: PRO, SP 8/2, pt. III, fols. 105-06; Portland MSS, Pw A 2148. See also Feiling, *Tory Party*, p. 226; Foxcroft, *Halifax*, I: 501-02.

29. Lord Wharton's proposal after the revolution that no newly created peer be allowed to sit in the House of Lords, except by permission of both houses, should be considered in this context. See G. F. Trevallyn Jones, *Saw-Pit Wharton: The Political Career from 1640 to 1691 of Philip, fourth Lord Wharton* (Sydney, 1967), p. 260.

30. This process can easily be traced in PRO, SP 44/164, fols. 414-17 *passim*.

31. Earl of Middleton to Earl of Derby, 16 August 1687, BM, Add. MSS 41,804, fol. 308.

32. Note by first Earl of Dartmouth, Burnet, *History*, III:193. See also rough draft of a letter from [Earl of Northampton to Earl of Middleton?], 7 October 1687, Northampton MSS, Bundle 1108, Castle Ashby, Northamptonshire, England.

33. Winston S. Churchill, *Marlborough, His Life and Times*, 4 vols. (London, 1933), I:245. See also Roger Morrice MS, Q, fol. 220, Dr. Williams's Library, London, England. This is the second volume of Roger Morrice's The Entring Book, Being an Historical Register of Occurrences from April, Anno 1667, to April 1691 (hereinafter cited as Morrice, Entring Book).

34. PRO, SP 44/174, fols. 415, 428; Morrice, Entring Book, II, fols. 167, 170; Barrillon to Louis XIV, 17 November 1687, PRO 31/3 (Baschet's Transcriptions), fol. 173.

35. Reresby, *Memoirs*, p. 487.

36. Van Citters to the States General, 12 December 1687, BM, Add. MSS 34,510 (Mackintosh Transcriptions), fols. 65-66; Macaulay, *History*, II:974.

37. A fairly comprehensive list of those dismissed from the lieutenancies in 1687 is to be found in [George Edward Cokayne], *The Complete Peerage*, ed. Vicary Gibbs, 13 vols. (London, 1910-59), II:656-57.

38. John P. Kenyon, *Robert Spencer, Earl of Sunderland, 1641-1702* (London, 1958), p. 173.

39. Andrew Browning, "Parties and Party Organization in the Reign of Charles II," *Transactions of the Royal Historical Society*, 4th ser. XXX (1948):32; Turner, *James II*, p. 328.

40. See, for instance, Morrice, Entring Book, II, fol. 201; newsletter to Sir William Trumbull, 11 November 1687, HMC 75, *Downshire*, I, pt. I:276; Gabriel Hastings to Earl of Huntingdon, 23 November 1687, Hastings MSS, Box 50, 5296, Huntington Library, San Marino, California.

41. Feiling, *Tory Party*, p. 218; François A. J. Mazure, *Historie de la Revolution de 1688 en Angleterre*, 3 vols. (Paris, 1825), II:303.

42. Barrillon to Louis XIV, 17 November 1687, PRO 31/3 (Baschet's Transcriptions), fol. 173; Henry Horwitz, *Revolution Politicks: The Career of Daniel Finch, Second Earl of Nottingham, 1647-1730* (Cambridge, 1968), p. 47.

43. James [Johnstone?] to Honoured Sir, 17 November 1687, Portland MSS, Pw A 2099.

44. Edward Wilson to Sir D. F[leming], 25 November 1687, HMC 25, *Le Fleming*, p. 206.

45. Turner, *James II*, p. 331. See also ? to Hon'd Sir, 8 December 1687, Portland MSS, Pw A 2111; Earl of Danby to William of Orange, 27 March 1688, PRO, SP 8/1, pt. II, fols. 197-98.

46. Kenyon, *Nobility in the Revolution*, p. 6. See also Esmond S. De Beer, "The House of Lords in the Parliament of 1680," *Bulletin of the Institute of Historical Research* XX (1943-45):23.

47. Arthur Stanley Turberville, *The House of Lords in the Reign of William III* (Oxford, 1913), pp. 122-23.

48. Pinkham, *Respectable Revolution*, p. 132; J. H. Plumb, *The Growth of Political Stability in England, 1675-1725* (London, 1967), p. 26; Ashley, *Glorious Revolution*, p. 175.

49. H. John Habakkuk, "English Landownership, 1680-1740," *Economic History Review* X (1989-40):10-11; Gerald E. Mingay, *English Landed Society in The Eighteenth Century* (London, 1963), pp. 61, 71.

50. A[ndrew] N[ewport] to Lord Herbert of Cherbury, 19 May 1688, PRO, 30/53/8, fol. 60; Morrice, Entring Book, II, fols. 239, 253.

51. Cited by Ashley, *Glorious Revolution*, p. 105.

Notes to Chapter III

1. [Henry Sidney] to Prince of Orange, 25 May [1688], Dalrymple, *Memoirs*, II, app. I:227-28; Baxter, *William III*, pp. 231-32.
2. Admiral Herbert to Prince of Orange, 25 May [1688], Dalrymple, *Memoirs*, II, app. I:225.
3. Thomas C. Nicholson and Arthur Stanley Turberville, *Charles Talbot, Duke of Shrewsbury* (Cambridge, 1930), p. 26.
4. Horwitz, *Revolution Politicks*, pp. 52-53.
5. Foxcroft, *Halifax*, I:494-95.
6. Baxter, *William III*, pp. 225-26.
7. Philippe Johann Hoffmann to Emperor Leopold I, 14 June 1688, Campana de Cavelli, *Les Derniers Stuarts*, II:205.
8. See Pinkham, *Respectable Revolution*, pp. 167-68.
9. Baxter, *William III*, pp. 233-34.
10. Burnet, *History*, III:283, 303-05.
11. In William Bentinck's opinion the aftermath of the Monmouth rebellion did have bearing on the reluctance of many to join the prince during the first week or so after he landed. See the note in Bentinck's hand concerning the progress of events between 5-16 November 1688, Portland MSS, Pw A 2230.
12. Burnet, *History*, III:303; Browning, *Danby*, I:387.
13. See the memorandum in the hand of Admiral Arthur Herbert, c. October 1688, Portland MSS, Pw A 2202.
14. Burnet, *History*, III:304-05.
15. See Earl of Danby's instructions for a messenger to the Prince of Orange, [20 November 1688], Browning, *Danby*, II:139-41.
16. Earl of Danby to Earl of Chesterfield, [September?] 1688, and Earl of Chesterfield to Earl of Danby, [September? 1688], BM Add. MSS 19,253 fols. 167-69 (*Letters of Philip, Second Earl of Chesterfield* [London, 1835], pp. 336-39).
17. Samuel Weller Singer, ed., *The Correspondence of Henry Hyde, Earl of Clarendon, and of his Brother, Laurence Hyde, Earl of Rochester; with the Diary of Lord Clarendon from 1687 to 1690*, 2 vols. (London, 1828), II:208 (hereinafter cited as *Diary of Clarendon*).
18. [Thomas Osborne, first Duke of Leeds], *Copies and Extracts of Some Letters Written to and from the Earl of Danby (now Duke of Leeds) in the Years 1676, 1677, and 1678* (London, 1710), pp. vi-vii. There is a considerable literature pertaining to the meeting at Whittington. See Henry Kirke, "The Revolution House at Whittington," *Journal of the Derbyshire Archaeological and Natural History Society* XXXVI (1914):1-8; *Notes and Queries*, 7th ser., V (1888):436; P. Cummingl, "The Revolution House at Whittington, Derbyshire," *The Everyday Book and Table Books*, ed. William Hone, 3 vols. (London, 1838), III:514-20; Samuel Pegge, *A Narrative of What Passed at the Revolution House at Whittington, County of Derby, in the Year 1688* (Nottingham, 1788). See also Samuel Pegge to Hayman Rooke, ? 1788 and 15 January

1789, Derbyshire Collection 844, fols. 225, 234, Derby Public Library, Derby, England.

19. The loyalist Ailesbury characterized his cousin Delamer as being a "person of an implacable spirit against the King and crown and of a most sour temper of mind." Thomas, Earl of Ailesbury, *Memoirs of Thomas Earl of Ailesbury*, ed. William Edward Buckley, 2 vols. (London, 1890), I:133. As might be expected, the Earl of Clarendon was hardly more charitable. Singer, ed., *Diary of Clarendon*, II:229.

20. Burnet, *History*, III:278-79; Lord Churchill to Prince of Orange, 4 August 1688, HMC 8, 9th Rep., pt. II, *Morrison*, p. 460.

21. Burnet, *History*, III:279. See also John Knox Laughton, ed., *Memoirs Relating to the Lord Torrington* (London, 1889), p. 27.

22. Jones, *Revolution*, pp. 230-31; Feiling, *Tory Party*, p. 227; Ogg, *James II and William III*, pp. 202-03.

23. Burnet, *History*, III:282.

24. See Princess Anne to Prince of Orange, 18 November [1688], Beatrice Curtis Brown, ed., *The Letters and Diplomatic Instructions of Queen Anne* (London, 1935), pp. 43-44.

25. See, for instance, Princess Anne to Princess of Orange, 20 March 1688, *Ibid.*, pp. 35-36; Singer, ed., *Diary of Clarendon*, II:199.

26. Singer, ed., *Diary of Clarendon*, II:189, 191, 194, 199.

27. [Colin Lindsay], Earl of Balcarras, *An Account of the Affairs of Scotland Relating to the Revolution in 1688* (Edinburgh, 1754), p. 15; Ailesbury, *Memoirs*, I:179-80; F. Elrington Ball, "His Part in the Revolution, 1688-89," HMC 36, n. s., *Ormonde*, VIII:xix-xx. See also Charles Dalton, ed., *English Army Lists and Commission Registers, 1661-1714*, 6 vols. (London, 1894), II:10, 12, 19, 135.

28. Efforts were made to secure support in the navy as well as in the army. See Laughton, ed., *Memoirs Relating to Torrington*, p. 27; Feiling, *Tory Party*, p. 227.

29. See the short biographical sketch in Wolley's historical collections for Derbyshire, BM, Add. MSS 6670, fol. 680.

30. Scarsdale was in London both for the trial of the seven bishops and for the installation of the Duke of Ormonde as Chancellor of Oxford, White Kennet, *Complete History of England*, 3 vols. (London, 1706), III:485; Anthony à Wood, *The Life and Times of Anthony Wood, Antiquary, at Oxford, 1632-1695, Described by Himself*, ed. Andrew Clark, 5 vols. (Oxford, 1895), III:275. It might be noted that Scarsdale's second in command before he lost his regiment, Colonel Thomas Langton, was deeply involved in the army plotting. Jones, *Revolution*, pp. 230-31.

31. The necessary warrant was issued to the Earl of Derby on 18 October 1688, PRO, SP 44/165, fol. 118.

32. See Western, *Monarchy and Revolution*, pp. 52-53. See also John Seacome, *The History of the House of Stanley* (Preston, 1793), p. 404.

33. "A Diary or memoty where my Lord Derby has been each day, with some observations of what he hath transacted on several accounts, and how corresponded, since the day before Michaelmas last, 1688,"

Kenyon MSS, Gredington, Shropshire, England (HMC 35, *Kenyon*, pp. 198-202).

34. *Ibid.*, p. 200. For indications of Derby's dependence upon the Duke of Ormonde during the revolutionary period, see two letters from the Earl of Derby to Duke of Ormonde, 19 December 1688, BM, Add. MSS 33,589, fols. 302, 304. See also the note by Lord Dartmouth in Burnet, *History*, III:407; Ball, "His Part in the Revolution," HMC 36, n. s., *Ormonde*, VIII:xx.

35. Foxcroft, *Halifax*, II:209; James Stanier Clarke, *The Life of James II*, 2 vols. (London, 1816), II:232; John R. Western, *The English Militia in the Eighteenth Century* (London, 1965), pp. 61-62.

36. For a full analysis of Bishop Compton's part in expanding the conspiracy, see David H. Hosford, "Bishop Compton and the Revolution of 1688," *Journal of Ecclesiastical History* XXIII (1972):209-18.

37. Carpenter, *Protestant Bishop*, pp. 60, 372-73.

38. Morrice, Entring Book, II, fols. 374-75. The Entring Book is a particularly full and reliable source for information relating to the rising at Nottingham, especially with respect to the activities of the Dissenters, Lord Delamer and the Earl of Devonshire. Throughout his life Morrice was closely connected with Nonconformist and Whig circles. He was ejected from the parish of Duffield, Derbyshire, shortly after the Restoration, which may explain his special interest and connection with the area just north of Trent. Arnold G. Matthews, *Calamy Revised, Being a Revision of Edmund Calamy's Account of the Ministers and Others Ejected and Silenced, 1660-62* (Oxford, 1934), p. 63. For the cover story circulated to explain Bishop Compton's absence from London, see newsletter to John Ellis, 29 September 1688, George J. W. Agar Ellis, Lord Dover, ed., *Letters Written During the Years 1686, 1687, 1688, and Addressed to John Ellis, Esq.*, 2 vols. (London, 1831), II:224; Singer, ed., *Diary of Clarendon*, II:188, 191; John Bramston, *The Autobiography of Sir John Bramston, K. B.*, ed. Lord Braybrooke (London, 1845), pp. 318, 320.

39. Earl of Danby to Countess of Danby, 2 October 1688, Browning, *Danby*, II:136-37; same to Earl of Chesterfield, ? September 1688, *Letters of Philip, Second Earl of Chesterfield*, pp. 336-37. See also Pinkham, *Respectable Revolution*, pp. 139-40.

40. Burnet, *History*, III:283.

41. Bolingbroke was among those peers who had been prepared to stand bail for the seven bishops. Presumably Compton had had contact with him in that connection, since the bishop played a particularly active role in organizing assistance for his brethren in the Tower. Bishop of London to [Archbishop of Canterbury, 12 June 1688], John Gutch, *Collectanea Curiosa*, 2 vols. (London, 1781), I:356-57.

42. Accounts of Charles, Earl of Dorset, entry for 17 September 1688, Sackville MSS, U 269, A 7/13, Kent Archives Office, Maidstone, England. It is likely that Dorset had been associated with the opposition for some time. With Halifax, Danby, Shrewsbury, Lumley, and Sidney, he was singled out for an anonymous letter in January, 1688,

threatening death if immediate reconciliation with the king were not effected. Anonymous letter to Earl of Danby endorsed as having been received 28 January 1687, when similar letters were also received by Shrewsbury, Dorset, Halifax, and Sidney, BM, Add. MSS 28,053, fol. 345.

43. The Earl of Manchester may already have been initiated into the plot; he had just returned from Holland where he was supposed to have met with William. Arthur Collins, *The Peerage of England*, 5 vols. (London, 1756), II:81.

44. See the hint that Delamer knew or at least suspected that a point of crisis was near. "His Lordship's Advice to His Children," dated 20 September 1688, in Henry Booth, Earl of Warrington, *The Works of the Right Honourable Henry, Late Lord Delamer and Earl of Warrington* (London, 1694), pp. 1-35. This essay would seem to have been written too early for the Bishop of London yet to have approached Delamer.

45. See Earl of Danby to Countess of Danby, 2 October 1688, and Earl of Devonshire to Earl of Danby, 1 October 1688, Browning, *Danby*, I:136-37.

46. [Leeds], *Letters Written to and from the Earl of Danby*, pp. vi-vii.

47. See Morrice, Entring Book, II, fol. 303.

48. Reresby, *Memoirs*, pp. 514-15.

49. See [Sarah Churchill, Duchess of Marlborough], *An Account of the Conduct of the Dowager Duchess of Marlborough, From Her First Coming to Court, to the Year 1710* (London, 1742), p. 17.

50. See "Draft of a petition giving particulars of a dispute between the Earl of Derby and Lord Delamer," which details the activities of the former between October and December, 1688, Kenyon MSS, #642 (printed with omissions HMC 35, *Kenyon*, pp. 205-06).

51. Apparently for safety's sake Devonshire sent his eldest son and heir out of the country at the time of the revolution. Lord Cavendish to Lady Cavendish, 29 August 1688, Devonshire MSS, 51.0, Chatsworth, Derbyshire, England.

52. Browning, *Danby*, I:390.

53. Earl of Danby to Countess of Danby, 2 October 1688, *Ibid.*, II: 136-37.

54. Jones, *Revolution*, pp. 230-31, 295; G. F. T. Jones, *Wharton*, p. 258.

55. See, for instance, Earl of Danby to Countess of Danby, 2 October 1688, and also Danby's instructions for a messenger to the Prince of Orange, [20 November 1688], Browning, *Danby*, II:136-37, 139-41.

56. D'Arcy had lost his commission as a colonel in the army and was forbidden the king's presence because of his votes in the House of Commons in 1685. George Duckett, "King James the Second's Proposed Repeal of the Penal Laws and Test Act in 1688," *Yorkshire Archaeological and Topographical Journal* V (1879):446.

57. G. F. T. Jones, *Wharton*, p. 258.

Notes to Chapter IV

1. Jones, *Revolution*, p. 43.
2. John N. L. Baker, "England in the Seventeenth Century," *An Historical Geography of England*, ed. H. C. Darby (Cambridge, 1951), p. 441; Jonathan D. Chambers, *Nottinghamshire in the Eighteenth Century* (London, 1966), pp. 82-83; Alfred C. Wood, "A Note on the Population of Nottingham in the Seventeenth Century," *Transactions of the Thoroton Society* XL (1936):109-13; Alfred C. Wood, "A Note on the Population of Six Nottinghamshire Towns in the Seventeenth Century," *Ibid.*, XLI (1937):18-26.
3. See Duke of Newcastle to Earl of Sunderland, 18 July 1688, PRO, SP 31/4, fol. 70.
4. The descriptions of three travellers who visited the city in the reigns of Charles II, William III, and George I are particularly informative. The observations of the first, Thomas Baskerville, are recorded in a notebook printed in HMC 29, *Portland*, III:308. The commentary of Celia Fiennes, who passed through Nottingham just before the end of the century, is to be found in Christopher Morris, ed., *The Journeys of Celia Fiennes* (London, 1947), pp. 72-73. A particularly full description is included in Daniel Defoe, *A Tour Through the Whole Island of Great Britain* (London, 1962), pp. 142-46.
5. John Potter Briscoe, "History of the Trent Bridges at Nottingham," *Transactions of the Royal Historical Society*, n.s. II (1873):213.
6. In this connection see Joseph H. Sacret, "The Restoration Government and Municipal Corporations," *English Historical Review* XLV (1930):232-59.
7. Duncan Gray, *Nottingham Through 500 Years* (Nottingham, 1960), pp. 97-103; Alfred C. Wood, *A History of Nottinghamshire* (Nottingham, 1947), pp. 209-11. See also the records of the corporation for this period, which are partially printed in W. T. Baker, ed., *Records of the Borough of Nottingham*, 7 vols. (London, 1900), V:232 ff. William Sacheverell, *The Case of the Corporation of Nottingham*, reprinted in Charles Deering, *Nottinghamia Vetus et Nova* (Nottingham, 1757), pp. 280-85.
8. This charter is printed in Baker, ed., *Records*, V:49-59.
9. John Millington to Marquess of Halifax, 18 March 1684, Spencer MSS, Halifax Correspondence, Box 6, Althorp, Northamptonshire, England. George Duckett, *Penal Laws and Test Act* (London, 1882, 1883), 1883:126-27 (hereinafter referred to as volume II and the 1882 publication as volume I).
10. Duckett, *Penal Laws and Test Act*, II:126-27; see also Morrice, Entring Book, II, fol. 199.
11. Samuel Sanders to Earl of Huntingdon, 19 October 1687, Hastings MSS, HA 10668.
12. See same to same, 8 October 1687, *Ibid.*, HA 10667.
13. Corporation of Nottingham MSS, 3455 (Hall Book, 1687-88),

fols. 22, 26, 32 (Baker, ed., *Records*, V:336-39).

14. Earl of Sunderland to Duke of Newcastle, 31 January 1688, PRO, SP 44/56, fol. 402.

15. See Morrice, Entring Book, II, fol. 247; Edward Roberts to George Langford, 20 November 1688, Thomas Bailey, *Annals of Nottinghamshire*, 4 vols. (London, n. d.), III:1031-32; Earl of Kingston to Earl of Nottingham, 15 July [16]90, Violet W. Walker, ed., "The Confiscation of Firearms in Nottingham in Charles Harvey's Mayoralty, 1689-1690," *Thoroton Society Record Series* XXI (1962):23.

16. A. Bernard Clarke, "Notes on the Mayors of Nottingham, 1600-1775," *Transactions of the Thoroton Society* XLI (1937):58; Gray, *Nottingham*, p. 97; Wood, *Nottinghamshire*, p. 209; Lacey, *Dissent*, p. 152.

17. James R. Jones, "James II's Whig Collaborators," *The Historical Journal* III (1960):65-73. The substance of the analysis that follows is based upon the arguments of this article.

18. In general, see the discussion in Lacey, *Dissent*, pp. 180-208.

19. For those voting against surrender in 1682, see Corporation of Nottingham MSS, 3449 (Hall Book, 1681-82), fol. 16. For the refusal of Thomas Twigg to accept appointment to the common council in 1688, see *Ibid.*, 3455 (Hall Book, 1687-88), fol. 32 (Baker, ed., *Records*, V:339). A number of Dissenters appointed to the corporation at Leicester also refused to serve. [Sir] Henry Beaumont to Earl of Huntingdon, 10 April [16]88, Hastings MSS, HA 664.

20. Newsletter to John Squire, 14 June 1684, *Calendar of State Papers Domestic*, 1684-85:54. See also Wood, *Nottinghamshire*, p. 211.

21. Jones, "James II's Whig· Collaborators," p. 69; Jones, *Revolution*, pp. 139-40.

22. Jones, "James II's, Whig Collaborators," p. 70. The fines of Sherwin and Sacheverell were the most severe meted out. For the Earl of Devonshire, see Thomas B. Howell, ed., *A Collection of State Trials*, 33 vols. (London, 1809-26), XI:1369-70.

23. Jones, *Revolution*, p. 140.

24. Lacey, *Dissent*, p. 209.

25. The alderman in question, Charles Harvey, had come to Nottingham from Lincolnshire and was first made a burgess when appointed to the common council in 1688. Walker, ed., "The Confiscation of Firearms in Nottingham in Charles Harvey's Mayoralty," p. 21; Gray, *Nottingham*, p. 108. For a similar situation at Leicester, see William Palmer and Charles Byerley to Earl of Huntingdon, 9 April 1688, Hastings MSS, HA 9844.

26. Nathan Wright to George Langford, 12 May 1688, Corporation of Nottingham MSS, 4962, c/2. See also *Ibid.*, 3455 (Hall Book, 1687-88), fol. 37 (Baker, ed., *Records*, V:338).

27. Corporation of Nottingham MSS, 3455 (Hall Book, 1687-88), fol. 61 (Baker, ed., *Records*, V:341-42). See also Gray, *Nottingham*, p. 105.

28. For the negotiations about the new charter, reference should be made to the extensive correspondence between Mayor George Langford

and Deputy Recorder Nathan Wright of which the letters directed to Wright are contemporary copies. [Langford] to [Wright], 23 May 1688, Wright to Langford, 27 May 1688, Langford and others to Wright, 26 June 1688, Wright to Langford, 28 June 1688, Corporation of Nottingham MSS, 4692, c/3-c/6. Enclosure from letter of Wright to Langford, 27 May 1688, *Ibid.*, 4752. Two letters missing from this series are printed in Deering, *Nottinghamia*, pp. 255-56: Wright to Langford, 21 June 1688, and Langford and others to Wright, 23 June 1688.

29. See the instructions for preparing a charter incorporating Nottingham, dated 31 July 1688, PRO, SP 44/338, fols. 44-46.

30. Gray, *Nottingham*, p. 106. See also three letters from Nathan Wright to George Langford on this subject, 4 and 13 September 1688 and 1 March 1689, Corporation of Nottingham MSS, 4756, 4759, and 4692, c/8.

31. Corporation of Nottingham MSS, 3456 (Hall Book, 1688-89), fol. 5 (Baker, ed., *Records*, V:350-51). The charter issued by James II is printed in Baker, ed., *Records*, V: 79-85. That the majority of those enfranchised would dissociate themselves from the Michaelmas election was a reaction that had been anticipated. See Nathan Wright to George Langford, 28 June 1688, Corporation of Nottingham MSS, 4692, c/6.

32. See the proclamation issued by James II on 17 October 1688, "For Restoring Corporations to their Ancient Charters and Liberties," and see the order in council of the same date, which makes note of the exceptions. James Lindsay, Earl of Crawford, and Robert Steele, eds., *Tudor and Stuart Proclamations, 1485-1714*, 2 vols. (Oxford, 1910), I:470. See also Jones, *Revolution*, p. 263.

33. Nottingham did not have its original charter restored until 1692; it was then decided that the surrender of 1682 had been illegal. Gray, *Nottingham*, pp. 107, 111; Wood, *Nottinghamshire*, p. 212.

34. J. H. Plumb, "Elections to the Convention Parliament of 1688-9," *Cambridge Historical Journal* V (1937):238. However, Professor Plumb is mistaken when he cites Nottingham as an obvious instance of a town in which confusion and turmoil resulted from the changeover in municipal officials.

35. Corporation of Nottingham MSS, 3455 (Hall Book, 1687-88), fol. 69. See also copies of letters sent by George Langford to Mr. Tomlinson, 27 August 1688, and to [Nathan Wright], 8 September 1688, *Ibid.*, fols. 4751, 4758. See also Chambers, *Nottinghamshire*, pp. 30-31; Duckett, *Penal Laws and Test Act*, II:244-45.

36. Corporation of Nottingham MSS, 3456 (Hall Book, 1688-89), fol. 15.

37. Of particular interest in this connection is the letter of Edward Roberts, secretary to James II, to George Langford, 20 November 1688, Bailey, *Annals*, III: 1031-32.

38. For changes in the charter of East Retford, see the warrant of 11 March 1685, PRO, SP 44/70, fols. 155-56. For changes in the Newark charter, see C. Guy Parsloe, "The Growth of a Borough Constitution: Newark-on-Trent, 1549-1688," *Transactions of the Royal Historical*

Society, 4th ser. XXII (1940):197; Cornelius Brown, *The Annals of Newark-Upon-Trent* (London, 1879), p. 196. Reference to the clause in question is also to be found in Corporation of Newark MSS, Minutebook (1675-1835), fol. 20.

39. See Duckett, *Penal Laws and Test Act*, II:127-28.

40. The Duke of Newcastle reputedly threatened the corporation with a "regulation" if they would not promise to choose representatives for parliament who favored repeal. Given the replies to the three questions, it seems probable that some alteration of personnel followed. See Edward Wilson to Marquess of Halifax, 10 July 1688, Devonshire MSS, 21.57.

41. Copies of the governmental directives, dated 24 and 25 February 1688, are to be found in the Corporation of Newark MSS, Minutebook (1675-1835), fol. 20. They are printed with incorrect dates in William Dickinson, *The History and Antiquities of the Town of Newark* (London, 1819), pp. 387-88.

42. Minutes of the town council for ? April and 29 September 1688, Corporation of Newark MSS, Minutebook (1675-1835), fol. 21.

43. Duckett, *Penal Laws and Test Act*, II:245.

44. Parsloe, "Growth of a Borough Constitution," p. 197.

45. The charter is printed in Robert Simpson, *The History and Antiquities of Derby*, 2 vols. in one (Derby, 1826), pp. 117-154. See also *Ibid.*, p. 116; William Hutton, *The History of Derby* (London, 1791), p. 238.

46. Andrew Browning and Doreen Milne, "An Exclusion Bill Division List," *Bulletin of the Institute of Historical Research* XXIII (1950): 210. See also the copy of a letter from [John Coke and others] to Sir Lionell Jenkins, 19 July 1683, Cowper MSS, Bundle 98, Melbourne Hall Derbyshire, England (HMC 23, *Cowper*, II:344).

47. Earl of Sunderland to Corporation of Derby, 2 January 1688, BM, Add. MSS 6669, fol. 232. The three questions were never directly posed to the corporation. See Duckett, *Penal Laws and Test Act*, I:168.

48. The reports in question are to be found in the Hastings Collection at the Huntington Library. The following are of particular value: George Vernon to Earl of Huntingdon, 31 January 1688, HA 371; George Fletcher to Earl of Huntingdon, 21 March 1688, HA 3227; John Bagnold to same, 16 April 1688, HA 12974; same to same, 25 April 1688, HA 12978; Vernon to same, 6 August 1688, HA 670; Bagnold to same, 30 August 1688, HA 12980; Vernon to same, 19 August 1688, HA 1043; same to same, 9 September 1688, HA 1163; same to same, [September? 1688], HA 3229.

49. An undated list of the members of the Derby corporation, including those men to be dropped and those to be added, is to be found in the Hastings MSS, unsorted local materials.

50. [Sir] H[enry] Beaumont to Earl of Huntingdon, 17 July [16]88, Hastings MSS, HA 667. See also same to same, 10 April [16]88, *Ibid.*, HA 664; Charles Byerley to same, 19 October 1687, *Ibid.*, HA 1162.

51. All freemen of the town could vote; there were about seven hun-

dred common burgesses in the early eighteenth century. See Simpson, *Derby*, p. 191; Hutton, *Derby*, p. 119.

52. See Duckett, *Penal Laws and Test Act*, I:407; Earl of Sunderland to Earl of Huntingdon, 13 September 1688, Hastings MSS, HA 12545 (HMC 78, *Hastings*, II:187-88).

53. For information pertaining to the religious complexion of the two counties in question, the following sources have proved helpful: John C. Cox, *Three Centuries of Derbyshire Annals*, 2 vols. (London, 1890), I:292-95, 301, 306-07; John C. Cox, "Ecclesiastical History," *The Victoria County History of Derby*, II:75; John C. Cox, "Ecclesiastical History," *The Victoria County History of Nottingham*, II:75; Everard L. Guilford, "Nottinghamshire in 1676," *Transactions of the Thoroton Society* XXVIII (1924):106-13; H. Hampton Copnall, ed., *Nottinghamshire County Records* (Nottingham, 1915), p. 136; G. Lyon Turner, ed., *Original Records of Early Nonconformity under Persecution and Indulgence*, 2 vols. (London, 1911), II:700-25; Wood, *Nottinghamshire*, p. 205.

54. See the addresses printed in the *London Gazette*, 19-23 May 1687; 15-19 September 1687; 29 September-3 October 1687. In connection with the strain of disquiet, see Samuel Sanders to Earl of Huntingdon, 19 October and 19 December 1687, Hastings MSS, HA 10668-69. See also Lacey, *Dissent*, pp. 184-85.

55. For an evaluation of the Bishop of Lichfield's position at the time of the second declaration of indulgence and petition of the seven bishops, see Earl of Clarendon to Princess of Orange, 21 May 1688, HMC 45, *Buccleugh*, II, pt. I:32. See also Thomas, Bishop of Carlisle to Sir Daniel Fleming, 2 June 1688, HMC 25, *Le Fleming*, p. 210.

56. A detailed report of this affair is contained in Edward Wilson to Marquess of Halifax, 25 April 1687, Devonshire MSS, 21.56. Unfortunately, it is impossible to determine what effect, if any, this injunction had because the records of presentment for the county stop in 1686. Copnall, ed., *Nottinghamshire County Records*, p. 136.

57. The dilemma confronting clergymen of a more timorous sort is clearly revealed in the letter of Rev. Theophilus Brookes of Foremark to Earl of Huntingdon, 2 June 1688, HMC 78, Hastings, II:184-85. See also Rev. Richard Hatton to Roger Kenyon, 30 May 1688, Kenyon MSS, 619 (HMC 35, *Kenyon*, pp. 190-91).

58. See Luttrell, *Historical Relation*, I:442; Bishop of Carlisle to Bishop of Ely, 4 June 1688, Tanner MS 28, fol. 50, Bodleian Library, Oxford, England (Gutch, *Collectanea Curiosa*, I:334-35); Leftwich Oldfield to Roger Kenyon, 3 June 1688, Kenyon MSS 621 (partially printed HMC 35, *Kenyon*, p. 191); Andrew Newport to Lord Herbert of Cherbury, 9 June 1688, PRO 30/53/8, fol. 63.

59. See the case of Archdeacon John Gery, chaplain to the Earl of Huntingdon. John Gery to Earl of Huntingdon, 12 August and 3 September 1688, Hastings MSS, HA 3993, 3997; John Onebye to Earl of Huntingdon, 7 September 1688, *Ibid.*, HA 9779 (printed in HMC 78, *Hastings*, II:187).

60. Lacey, *Dissent*, pp. 155-56. See also Reresby, *Memoirs*, p. 452; Matthew Henry Lee, ed., *Diaries and Letters of Philip Henry, M.S. of Broad Oak, Flintshire* (London, 1882), p. 328.

61. George Vernon to Earl of Huntingdon, 19 August 1688, Hastings MSS, HA 1043.

62. See the *London Gazette*, 8-12 March 1688.

63. See the copy of a letter from the Bishop of Chester to the mayor of Wigan, 31 May 1687, BM, Add. MSS 4164, fol. 153. For Leicester, see Nathan Wright to Earl of Huntingdon, 19 October 1687, Hastings MSS, HA 13676; Joseph Cradock to same, 28 May 1688, *Ibid.*, HA 1703.

64. George Vernon to Earl of Huntingdon, received 8 June 1688, Hastings MSS, HA 372; same to same, 1 July 1688, *Ibid.*, HA 373 (partly printed HMC 78, *Hastings*, II:185).

65. For Leicester, see the three letters from Sir Henry Beaumont to the Earl of Huntingdon, ? May, 15 August, 29 August 1688, Hastings MSS, HA 662, 668, 669.

66. George Vernon to Earl of Huntingdon, 6 and 19 August 1688, Hastings MSS, HA 670, 1043. For some indication of Robert Wilmot's political orientation, see J. Degge to Earl of Rutland, 20 February 1685, HMC 24, *Rutland*, II:86-87.

67. Duckett, *Penal Laws and Test Act*, II:121. There were, of course, Dissenters among the Nottinghamshire gentry, although they probably were occasional conformers. See, for instance, Samuel Sanders to Earl of Huntingdon, 19 October 1687, Hastings MSS, HA 10668.

68. See the comment in Paul C. Vellacott, ed., "The Diary of a Country Gentleman in 1688," *Cambridge Historical Journal* II (1926): 54.

69. Edward Wilson to Marquess of Halifax, 10 July 1688, Devonshire MSS, 21.57. See also Nathan Wright to George Langford, 7 July 1688, Corporation of Nottingham MSS, 4745; George Vernon to Earl of Huntingdon, 6 August 1688, Hastings MSS, HA 670.

70. In this connection see Reresby, *Memoirs*, p. 522; Richard Lapthorne to Richard Coffin, 6 and 13 October 1688, HMC 4, 5th Rep., pt. I, *Pine-Coffin*, 379.

71. After the revolution there were only two non-jurors among the beneficed clergy of Nottinghamshire and apparently no more in Derbyshire. Cox, "Ecclesiastical History," *Victoria County History of Nottingham*, II:75; Anchitell Grey to Sir Phillip Gell, 9 July 1689, Gell MSS, Box 98, bundle marked "Letters to Sir Phillip Gell," Newnham Hall, Northamptonshire, England.

Notes to Chapter V

1. In 1685, for instance, Coke could first consider standing for parliament from the county of Leicester and then opt to sit for the borough of Derby. See two letters of Earl of Ailesbury to Earl of Rutland, 14 and 22 February 1685, HMC 24, *Rutland*, II:85, 87.

2. Those peers with significant influence in one or both counties included the Duke of Newcastle, the Marquess of Halifax, the Earls of Devonshire, Rutland, Scarsdale, Chesterfield, Huntingdon, Clare, Kingston, and Lords Ferrers, Lexington, and Byron.

3. John Millington to Marquess of Halifax, 23 March 1685, and Duke of Newcastle to same, 13 April 1685, Spencer MSS, Halifax Correspondence, Box 6.

4. Lexington received a pass to travel overseas on 15 December 1686, PRO, SP 44/70, fol. 258. See also Luttrell, *Historical Relation*, I:381. According to Clarendon he returned to England just in time for the critical vote in the Lords concerning the vacancy of the throne. Singer, ed., *Diary of Clarendon*, II:261. Kingston apparently left England sometime after March 1687, PRO, SP 44/337, fol. 249. According to his accounts, he was in Venice in July 1688, and a chance reference in a letter of Lord Cavendish would indicate that he had arrived in Brussels by mid-November. See the accounts of the Earl of Kingston, BM, EG. 3526, fols. 60-70; Lord Cavendish to Lady Cavendish, 18 November [1688], Devonshire MSS, 51.2.

5. The Earl of Huntingdon supported exclusion but then shifted ground and became an ultra-loyal supporter of the throne.

6. 1685 was one of the few years when Lord Byron's name appears in the commission of the peace. Libri Pacis, 10 October 1685, PRO, C193/12/5.

7. According to Clarendon this sort of tactic was used in a number of instances. Singer, ed., *Diary of Clarendon*, II:261. See also *Journals of the House of Lords*, XIV:107-08, 113, 116, 118.

8. Sir Keith Feiling ranks the Earl of Clare among such Whig oriented peers as the Earls of Dorset and Anglesey. Feiling, *Tory Party*, p. 232.

9. Halifax's country seat was located at Rufford, midway between Mansfield and Tuxford, while Chesterfield's principal residence was at Bretby in the southern tip of Derbyshire.

10. See Haley, "A List of English Peers," and Hosford, "The Peerage and the Test Act."

11. Earl of Sunderland to Duke of Newcastle, 8 March 1688, PRO, SP 44/56, fol. 408. See also Morrice, Entring Book, II, fol. 246.

12. Wood, "Revolution of 1688 in the North of England," pp. 79-80. The following letters provide some interesting insights into aspects of the Duke of Newcastle's character and royalist commitment: Duke of Newcastle to Earl of Danby, 5 December 1687, Portland MSS, Pw 1, fol. 547; same to Earl of Sunderland, 5 June 1688, PRO, SP 31/4, fol. 40; William Chiffinch to Duke of Newcastle, 19 June 1688, BM,

Loan 29/236, fol. 426. See also Reresby, *Memoirs*, p. 545.

13. J. H. Plumb, "Political History, 1530-1885," *The Victoria County History of Leicester*, II:119-20.

14. See, for instance, the letter of G. Palmer to [someone in the Earl of Huntingdon's service], 10 November 1688, Huntingdon Letters, 14D32/4/10, City of Leicester Museum and Art Gallery, Leicester, England.

15. The letter instructing Newcastle to put the questions was dispatched from London by the Earl of Sunderland on 25 October 1687, PRO, SP 44/56, fol. 389. The complete returns for the county, including the municipal corporations, are printed in Duckett, *Penal Laws and Test Act*, II:119-28.

16. See Morrice, Entring Book, II, fol. 214.

17. *Ibid.*

18. See George Vernon to Earl of Huntingdon, 31 January 1688, Hastings MSS, HA 371.

19. The complete report is printed in Duckett, *Penal Laws and Test Act*, I:164-8.

20. A clause of dispensation ws added to all commissions of the peace for Derbyshire in September 1687. PRO, IND 4215, fol. 180. Thomas Eyre of Hassop and Basil and William Fitzherbert of Norbury are identified as Catholics in the return itself; Sir Henry Hunloke was clearly of that faith also. See Sir Henry Hunloke to Earl of Huntingdon, 14 July 1688, Hastings MSS, HA 10669 (HMC 78, *Hastings*, II:186). See also John C. Cox, "Political History," *The Victoria County History of Derby*, II:139.

21. Samuel Sanders to Earl of Huntingdon, 19 December 1688, Hastings MSS, HA 10669.

22. See the lists of deputy lieutenants approved by the board of regulators for Nottinghamshire (4 February 1688) and Derbyshire (16 February 1688), PRO, SP 44/165, fols. 13, 19. In the former instance direct comparison may be made with those identified as deputies in the return for the county printed in Duckett, *Penal Laws and Test Act*, II: 123. But in the latter case reference must be made to a list submitted to Lord Preston as an enclosure to a letter dated 1 November 1688, Preston MSS, Miscellania, fol. 120, Netherby, Cumberland, England. The letter itself, from Sir Henry Hunloke and George Vernon, is to be found *Ibid.*, Letters from England, etc., fol. 1.

23. A relatively elderly man for the period (aged 65), Molineux does not seem to have figured prominently in local politics, nor had he been a member of the commission of the peace during the preceding ten years. See PRO, C193/12/4, fols. 90-92; PRO, C193/12/5, fols. 108-11. He was, however, married to a sister of Sir Scrope Howe.

24. See Duckett, *Penals Laws and Test Act*, II:122. Both these men had already been added to the commission of the peace in Nottingham. A clause of dispensation had been put into effect for the county in August 1687, which was a month earlier than Derbyshire. PRO, IND 4215, fol. 178.

25. See Wood, *Nottingham*, pp. 208, 211. Reference should also be made to the valuable series of letters from John Millington the Marquess of Halifax, which provide clear insights into the politics of the county between 1681 and 1685. Spencer MSS, Halifax Correspondence, Box 6.

26. Anchitell Grey needs no introduction. Perhaps the clearest indication of the political orientation of Maurwood and Sanders is to be seen in their attempt, in combination with others of similar outlook, to promote the candidacy of Grey and William Sacheverell in the election of 1685. J. Degge to Earl of Rutland, 20 February 1685, HMC 24, *Rutland*, II:86-87. Sanders had the backing of the crown as a candidate for parliament from the borough of Nottingham when it seemed that an election would be held in the autumn of 1688. Earl of Sunderland to Duke of Newcastle, 13 September 1688, PRO, SP 44/56, fol. 432; Duke of Newcastle to L. Collin, 17 September 1688, Portland MSS, Pw 1, fol. 656. His correspondence with the Earl of Huntingdon would indicate that he should be classed a Whig collaborator. In particular, see Samuel Sanders to Earl of Huntingdon, 19 December 1688, Hastings MSS, HA 686.

27. In the case of Derbyshire at least two men, John Spateman and Thomas Woolhouse, included in the commission of the peace were open adherents of Presbyterianism. See George Vernon to Earl of Huntingdon, 19 August 1688, Hastings MSS, HA 1043. See also Charles Prior, "The Spatemans of Roadnook," *Journal of the Derbyshire Archaeological and Natural History Society* XXXVII (1915):50.

28. George, "Parliamentary Elections and Electioneering in 1685," p. 173.

29. John Millington to Marquess of Halifax, 31 March 1683 and 16 March 1685, Spencer MSS, Halifax Correspondence, Box 6; Earl of Sunderland to Duke of Newcastle, 19 March, 1685, PRO, SP 44/56, fol. 188.

30. [Sir] H[enry] Beaumont to Earl of Huntingdon, [? May 1688], Hastings MSS, HA 662.

31. See, for instance, the letter of John Bennett to Earl of Huntingdon, 19 January 1688, *Ibid.*, HA 686.

32. Morrice, Entring Book, II, fol. 247; returns from royal agents in Nottinghamshire, September 1688, Duckett, *Penal Laws and Test Act*, II:224-45; Edward Wilson to Marquess of Halifax, 10 July 1688, Devonshire MSS, 21.57. The attempt by Sacheverell's biographer to suggest that he, like the Earl of Sunderland, was attempting to lure the king to disaster by his cooperation is a bit of special pleading on the part of an embarrassed descendent. George Sitwell, *The First Whig* (Scarborough, 1894), p. 173.

33. An interesting commentary on this phenomenon is contained in the letter of John Millington to Marquess of Halifax, datelined Derby, 27 July 1681, Spencer MSS, Halifax Correspondence, Box 6.

34. This was a situation common to many counties and much more the rule than the conditions prevailing in Nottinghamshire. Morrice, Entring Book, II, fol. 245.

35. Sir Henry Hunloke to Earl of Huntingdon, 14 July 1688, Hastings MSS, HA 10669.

36. See the note pertaining to an order of the House of Commons, dated 1689, HMC 8, 9th Rep., pt. II, *H. C. Pole-Gell*, 399. For Fitzherbert compare the comments in the following: Duckett, *Penal Laws and Test Act*, I:166; letter of George Vernon to Earl of Huntingdon, 6 August 1688, Hastings MSS, HA 670.

37. Gell, in fact, asked to be excused on the basis of age and ill-health. Geo. Fletcher to Earl of Huntingdon, 28 May 1688, Hastings MSS, HA 3228.

38. See [Sir] Henry Hunloke and George Vernon to [Lord Preston], 1 November 1688, Preston MSS, Letters from England, etc., fol. 1.

39. The Earl of Huntingdon's absence also created difficulties in Leicestershire. See John Gery to Earl of Huntingdon, 3 and 28 April 1688, Hastings MSS, HA 3990-91; Gervase Jaques to Earl of Huntingdon, 26 May 1688, *Ibid.*, HA 7789; [Sir] H[enry] Beaumont to same, [? May 1688], *Ibid.*, HA 662.

40. Compare the list of justices approved in London with that naming the men who actually took the qualifying oath of office. Duckett, *Penal Laws and Test Act*, II:294; Cox, *Derbyshire Annals*, I:37-50. See also three letters in the Hastings MSS at the Huntington Library: Ch[arles] Byerly to Earl of Huntingdon, 23 May 1688, HA 12979; George Vernon to same, 8 June and 6 August 1688, HA 372, HA 670; see also Earl of Sunderland to Sir Simon Degge, 23 October 1688, PRO, SP 44/97, fol. 2.

41. See James II to Earl of Huntingdon, 22 September 1688, Hastings MSS, HA 7164 (HMC 78, *Hastings*, IV:220); Robert Wilmot to same, 27 October 1688, *Ibid.*, HA 12983. See also [Sir] Henry Hunloke and George Vernon to [Lord Preston], 1 November 1688, cited in note 38.

42. Western, *English Militia*, pp. 23, 50.

43. That James discouraged musters is clearly indicated in the letter of Earl of Lindsey to James II, 27 September 1688, PRO, 31/4, fols. 78-79. See also Lord Aston to Earl of Sunderland, 29 September 1688, *Ibid.*, fol. 82; Earl of Sunderland to Earl of Bath and Earl of Bristol, 25 May 1687, PRO, SP 44/56, fol. 373.

44. Western, *English Militia*, p. 63.

45. Lord Teynham to Earl of Sunderland, 8 October 1688, PRO, SP 31/4, fol. 101; Earl of Lindsey to same, 22 October 1688, *Ibid.*, fol. 191: G. Palmer to [someone in the Earl of Huntingdon's service] 10 November 1688, Huntingdon Letters, 14D32/4/10, City of Leicester Museum and Art Gallery, Leicester, England; Sir Henry Hunloke to Earl of Huntingdon, 14 July 1688, Hastings MSS, HA 10669.

46. Jones, *Revolution*, p. 107.

47. See Earl of Sunderland to Earl of Huntingdon, 13 September 1688; Jacques Gervase to Earl of Huntingdon, 4 September 1688; [Sir] H[enry] Beaumont to Earl of Huntingdon, 29 August 1688, Hastings MSS, HA 12545, HA 7794, HA 669.

Notes to Chapter VI

1. Warrington, "Reasons Why King James Ran Away from Salisbury," p. 56.
2. Foxcroft, *Halifax*, II:5; Kenyon, *Sunderland*, p. 218; Turner, *James II*, pp. 414, 427.
3. Luttrell, *Historical Relation*, I:461, 464; newsletter, 6 October 1688, HMC 25, *Le Fleming*, p. 213. See also the pass issued to Lovelace to travel abroad, 2 September 1688, PRO, SP 44/70, fol. 309, and see the warrant for his arrest, 27 September 1688, PRO, SP 44/338, fol. 103.
4. Marquis d'Albeville to Earl of Middleton, 11 October 1688, BM, Add. MSS 41,816, fol. 230.
5. See Ralph Cole and John Duck to Earl of Sunderland, 26 October 1688, PRO, SP 31/4, fol. 191; Earl of Middleton to Duke of Newcastle, 30 October 1688, PRO, SP 44/97, fol. 8; John Reresby to Lord Preston, 5 November 1688, HMC 6, 7th Rep., app. I, *Sir F. Graham*, p. 413; Duke of Newcastle to [Earl of Middleton], 6 and 14 November 1688, BM, Add. MSS 41,805, fols. 142, 212-13.
6. Turner, *James II*, p. 422.
7. See contemporary comment to this effect: Unknown to J[ames] Harrington, 27 September [1688], BM, Add. MSS 36,707, fol. 42; transcriptions of three letters from van Citters to the States General, 5, 12, and 16 October 1688, BM, Add. MSS 32,515, fols. 104-05, 108, 115; newsletter to Sir Sackville Crow, 9 October 1688, BM, Add. MSS 38,175, fols. 140-41; newsletters of 11 October and 6 November 1688, HMC 25, *Le Flemming*, pp. 214, 218.
8. See Earl of Sunderland to Lord Fairfax, 29 September 1688, PRO, SP 44/56, fol. 444; same to Duke of Newcastle, 6 October 1688, *Ibid.*, fol. 449; Earl of Middleton to Duke of Newcastle, 30 October 1688, PRO, SP 44/97, fol. 8.
9. Marquis d'Albeville to Earl of Middleton, 15 October 1688, BM, Add. MSS 41,816, fol. 238.
10. See V. R. to Sir John Newton, 8 November 1688, HMC 4, 5th Rep., app. I, *Ellacombe*, p. 324; Earl of Middleton to Lord Langdale, 10 November 1688, PRO, SP 44/97, fol. 14; Lord Preston to Duke of Newcastle, 13 November 1688, Preston MSS, Letter Book, vol. 8 (HMC 6, 7th Rep., app. I, *Sir F. Graham*, p. 348). See also Philippe Johann Hoffmann to Emperor Leopold I, 15 November 1688, Campana de Cavelli, *Les Derniers Stuarts*, II:315.
11. Letters to this effect went out from the Earl of Sunderland to the lord lieutenants concerned on 30 October 1688, PRO, SP 44/97, fols. 6-8.
12. Warrington, "Reasons Why King James Ran Away from Salisbury," p. 57.
13. Earl of Danby to Countess of Danby, 2 October 1688, Browning, *Danby*, II:36-37; Clarke, *Life of James the Second*, II:205-06; "The Last & Present Quarters of the Horse and Dragoons" and "The Last and

Present Dispositions of the Foot," both dated July 1688, BM, Add. MSS 38,695, fol. 27. See also Ashley, *Glorious Revolution*, pp. 154-55.

14. Considerable information about the garrisons in the north is to be found in Browning, *Danby*, I:401, 417. For the decision to leave Scarborough undefended, see Lord Belasys to Duke of Newcastle, 27 October 1688, BM, Loan 29/236 (Portland MSS, Vere and Cavendish papers), fol. 434. The number of regulars in the garrison at Chester is difficult to determine because it served as a way station for regiments being transferred from Ireland. See Peter Shakerley to William Blathwayt, 6 October 1688, HMC 39, *Hodgkin*, p. 73; see also same to [Lt. General Robert Werden?], 13 December 1688, BM, Add. MSS 38,695, fol. 103. The last letter cited speaks of a garrison consisting of a regiment of foot and some dragoons, but this includes eight or nine companies of foot brought to Chester at the end of November by Colonel Gage. Generally, see Clarke, *Life of James the Second*, II:191.

15. Gertrude Ann Jacobsen, *William Blathwayt* (New Haven, 1932), p. 229. See also [William] Blathwayt to Duke of Newcastle, 1 November 1688, Godfrey Davies, "Letters on the Administration of James II's Army," *Journal of the Society for Army Historical Research* XXIX (1951):82.

16. Professor Browning estimates that there were about three hundred men organized into six companies, but there appears to have been a seventh which escaped his notice. Browning, *Danby*, I:402.

17. The materials relating to the Duke of Newcastle's regiment are widely scattered, but the following are among the more important documents: Newcastle's commission, dated 29 September 1688, Portland MSS, Pw 1, fol. 161; accounts for the regiment, *Ibid.*, fol. 332; Duke of Newcastle to [Earl of Sunderland], 1 and 4 October 1688, PRO, SP 31/4, fols. 86, 89; Earl of Sunderland to Duke of Newcastle, 4 October 1688, PRO, 44/56, fol. 448; Newcastle's commission as lord lieutenant of Yorkshire, 11 October 1688, *Ibid.*, fol. 108; Earl of Sunderland to Duke of Newcastle, 11 October 1688, BM, Loan 29/236 (Portland MSS, Vere and Cavendish papers), fol. 432; Lord Langdale to Earl of Middleton, 23 November 1688, BM, Add. MSS 41,805, fol. 271. See also Dalton, ed., *English Army Lists*, II:175.

18. Although they did not arrive in time, regiments of foot and horse were actually summoned from Ireland for this purpose. Earl of Middleton to Lord Preston, 21 November 1688, PRO, SP 44/97, fol. 19.

19. See the harsh evaluation of the duke's performance made by Professor Turberville. Arthur Stanley Turberville, *A History of Welbeck Abbey and Its Owners*, 2 vols. (London, 1938), I:212.

20. See Reresby, *Memoirs*, pp. 517, 545. See also White Kennet, *Memoirs of the Family of Cavendish* (London, 1708), pp. 24-25.

21. Others given commissions who figured prominently in the rising at York were Lord Fairfax, Christopher Tankard, Tobias Jenkins, and Sidney Wortley. The list of deputies Newcastle submitted to the king is to be found in PRO, SP 31/4, fol. 124. The covering letter from the duke to the Earl of Sunderland, 14 October 1688, is located separately in the

same series, *Ibid.*, fol. 136. Goodrick and D'Arcy seem to have been particularly adept at pulling the wool over Newcastle's eyes. Reresby, *Memoirs*, p. 545; Duke of Newcastle to Earl of Middleton, 14 November 1688, BM, Add. MSS 41,805, fol. 212.

22. Reresby, *Memoirs*, p. 525; Lord Preston to Duke of Newcastle, 13 November 1688, Preston MSS, Letter Book, vol. 8, (HMC 6, 7th Rep., app. I, *Sir F. Graham*, p. 348); Sir John Reresby to Lord Preston, 9 November 1688, printed *Ibid.*, 415.

23. Earl of Lindsey to Earl of Middleton, 27 October 1688, BM, Add. MSS 41,805, fol. 85.

24. See, for instance, the detailed information contained in a newsletter to the Earl of Derby, 13 November 1688, Kenyon MSS, 643.

25. Reresby, *Memoirs*, p. 524.

26. Kennet, *Family of Cavendish*, p. 25; Laurence Echard, *The History of the Revolution, and the Establishment of England in the Year 1688* (London, 1725), pp. 170-72.

27. See draft of Danby's instructions for a messenger to the Prince of Orange, [20 November 1688], Browning, *Danby*, II:139-41.

28. See the deposition of Lieutenant John Gorman, who spoke to Delamer on November 16 at Manchester, [19 November 1688], BM, Add. MSS 41,805, fols. 232-33. A transcript of Gorman's testimony was dispatched to the king at Salisbury, with a covering letter from Lord Preston to the Earl of Middleton, 19 November 1688, HMC 6, 7th Rep., app. I, *Sir F. Graham*, p. 349.

29. A concise summary of the maneuvering before the seizure of York is to be found in Browning, *Danby*, I:396. See also Reresby, *Memoirs*, pp. 525-27; Sir John Reresby to Lord Preston, 17 November 1688, Preston MSS, Letters from England, etc., fols. 65-67. The notices about the meeting at York were sent out to the gentry on 13 November, which gives some indication as to the latest possible date by which the revised plans for the northern risings were completed. Also of interest is the fact that the conspirators at York had to dispatch one of their number, John D'Arcy, to persuade the Duke of Newcastle that his presence was necessary at the meeting. See Duke of Newcastle to [Earl of Middleton?], 21 November 1688, BM, Add. MSS 41,805, fols. 243-44.

30. Delamer has left an interesting commentary on this matter which is particularly critical of the conservative "revolutionaries" at York. Warrington, "Reasons Why King James Ran Away from Salisbury," pp. 64-67.

31. See the comments to this effect in Wood, "Revolution of 1688 in the North of England," p. 82; Browning, *Danby*, I:397.

32. Extensive documentation is available on this question. The following items make the point most clearly: The deposition of Lieutenant John Gorman, [19 November 1688], BM, Add. MSS 41,805, fols. 232-33; a series of letters to Philip Froude from John Franidys, postmaster at Derby, William Rathbone, postmaster at Lichfield, and C. R[eynolds], postmaster at Nottingham, all dated 21 November 1688, BM, Add. MSS 41,805, fols. 240, 254-55, 258-59. See also the document endorsed "Intel-

ligence from Burton, Derby, and Nottingham," 21 November 1688, *Ibid.*, fol. 245; Peter Shakerley to Lieutenant General [Robert] Werden, 21 November 1688, BM, Add. MSS 38,695, fol. 86.

33. [Arthur Mainwaring], *The King of Hearts* (London, 1690).

34. A manuscript copy of the declaration is to be found in BM, Add. MSS 41,805, fol. 222. Possibly this is the actual document posted on the market cross at Warrington, which was dispatched to London with a covering letter from the postmaster, Peter Naylor, to Philip Froude, 21 November 1688, *Ibid.*, fols. 260-61. Printed versions of the declaration subsequently appeared of which a copy is to be seen in the John Rylands Library, R10618, Manchester, England.

35. An interesting list of those members of the Lancashire gentry suspected of being Roman Catholics includes well over 150 names; it was probably drawn up in the last decade of the seventeenth century. Kenyon MSS, DDKe 7/31, Lancashire Record Office, Preston, England.

36. R[oger] F[leming] to Sir Daniel Fleming, 22 November 1688, MS Don. C39, fol. 2, Bodleian (HMC 25, *Le Fleming*, p. 221). For rumors in London about the Earl of Derby, see Earl of Nottingham to Viscount Hatton, 24 November 1688, BM, Add. MSS 29,594, fol. 135. For general background on the earl's role in the revolution, see the diary of Lord Derby's activities, HMC 35, *Kenyon*, 200-02; Lord Delamer to Earl of Derby, 10 December 1688, *Ibid.*, p. 210; Lord Preston to same, 19 November 1688, Preston MSS, Letters from Paris to Foreign Ministers, 1682, and Dispatches to Lords Lieutenant in 1688, section II, fol. 10 (hereinafter this bound volume of manuscripts will be referred to as Dispatches to Lords Lieutenant in 1688).

37. See J. Colley to William Adams, 24 November 1688; [Viscount] C[holmondeley] to same, 25 December 1688, both letters in Cholmondeley MSS, DCH/K/10, Cheshire Record Office, Chester, England. See also the deposition of Lieutenant John Gorman cited in note 28.

38. Some basis for this generalization can be clearly established in several cases. For Samuel Finney of Fulshaw and Captain Thomas Latham, see Samuel Finney III, MS "History of the Parish of Wilmslow," [1785], DFF/38/35, fols. 52-53, Cheshire Record Office. There was a particularly close association between Delamer and John Mainwaring, eldest son of Sir Thomas Mainwaring of Over Peover. Of interest in this connection is the entry for 18 November 1688, in Colonel [Roger] Whitley's Diary, 1684-1697, Mainwaring MS 31, fol. 99, John Rylands Library. Nathaniel Booth, Delamer's uncle, was quite active in raising men and money to support his nephew's venture, *Calendar of Treasury Papers.* 1557-1695: 42-43. Sir Robert Duckenfeld's family had linked political fortunes with the Booths since the time of the civil wars. Among other members of the Cheshire gentry who can specifically be identified as participants are John Egerton, Thomas Warburton, William Lawton, Randolph Holme, Henry Brooke, Thomas Minshall, and, possibly, Sir John Bland. See Peter Shakerley to Lieutenant General [Robert] Werden, 21 November 1688, BM Add. MSS 38,695, fol. 86; newsletter to [Sir Daniel Fleming], ? November 1688, MS Don.

C39, fol. 11, Bodleian; Henry Kirke, ed., "Dr. Clegg, Minister and Physician in the 17th and 18th Centuries," *Journal of the Derbyshire Archaeological and Natural History Society* XXXV (1913):10.

39. See Kenyon, *Nobility in the Revolution*, p. 5; Lawrence Stone, *The Crisis of the Aristocracy, 1558-1641* (Oxford, 1965), p. 199.

40. This was a company of foot from Lord Montgomery's regiment, the bulk of which was stationed at Hull. The commander of the unit was Captain Richard Leigh, and it was his second, Lieutenant John Gorman, who was dispatched immediately thereafter to London with a report of what was happening. See note 28; see also T. J[ackson] to Charles Jackson, 17 November 1688, HMC 6, 7th Rep., app. I, *Sir F. Graham*, p. 416. The information in this letter confirms that contained in Gorman's deposition on a number of important points.

41. Morrice, Entring Book, II, fol. 326. The following letters provide specific details about Delamer's march from Bowden Downs to Nottingham: R. H. to [Lord Preston?], 20 November 1688; Lord Aston to Lord Preston, 21 November 1688; [Lady Aston] to Lady Abergaveny, same date; Peter Naylor to same, same date, BM, Add. MSS 41,805, fols. 234, 238, 246-48, 254-55, 260-61.

42. Wood, *Life and Times*, III:284. For typically exaggerated reports of the size of Delamer's following, see [Robert Price] to Duke of Beaufort, 22 November 1688, MS Carte 130, fol. 307, Bodleian; newsletter, 20 November 1688, MS Don. C38, fol. 362, Bodleian.

43. See Warrington, "Reasons Why King James Ran Away from Salisbury," p. 64. Godolphin made a similar point when he commented that "the noyse of their [Delamer and his party] being together in armes is perhaps the worst consequence of any thing they are like to doe." Earl of Godolphin to Earl of Middleton, 23 November 1688, BM, Add. MSS 41,805, fols. 275-76.

44. Included in this latter category was the sculptor Gaius Gabriel Cibber, whose son accidentally met with his father among the troops at Nottingham, exchanged places with him and later recorded aspects of his experiences in his autobiography. Colley Cibber, *An Apology for the Life of Mr. Colley Cibber*, ed. Edmund Bellchambers (London, 1822), p. 41.

45. Sir William Russel, Bt., came from Chippenham, Cambridge; he was not a near relation of the Bedford Russells, and his connection with the movement is somewhat obscure. For general information pertaining to those assembled at Derby, see "Intelligence from Burton, Derby, and Nottingham," 21 November 1688, BM, Add. MSS 41,805, fol. 245; newsletter to [Sir Daniel Fleming], 24 November 1688, MS Don. C39, fol. 9, Bodleian.

46. After the arrival of both Delamer and Devonshire at Nottingham, their joint force was estimated at a total strength of about six hundred horse of which almost four hundred had been brought in by the Cheshire contingent. C. R[eynolds] to Philip Froude, 21 November 1688, BM, Add. MSS 41,805, fols. 249-50. See also Morrice, Entring Book, II, fol. 375. Most local histories inflate the number of horse with Devonshire

to five hundred but provide no evidence in substantiation. See, for instance, Stephen Glover, *The History of the County of Derby*, ed. Thomas Noble, 2 vols. (Derby, 1829), II:383-84.

47. This declaration has been printed many times and is most accessible in *A Collection of State Tracts Published on Occasion of the Late Revolution in 1688 and during the Reign of King William III*, 3 vols. (London, 1705-07), I:438. It is almost always dated 21 November 1688, but this is clearly a mistake since Devonshire had arrived at Nottingham by the evening of 20 November. See also Kennet, *Family of Cavendish*, p. 25.

48. John Coke to Francis Thacker, 24 November 1688, Cowper MSS, Bundle 98 (partly printed HMC 23, *Cowper*, II:344-45); Earl of Devonshire to Earl of Danby, Nottingham, 20 November 1688, Browning, *Danby*, II:139-40.

49. Lord Preston to Duke of Newcastle, 19 November 1688, HMC 6, 7th Rep., app. I, *Sir F. Graham*, p. 349. Duke of Newcastle to [Lord Preston], 21 November 1688, BM, Add. MSS 41,805, fols. 243-44.

50. Earl of Devonshire to Earl of Danby, 20 November 1688, Browning, *Danby*, II:139-40. See also "Intelligence from Burton, Derby, and Nottingham," BM, Add. MSS 41,805, fol. 245. Danby himself had sent word to the Earl of Abingdon suggesting that he join the group at Nottingham, but the latter had already gone to the prince directly. Browning, *Danby*, II:141; Luttrell, *Historical Relation*, I:476.

51. Morrice, Entring Book, II, fol. 370. The names have been ommitted in the relevant entry, but internal evidence makes it clear that the reference is to Delamer and Devonshire.

52. Deering, *Nottinghamia*, pp. 260-61. Although Deering's account of the matter was drawn up more than twenty years later, it was based upon the recollections of eyewitnesses to the event. In other respects his narrative concerning Nottingham and the revolution appears trustworthy when it can be compared with contemporary source material.

53. See Edward Roberts, secretary to James II, to George Langford, 20 November 1688, Bailey, *Annals*, III:1031-32. In connection with the issuance of writs for a parliament that was never to meet, yet another appeal for the support of the Nottingham Dissenters was made by the central government in the first days of December. Same to same, 3 December 1688, *Ibid.*, p. 1034. The records of the corporation are a virtual blank from 4 November until the end of the first week in December. The corporation then involved itself officially in the proceedings at Nottingham only to the extent of raising funds to help defray the charges of providing a guard for Princess Anne. Corporation of Nottingham MSS, 3456 (Hall Book, 1688-89), fols. 14, 23.

54. A printed copy of the declaration is to be found in PRO, SP 31/4, fol. 305; it is also printed in John Blackner, *The History of Nottingham* (Nottingham, 1815), pp. 376-77. Although dated 22 November 1688 in its printed form, the available evidence points to the conclusion that it was not made public until 24 November. In general see Deering, *Nottinghamia*, pp. 260-61.

55. Printed in HMC 35, *Kenyon*, p. 208.

56. Lord Delamer to Prince of Orange, 1 December 1688, PRO, SP 8/2, pt. II, fols. 65-66 (Japikse, ed., *Correspondentie*, pt. II, vol. III (28):72). See also Dr. George Hicks to Arthur Charlett, 1 December 1688, Ballard MS 12, fol. 42, Bodleian; Morrice Entring Book, II, fols. 332, 337, 342.

57. Duke of Beauford to [Earl of Middleton], 28 November 1688, BM, Add. MSS 41,805, fol. 293. See also Kenyon, *Nobility in the Revolution*, pp. 17-18.

58. William of Orange to Lord Delamer, 2 December 1688, Stamford MSS, Dunham Massey Hall, Cheshire, England; Earl of Stamford to Prince of Orange, 5 December 1688, PRO, SP 8/2, pt. II, fols. 71-72 (Japikse, ed., *Correspondentie*, pt. II, vol. III (28):72). See also Nathaniel Pinney to Hester Pinney, 3 December 1688, Geoffrey Nuttal, ed., *Letters of John Pinney, 1679-1699* (London, 1939), p. 60.

59. A. A. Mitchell, "The Revolution of 1688 and the Flight of James II," *History Today* XV (1965):500. It is interesting to note that the onset of James's famous nosebleeds apparently coincided with receipt of the news that Delamer was in arms and expected to be joined by other peers. See Earl of Middleton to Lord Preston, 21 November 1688, PRO, SP 44/97, fol. 19.

60. Earl of Devonshire to Earl of Danby, 24 November 1688, HMC 8, 9th Rep., pt. II, *Morrison*, p. 460; Bentinck's journal of events, Portland MSS, Pw A 2231 (Japikse, ed., *Correspondentie*, pt. I, vol. II [24]:629).

61. The agent involved was one Coronet [Richard?] Gee, whose family belonged to the class of lesser gentry in Leicestershire. See Dalton, ed., *English Army Lists*, I:125, 248. See also newsletter to Roger Kenyon, 29 November 1688, Kenyon MSS, 648 (HMC 35, *Kenyon*, 209).

62. Earl of Devonshire to Lord ?, 28 November 1688, HMC 8, 9th Rep., pt. II, *Morrison*, p. 460. Information pertaining to this regiment, its officers, movements, expenses, supply and the like is drawn from manuscript material at Melbourne Hall (Cowper MSS) unless otherwise noted. The relevant documents, which were largely ignored by the Historical Manuscripts Commission in the nineteenth century, consist of accounts kept by John Wright for the regiment as a whole and by Issac Deprepetit for the troop under the direct command of Lieutenant Colonel John Coke. Of particular interest are those items endorsed as follows: "John Wright account of money receiv'd & disburst for ye troops in Nottinghamshire;" "Received by my Lord Devonshire and his order of Publick money;" "An account of money received out of ye Publick revenue by My Ld Devonshire;" "Novem: ye 28, 1688, An account of ye Money received of ye officers of ye Revinue & the disbursements by Mr. John Wright;" "An account of money received by Myld Devonshire and his order out of ye Publick revenue for ye expedition in ye Late Revolution." These manuscripts are in a bundle marked "A" in the safe in the muniment room. "A generall account of ye Money Received of ye Lieutenant Cololl Coke by me I. Deprepetit from ye 27

of November, 1688, to ye 20th of February, 1688/9;" "An account generall of ye Lieut Cololl Coke's Money for ye use of his troop from ye 28 of November, 1688, to ye 16 of March 1688/9;" "An account of what the Souldiers had to fitt ym out;" and "An account concerning the affairs of ye Regiment." These manuscripts are in bundle 119 in the safe in the muniment room. See also "Deprepetit's account of disbursements to Colonel John Coke, 8 December, 1688 to [13 January, 1689]" and "Deprepetit's account [to John Coke], 27 November, 1688," HMC, *Cowper*, II:348-50, 345.

63. See John Coke to Francis Thacker, 24 November 1688, Cowper MSS, Bundle 98 (partly printed HMC 23, *Cowper*, II:344-45).

64. Interestingly, Coke was the only representative from Derbyshire to vote against making William and Mary joint sovereigns in place of James II. Feiling, *Tory Party*, p. 496. The dilemma of the Tory gentry in general is well summed up in Bramston, *Autobiography*, p. 338.

65. For Hutchinson see Blackner, *History of Nottingham*, p. 337.

66. Morrice, Entring Book, II, fols. 370-71; Sitwell, *The First Whig*, p. 176. Despite his earlier willingness to collaborate with James, Sacheverell apparently was taken into the plans for the rising at Nottingham. His failure to make an appearance there contributed to his defeat when he stood for election to the Convention Parliament from Derbyshire, although he was subsequently able to obtain a seat at Heytesbury, Wiltshire. [Edward Harley?] to Robert Harley, 19 January 1689, BM, Add. MSS 40,621, fol. 3.

67. Philip Prime, for instance, was not only a Dissenter himself but managed to raise an entire troop of horse among Derbyshire Nonconformists. Morrice, Entring Book, II, fol. 392. Others who can be specifically identified as supporters of the rising not mentioned in the text include Purey Cust, son of Sir Richard Cust, a Whig of Lincolnshire; Thomas Hartop, possibly a connection of the Nonconformist radical Sir John Hartop of Leicestershire; Charles White, probably the son of the prominent Nottinghamshire Whig John White of Tuxford; Richard Roe; Edward Harvey; Thomas Wright; and Robert Milward.

68. It is unclear why Scarsdale was associated with this group, although possibly he felt more comfortable moving in the company of the Tory oriented Earl of Northampton rather than associating initially with Devonshire and Delamer.

69. The content of this message is summarized in Earl of Devonshire to Earl of Danby, 20 November 1688, Browning, *Danby*, II:139-40.

70. A somewhat confused and much amended account of the fortunes of this group is to be found in Wood, *Life and Times*, III:283-84.

71. The youngest and perhaps best known of the three Montagu brothers joining the movement was Charles, subsequently first Earl of Halifax, who rapidly rose to prominence as a leading Whig in the reign of William III.

72. Roger Jones to Viscount Hatton, 28 November 1688, BM, Add. MSS 29,563, fol. 342; John Selby and others to [Lord Preston], 26 November 1688, HMC 6, 7th Rep., app. I, *Sir F. Graham*, p. 418; news-

letter, 29 November 1688, MS Don. C39, fol. 28, Bodleian. A variation of the rumor concerning the regiment of royal dragoons seems also to have met up with Delamer on 27 November when he was in the vicinity of Birmingham. Morrice, Entring Book, II, fol. 337. See also Lt. Col. William Fleming to Roger Fleming, 30 November 1688, MS Don. C39, fol. 31, Bodleian; the relevant portion of the letter is not included in the extract printed in HMC 25, *Le Fleming*, p. 225.

73. See, for instance, the comments of Bishop Compton to Prince of Orange, 2 December 1688, PRO, SP 8/2, pt. II, fols. 69-70 (Dalrymple, *Memoirs*, II, app. I:335).

74. Newsletter, 29 November 1688, MS Don. C39, fol. 28, Bodleian.

75. Morrice, Entring Book, II, fol. 370; Duke of Newcastle to Lord Preston, 1 December 1688, HMC 6, 7th Rep., app. I, *Sir F. Graham*, p. 419. See also Lord Preston to Duke of Newcastle, same date, *Ibid.*, 350.

76. A clear statement of this intention is to be found in Earl of Devonshire to Lord ?, 28 November 1688, HMC 8, 9th Rep., pt. II, *Morrison*, p. 460.

77. See the newsletter to [Mr. Thornburgh, ? November, 1688], MS Rawlinson Letters 109, fol. 114, Bodleian. That this rumor had currency is confirmed by the dispatch of the imperial envoy Philippe Johann Hoffmann, 3 December 1688, Campana de Cavelli, *Les Derniers Stuarts*, II:338-39.

Notes to Chapter VII

1. See Herbert H. Rowen, "A Second Thought on Locke's First Treatise," *Journal of the History of Ideas* XVII (1956):130-32.

2. In particular see Princess Anne to the queen, "About Dec 2d, 1688," Galway of Serlby MSS, 12,740, University of Nottingham, Nottingham, England. See also [Marlborough], *Conduct*, 19.

3. Princess Anne to Prince of Orange, 18 November 1688, Brown, ed., *Letters of Queen Anne*, pp. 43-44; Burnet, *History*, III:335; [Marlborough], *Conduct*, p. 17.

4. See Lord Preston to Earl of Middleton, 24 November 1688, Preston MSS, Dispatches to Lords Lieutenant in 1688, Section II, fol. 13.

5. Earl of Middleton to Lord Preston, 25 November 1688, HMC 6, 7th Rep., app. I, *Sir F. Graham*, p. 419. See also Macaulay, *History*, III:1166.

6. Ailesbury, *Memoirs*, I:191; Burnet, *History*, III:335; [Marlborough], *Conduct*, p. 17.

7. See Bentinck's journal of events, 2/12 December 1688, Japikse, ed.,

Correspondentie, pt. I, vol. II (24):630; Samuel Pepys to Lord Dartmouth, 26 November 1688, HMC 20, *Dartmouth*, I:214; newsletter to Mr. Norton of Walden, 28 November 1688, BM, Add. MSS 34,487, fol. 40; Bishop of London to Earl of Danby, 2 December 1688, HMC 8, 9th Rep., pt. II, Morrison, p. 461.

8. Newsletter to [Arthur Charlett], 20 November [1688], Ballard MS 45, fol. 65.

9. Compton's biographer wrongly asserts that the bishop joined his nephew, the Earl of Northampton, at Castle Ashby and that they then proceeded to Nottingham together. Carpenter, *Protestant Bishop*, p. 133. For general information pertaining to this stage of the flight from London, see [Marlborough], *Conduct*, p. 17; and Ailesbury, *Memoirs*, I:191.

10. John Horton to Viscount Hatton, 2 December 1688, BM, Add. MSS 29,563, fol. 347; newsletter from London, 4 December 1688, MS Don. C39, fol. 36, Bodleian; [Mr. Sayre] to Mr. [Arthur] Charlett, n. d., Ballard MS 45, fol. 55.

11. See, for instance, the reaction of the queen as recorded in Bishop of London to Earl of Danby, 2 December 1688, HMC 8, 9th Rep., pt. II, *Morrison*, p. 461. See also newsletter to John Ellis, 27 November 1688, BM, Add. MSS 4194, fol. 49; unknown to James Harrington, 27 November [1688], BM, Add. MSS 36,707, fol. 49.

12. See the analysis in Carpenter, *Protestant Bishop*, p. 136. See also Philippe Johann Hoffman to Emperor Leopold I, 13 December 1688, Campana de Cavelli, *Les Derniers Stuarts*, II:365.

13. Earl of Devonshire to Prince of Orange, 2 December 1688; Bishop of London to same, 2 December 1688, PRO, SP 8/2, pt. II, fols. 67-70 (Dalrymple, *Memoirs*, II, app. I:334-35); Prince of Orange to Bishop of London, 5/15 December 1688, HMC 8, 9th Rep., pt. II, *Morrison*, pp. 460-61.

14. Shortly after her arrival Anne was to comment about the lack of news at Nottingham. Princess Anne to Sir Benjamin Bathurst, 3 December 1688, BM, Loan 51/71 (Bathurst MSS), fol. 19 (Brown, ed., *Letters of Queen Anne*, p. 45).

15. The Earl of Ailesbury gives an amusing account of one source of these rumors. Ailesbury, *Memoirs*, I:191. See also Cibber, *Apology*, pp. 46-47; "Draft summary of the Corporation of Nottingham's case for the restoration of arms . . . ," [summer, 1690?], printed in Walker, ed., "Confiscation of Firearms in Nottingham in Charles Harvey's Mayoralty, 1689-1690," p. 27.

16. See Dalton, ed., *English Army Lists*, II:171; Edmund Bohun, *The History of Desertion*, printed in *A Collection of State Tracts*, I:47.

17. Col. Roger Whitley's Diary, 1684-1697, entry for 27 November 1688, Mainwaring MS 31, fol. 99, John Rylands Library; Peter Shakerley to William Blathwayt, 21 November and 7 December 1688, BM, Add. MSS 38,695, fols. 86, 92; [William Denton to Sir Ralph Verney], 4 December 1688, HMC 6, 7th Rep., app. I, *Verney*, p. 502. See also George Ormerod, *The History of the County Palatine and City of Chester*, 3 vols. (London, 1819), I:211.

18. Diary of Lord Derby's activities, HMC 35, *Kenyon*, 201-02; Peter Shakerley to [Prince of Orange], 13 December 1688, BM, Add. MSS 38,695, fol. 103; same to Lt. Gen. Robert Werden, 15 December 1688, and enclosure of same date to be submitted to the Prince of Orange, *Ibid.*, fols. 104, 106.

19. Col. Roger Whitley's Diary, 1684-1697, entry for 19 December 1688, Mainwaring MS 31, fol. 100. Apparently this declaration was drawn up the preceding day. See HMC 4, 5th Rep., pt. I, *Cholmondeley*, 343.

20. Diary of Lord Derby's activities, HMC 35, *Kenyon*, pp. 201-02; Lt. Col. William Fleming to Roger Fleming, 29 November 1688, MS Don. C39, fols. 14-15 (partly printed in HMC 25, *Le Fleming*, p. 223).

21. Peter Shakerley to William Blathwayt, 24 December 1688, BM, Add. MSS 38,695, fol. 112. See also a newsletter from Chester to Sir Ri[chard] Ryvers, 26 December 1688, MS Carte 40, fol. 504, Bodleian.

22. For the religious complexion of the city of Chester, see the comment in Charles F. Mullett, "The Legal Position of English Protestant Dissenters, 1660-1689," *Virginia Law Review*, XXII (1936): 506.

23. Lord Delamer to Earl of Derby, 10 December [1688], Kenyon MSS, 653 (partly printed HMC 35, *Kenyon*, p. 210). See also the newsletter from Chester to Sir Ri[chard] Ryvers, 26 December 1688, MS Carte 40, fol. 504, Bodleian.

24. Chesterfield has left two fairly extensive commentaries on his attitudes and activities at the time. See Earl of Chesterfield to Marquess of Halifax, 16 December 1688, Spencer MSS, Halifax Correspondence, Box I, Althorp; entrybook of the Earl of Chesterfield, BM, Add. MSS 19,253, fols. 192-93 (*Letters of Philip, Second Earl of Chesterfield*, pp. 48-50).

25. See Morrice, Entring Book, II, fol. 371.

26. Apparently the association was the brainchild of Sir Edward Seymour. Foxcroft, *Halifax*, II:26.

27. Morrice, Entring Book, II, fol. 372. Among those peers signing were the Earls of Devonshire, Northampton and Manchester, the Bishop of London, Lords Grey de Ruthin, Carteret, Sherard, Cholmondeley, and, after some hesitation, the Earl of Scarsdale. As for those nobles refusing to engage, Lord Cullen had joined Anne in Leicestershire on her way north and Lord Ferrers had come in with Chesterfield after the princess arrived at Nottingham. Specific evidence concerning Lords Brooke and Digby—both of whom came from Warwickshire—and Lord Leigh of Staffordshire is not available, but presumably they either joined Anne's escort as she moved north from London or came to Nottingham after her arrival.

28. Morrice, Entring Book, II, fol. 371; Robert Wilmot to Sir John Gell, 19 December 1688, Gell MSS, ser. A, #37; [Rev. Theophilus?] Brookes to Earl of Huntingdon, 19 December 1688, Hastings MSS, HA 13420 (partly printed HMC 78, *Hastings* II:211).

29. For the replies of several of the individuals identified, see Duckett, *Penal Laws and Test Act*, I:166-67. See also "A List of the late Deputy

Leiftennts and Officers in the Militia [of Derbyshire]," enclosure to a letter from George Vernon and Sir Henry Hunloke to Lord Preston, 1 November 1688, Preston MSS, Miscellania, fol. 120.

30. See Duke of Newcastle to captains in the militia of Nottingham-shire, 5 December 1688, Preston MSS, Letters from England, etc., fol. 135.

31. [Rev. Theophilus?] Brookes to Earl of Huntingdon, 19 December 1688, Hastings MSS, HA 13420; [Countess of Huntingdon to same], 7 and 11 December 1688, HMC 78, *Hastings*, II:204, 206.

32. See again [Rev. Theophilus?] Brookes to Earl of Huntingdon, 19 December 1688, Hastings MSS, HA 13420; J[ohn] H[orton] to Viscount Hatton, 10 December 1688, BM, Add. MSS 29,563, fol. 359; Lord Sherard to John Coke, 19 December 1688, HMC 23, *Cowper*, II:345. The content of this letter would indicate that Coke and Sherard were the key figures involved in the management of the Leicestershire militia after it had been raised.

33. Morrice, Entring Book, II, fols. 369-70. Until her death shortly before the revolution, Sir Scrope Howe had been connected to the Earl of Rutland by marriage to his daughter Anne.

34. J[ohn] H[orton] to Viscount Hatton, 10 December 1688, BM, Add. MSS 29,563, fol. 359; [Earl of] W[estmorland] to same, 13 December 1688, BM, Add. MSS 29,563, fol. 372. See also the interesting and typical letter of excuse for failing to come to the aid of the king, Earl of Westmorland to [Earl of Middleton], 17 November 1688, *Ibid.*, 41,805, fol. 231; rough draft of warrant from [Earl of Northampton to Deputy Lieutenants of Warwickshire], ? December [1688], Northampton MSS, Bundle 1108.

35. Naturally enough effort was made to publicize Anne's arrival and the consequent influx of important men to Nottingham. *Great News from Nottingham. The Fifth of December, 1688* (Nottingham?, 1688).

36. See [Earl of Lindsey] to Countess of Danby, 10 December 1688, HMC 38, 14th Rep., app. IX, *Lindsey*, p. 452; Earl of Lindsey to Earl of Danby, 11 December 1688, HMC 22, 11th Rep., app. VII, *Leeds*, p. 28. Note is made of an "Address of the Lord Lieutenant, &c. of the County of Lincoln to the Prince of Orange," signed 13 December 1688, in HMC 22, 11th Rep., app. VII, *Waterford*, p. 76. Most of the Waterford MSS are now on deposit at the Northumberland Record Office, but this address numbers among several documents that have disappeared during the migrations of the collection following the compilation of the Historical Manuscripts Commission calendar in 1888.

37. "The Declaration of the Nobility and Gentry of the County of Stafford," [4 December 1688], *A Sixth Collection of Papers Relating to the Present Juncture of Affairs* (London, 1689), pp. 15-16. Appended to the text of the declaration itself is a short descriptive summary of subsequent events. See also Morrice, Entring Book, II, fol. 371.

38. See Bishop of London to Earl of Danby, 2 December 1688, HMC 8, 9th Rep., pt. II, Morrison, p. 461; Earl of Devonshire to same, 3 December [1688]; [Earl of] D[anby] to Bishop of London, 4 December

1688; same to Earl of Devonshire and Bishop of London, 4 December 1688. The last three letters cited are printed in Browning, *Danby*, II: 145-46.

39. Professor Browning makes no attempt to provide definite figures in this connection, and the estimate of ten thousand men made by Professor Wood is clearly an exaggeration. See Wood, "Revolution of 1688 in the North of England," p. 90.

40. Lumley had reached the county town of Durham by 5 December at the latest; given the distance involved he must have left York two or three days earlier. A combination of factors, including the absence of the Bishop of Durham, contributed to his success in raising men and organizing a petition for a free parliament. However, some controversy exists as to whether his achievement included securing the city of Newcastle for the prince. While contemporary newsletters and subsequent historical narratives generally state that he did, there is testimony of Sir Christopher Musgrave to the effect that Newcastle maintained a position of neutrality, refusing assistance from the Catholic commander of the garrison at Berwick as well as from Lord Lumley.

See Lord Lumley to Earl of Danby, 5 December 1688, HMC 22, 11th Rep., app. VII, *Leeds*, p. 27. For a report that Lumley actually secured the city of Newcastle, see Morrice, Entring Book, II, fol. 343. Considerably embellished and moved back to the month of November, the story later appears in John Brand, *The History and Antiquities of the Town and County of the Town of Newcastle upon Tyne*, 2 vols. (London, 1789), II:499. Evidence to the contrary—combined with additional information of value about Lumley's activity in Durham—is to be found in a letter from Sir Christopher Musgrave to Sir Daniel Fleming, 13 December 1688, HMC 25, *Le Fleming*, p. 228. The Wednesday referred to in this letter in connection with Lumley's offer of assistance to Newcastle is 5 December.

41. See Earl of Danby to Sir John Hanmer, 30 November 1688; same to same, 5 December 1688; Sir John Hanmer to [Earl of Danby], 4 December 1688, Browning, *Danby*, II:142-43, 147.

42. Earl of Danby to [Countess of Danby], 5 December 1688, *Ibid.*, p. 148.

43. This analysis is based largely on the conclusions of Professor Browning. In particular see *Ibid.*, I:409.

44. Besides Lumley's efforts in Durham, the earl was also closely connected with the unsuccessful attempt of Sir John Lowther to secure the capitulation of the garrison at Carlisle, to raise the militia of Westmorland and Cumberland, and to arrange for a declaration in support of a free parliament.

See Sir John Lowther, Richard Lowther, and others to Earl of Danby, 2 December 1688; Sir John Lowther to same, 5 and 12 December 1688, HMC 22, 11th Rep., app. VII, *Leeds*, pp. 27-28; Joseph Reed to Sir John Lowther, 6 December 1688, HMC 33, *Lonsdale*, p. 97. See also Browning, *Danby*, I:417-18; James Wilson, "Political History," *The Victoria County History of Cumberland*, II:298.

45. See [Earl of Danby] to Prince of Orange, 7 December 1688, Browning, *Danby*, II:149-50 and HMC 38, 14th Rep., app. IX, *Lindsey*, pp. 450-51. This was the first message from Danby that William acknowledged receiving; he ignored the earl's request. Prince of Orange to [Earl of Danby], 12/22 December 1688, Browning, *Danby*, II:150.

46. Browning, *Danby*, I:411-12. See also Earl of Danby to [Countess of Danby], 12 December 1688, *Ibid.*, II:152-53; Charles Bertie to Earl of Danby, 10 December 1688, HMC 38, 14th Rep., app. IX, *Lindsey*, p. 452. A reasonably detailed but somewhat unreliable account of this affair is contained in Reresby, *Memoirs*, pp. 557-58. Some additional light is shed on the matter by information contained in Ailesbury, *Memoirs*, I:195. With some minor discrepancies, the fullest recapitulation is to be found in Wood, "Revolution of 1688 in the North of England," p. 92.

47. See Bishop of London to [Earl of Danby], 5 December 1688; same to same, 8 December [1688], in Browning, *Danby*, II:146-47, 151.

48. See Earl of Devonshire to [Earl of Danby], 5 December 1688, *Ibid.*, p. 147.

49. Prince of Orange to Bishop of London, 5/15 December 1688, HMC 8, 9th Rep., pt. II, *Morrison*, pp. 460-61. This was the first word that had been received from William, but it is apparent that the insurgents had already considered the possibility of marching south toward Oxford. See the postscript of the letter from Lady Justinian Isham to Sir Justinian Isham, 6 December 1688, Isham MSS, IC 1431, Northampton Record Office, Northampton, England.

50. Earl of Devonshire to Earl of Danby, 8 December [1688], Browning, *Danby*, II:151. Among the Le Fleming newsletters not printed by the Historical Manuscripts Commission is one, dated 6 December 1688, which contains reference to fifteen hundred horse at Nottingham, MS Don. C39, fol. 49, Bodleian. There was also a great deal of misinformation in circulation such as the Dutch envoy's report that the northern lords were about to march south with a force of some ten thousand horse. Arnout van Citters to the States General, 7 December 1688, BM, Add. MSS 34,510 (Mackintosh transcriptions), fol. 190.

51. According to one of the peers involved, the force numbered three thousand horse and eight hundred foot by the time it reached Leicester. These figures would seem to be inflated, although not entirely impossible. Lord Grey de Ruthin to Viscount Hatton, [10? December] 1688, BM, Add. MSS 29,563, fol. 395. An estimate of two thousand horse is contained in another of the Le Fleming newsletters, 15 [December] 1688, MS Don. C39, fol. 62, Bodleian. In general the information in the Le Fleming newsletters is quite reliable. Yet another participant in the march to Oxford estimated that the army from Nottingham numbered three thousand horse and some foot by the time it reached its destination. ? Keirness to William Adames, 18 December 1688, Cholmondeley MSS, DCH/K/10, Cheshire Record Office.

52. For the personnel of Compton's troop, who collectively were estimated to be worth £100,000 per annum, see "The Names of those

Gentlemen who listed themselves under the Comand [sic] of the . . . Bishop of London . . . ," Isham MSS, IL 3982, Northampton Record Office. Among the numerous comments relating to Compton's role, see: Dr. [Thomas] Smith to Sir William Haward, 16 December 1688, *Letters Written by Eminent Persons in the Seventeenth and Eighteenth Centuries*, 2 vols. (London, 1813), I:51-52; unsigned fragment, [16 December 1688], and A[rthur] C[harlett] to Reverend Sr, 16 December 1688, both letters in MS Eng. Hist. C6, fols. 126, 127, Bodleian.

53. Ciber, *Apology*, p. 49.

54. See Chesterfield's entrybook, *Letters of Philip, Second Earl of Chesterfield*, p. 51; Earl of Chesterfield to Marquess of Halifax, 16 December 1688, *Ibid.*, p. 335. A day or two later Sir Gilbert Clarke of Derbyshire also left to return home. Although he had come in with Chesterfield originally, the circumstances of his leave-taking were less strained. See Robert Wilmot to Sir John Gell, 19 December 1688, Gell MSS, Series A, #37.

55. See [Issac] Deprepetit to Colonel John Coke, n. d.; account of disbursements, 8 December 1688 to [13 January 1689], both printed in HMC 23, *Cowper*, II:348-50. See also "An account of what the Souldiers had to fitt ym out," n. d., Cowper MSS, Bundle 119.

56. See the information contained in J[ohn] H[orton] to Viscount Hatton, 10 December 1688, BM, Add. MSS 29,563, fol. 359.

57. John Coke subsequently claimed that the expedition left him five hundred pounds out of pocket. See the first of two letters on a sheet endorsed "Copy of two letters to ye Duke of Devonshire about ye Regiments accounts and ye Leicesttershire [sic] excise money," n. d., Cowper MSS, Bundle A.

58. The purse circulated in Derby apparently did very well; that in Nottingham was less successful. See Morrice, Entring Book, II, fol. 371; Corporation of Nottingham MSS, 3456 (Hall Book, 1688-89), fols. 14, 23.

59. Something over two thousand pounds in hearth and excise tax money was taken in by agents of the Earl of Devonshire before the end of December. In general see "An Account of money received out of ye Publick revenue by Ld Devonshire," "An account of money received by myld Devonshire and his order out of ye Publick revenue for ye expedition in ye Late Revolution," "Novem: ye 28, 1688 An account of ye Money received of ye officers of ye Revinue & the disbarsements by Mr. John Wright," Cowper MSS, Bundle A; "A generall account of ye Money Received of ye Lieutenant Cololl Coke by me I. Deprepetit from ye 27 of November 1688 to ye 20th of February 1688/9," and also endorsed "Deprepetits Acct," *Ibid.*, Bundle 119. If the figures relating to John Coke's troop provide any kind of reliable guide, it cost thirty pounds per week to maintain a unit of about forty men. See "An account generall of ye Lieut Cololl Coke's Money for ye use of his troop from ye 28 of November 1688, to ye 26 of March 1688/9," *Ibid.*, Bundle 119; see also Morrice, Entring Book, II, fols. 370-71.

60. See [Arthur Charlett] to ?, 12 December 1688, MS Eng. Hist. C6,

fol. 124, Bodleian; Prince of Orange to [Duke of Ormond], 12 December 1688, MS Carte 40, fol. 502, Bodleian. A fairly detailed description of Anne's arrival and reception at the university is to be found in the diary of Dr. Thomas Smith, fellow of Magdalen College. MS Smith 141, fol. 39, Bodleian.

61. Cibber, *Apology*, 49; Morrice, Entring Book, II, fol. 423; R. Davies to John Wright, clerk to the Earl of Devonshire's troop, 22 December 1688 and I[ssac] Deprepetit to Captain [John] Coke, 30 December 1688, HMC 23, *Cowper*, II:345, 346-47; Dalton, ed., *English Army Lists*, II:247.

62. Morrice, Entring Book, II, fol. 371; Luttrell, *Historical Relation*, I:484; ? Keirnes to William Adams, 18 December 1688, Cholmondeley MSS, DCH/K/10; see also Kennet, *Family of Cavendish*, p. 26. Devonshire was not, however, among the group of peers that William assembled at Windsor on 17 December to discuss what should be done about the king's return to London. Dorothy Somerville, *King of Hearts* (London, 1962), p. 50.

63. Expecting to depart York on 12 December with six hundred horse, Danby thought that he would reach Oxford about 20 December. The substance of this paragraph is based largely on Browning, *Danby*, I: 411-18.

64. See the commentary in Morrice, Entring Book, II, fol. 359. This source singles out the counties of Stafford, Derby, and Nottingham as especially affected by the "invinsible feares." See also Ralph Thoresby, *The Diary of Ralph Thoresby, F. R. S.*, ed. Joseph Hunter, 2 vols. (London, 1830), I:188-89; [Rev. Theophilus?] Brookes to Earl of Huntingdon, 19 December 1688, Hastings MSS, HA 13420; Ralph Hassell and others to ? at Leeds, 17 December 1688, BM, Add. MSS 10,039, fol. 51; Major Francis Holdsworth to ?, 14 December 1688, HMC 39, *Hodgkin*, p. 75. See also the series of six letters coming in to Danby and others at York between 14 and 17 December 1688, HMC 22, 11th Rep., app. VII, *Leeds*, pp. 28-29.

65. Singer, ed., *Diary of Clarendon*, II:236; Morrice, Entring Book, II, fol. 371.

66. This group included the Earls of Scarsdale and Chesterfield and Lords Ferrers and Leigh in the upper chamber and John Coke, Robert Burdett, Lord Digby, Sir Roger Cave, and Sir Justinian Isham sitting for the boroughs of Derby, Lichfield, Warwick, Coventry, and Northampton, respectively. See "A list of those against making the Prince and Princess of Orange King and Queen," [5 February 1689], Feiling, *Tory Party*, pp. 496-98. See also *Journals of the House of Lords*, XIV:119.

67. The opposition of John Coke and the Earl of Scarsdale, among others of the Cockpit circle, to the revolutionary settlement was probably an outgrowth of Anne's displeasure with the trend of events. See Reresby, *Memoirs*, p. 551.

68. See Singer, ed., *Diary of Clarendon*, II:252-62, especially 261; Morrice, Entring Book, II, fols. 446-47, 451-52, 456, 459-62; *Journal of the House of Lords*, XIV:118-19.

Note to Chapter VIII

1. S. Arthur Strong, ed., *A Catalogue of Letters and Other Historical Documents Exhibited in the Library at Welbeck* (London, 1903), app. I, p. 212.

BIBLIOGRAPHY

I. MANUSCRIPT SOURCES

A. *Libraries and Archives*

Archives du Ministere des Affaires Étrangères. Paris, France.
   Correspondance Politique Angleterre, vols. 163-64.
British Museum. London, England.
   Additional MSS 4164; 4194; 6669; 10,039; 19,253; 28,053;
      29,563; 29,594; 32,515; 33,589; 34,487; 34,510; 34,515;
      36,703; 36,707; 38,175; 38,695; 40,621; 41,804; 41,805;
      41,814; 41,816.
   Egerton MSS 2621; 3526.
   Loan 29/236; 29/240; 51/71.
Bodleian Library. Oxford, England.
   Ballard MSS 12; 21; 45.
   Carte MSS 40; 130; 217.
   Donated MSS C/39.
   English History MSS C6.
   Rawlinson Letters 109.
   Smith MSS 141.

Tanner MSS 28; 150.
Wood's Diaries 32.
Cheshire Record Office. Chester, England.
Cholmondeley MSS.
Finney of Fulshaw MSS.
City of Leicester Museum and Art Gallery. Leicester, England.
Huntingdon Letters.
Derby Public Library. Derby, England
Derbyshire Collection 844.
Dr. Williams's Library. London, England.
Roger Morrice MS, Q.
Henry E. Huntington Library. San Marino, California.
Hastings Collection.
John Rylands Library. Manchester, England.
Legh of Lyme MSS.
Mainwaring MSS.
Kent Record Office. Maidstone, England.
Sackville MSS.
Lancashire Record Office. Preston, England.
Kenyon MSS.
Northamptonshire Record Office. Northampton, England.
Isham of Lamport MSS.
Newark Municipal Building, Newark, England.
Corporation of Newark MSS.
Nottingham Public Library. Nottingham, England.
Corporation of Nottingham MSS.
Public Record Office. London, England.
Baschet's Transcriptions, PRO 31/3.
Crown Office Docket Book, IND 4215.
Entry Books, SP 44.
King William's Chest, SP 8.
Libri Pacis, PRO C139/12/4-5.
Powis MSS, PRO 30/53/8.
State Papers Domestic (James II), SP 31.
University of Nottingham. Nottingham, England.
Galway of Serlby MSS.
Parkyns of Bunny MSS.
Portland (Welbeck Abbey) MSS.

B. *Privately Owned Manuscripts*

Cowper MSS. Marquess of Lothian, Melbourne Hall. Derbyshire, England.

Devonshire MSS. Duke of Devonshire, Chatsworth. Derbyshire, England.

Gell MSS. Lt. Col. John Chandos-Pole, Newnham Hall. Northamptonshire, England.

Kenyon MSS, Lord Kenyon, Gredington. Shropshire, England.

Northampton MSS. Marquess of Northampton, Castle Ashby. Northamptonshire, England.

Preston MSS. Sir Fergus Graham, Netherby. Cumberland, England.

Rutland MSS. Duke of Rutland, Belvoir Castle. Leicestershire, England.

Spencer MSS, Halifax Correspondence. Earl Spencer, Althorp. Northamptonshire, England.

Stamford MSS. Earl of Stamford, Dunham Massey Hall. Cheshire, England.

II. BOOKS

A. *Primary*

Ailesbury, Thomas, Earl of. *Memoirs of Thomas, Earl of Ailesbury*. Edited by William Edward Buckley. 2 vols. London, 1890.

Alphabetical Account of the Nobility and Gentrey . . . related unto the several counties of England and Wales. London, 1892.

Baker, W. T., ed. *Records of the Borough of Nottingham*. Vol. V. London, 1900.

Balcarras, Colin Lindsay, Earl of. *An Account of the Affairs of Scotland Relating to the Revolution in 1688*. Edinburgh, 1754.

Basset, Thomas and Thomas Fox. *The Proceedings and Tryal in the Case of the Most Reverend Father in God William Lord Archbishop of Canterbury*. London, 1689.

Bloxam, John R., ed. *Magdalen College and King James II, 1686-1688*. Oxford, 1886.

Bramston, John. *The Autobiography of Sir John Bramston, K. B.* Edited by Lord Braybrooke. London, 1845.

Brown, Beatrice Curtis, ed. *The Letters and Diplomatic Instructions of Queen Anne*. London, 1935.

Browning, Andrew, ed. *English Historical Documents, 1660-1714*. London, 1953.

Buckingham, John Sheffield, Duke of. *Works of John Sheffield, Earl of Mulgrave, Marquis of Normandy, and Duke of Buckingham*. London, 1729.

Burnet, Gilbert. *Bishop Burnet's History of His Own Time*. Vols. III-IV. Oxford, 1833.

Calendar of State Papers, Domestic Series, 1684-1685.

Calendar of Treasury Papers, 1557-1696.

Campana de Cavelli, Emilia, Marquise. *Les Derniers Stuarts à Sainte-Germain en Laye: Documents Inédits et Authentiques* Vol. II. Paris. 1871.

Catalogue of the Nobility and Principal Gentry (Said to be) in Arms with the Prince of Orange, and in several other Parts of England. London?, 1688.

Chamberlayne, Edward. *Angliae Notitia: Or the Present State of England*. London, 1687.

Cibber, Colley. *An Apology for the Life of Mr. Colley Cibber*. Edited by Edmund Bellchambers. London, 1822.

Clarke, James Stanier. *The Life of James the Second*. Vol. II. London, 1816.

Cobbett, William, ed. *Cobbett's Parliamentary History of England*. Vols. IV-V. London, 1808-09.

A Collection of the State Tracts Published on Occasion of the Late Revolution in 1688 and during the Reign of King William III. London, 1705-07.

Copnall, H. Hampton, ed. *Nottinghamshire County Records*. Nottingham, 1915.

Cox, John Charles, ed. *Three Centuries of Derbyshire Annals*. London, 1890.

Crawford, James Ludovic Lindsay, Earl of, and Robert Steele, eds. *Tudor and Stuart Proclamations, 1485-1714*. Vol. I. Oxford, 1910.

Dalrymple, John. *Memoirs of Great Britain and Ireland*. Vol. II. London, 1771.

Dalton, Charles, ed. *English Army Lists and Commission Registers, 1661-1714.* Vol. II. London, 1894.

Declaration of the Nobility, Gentry, and Commonalty at the Rendezvous at Nottingham. Nottingham?, 1688.

Defoe, Daniel. *A Tour Through the Whole Island of Great Britain.* London, 1962.

Dover, George J. W. Agar Ellis, Lord, ed. *Letters Written during the Years 1686, 1687, 1688, and Addressed to John Ellis, Esq. Vol. II. London, 1831.*

Duckett, George. *Penal Laws and Test Act.* London, 1882, 1883.

Echard, Laurence. *History of England.* Vol. III. London, 1718.

_____. *The History of the Revolution, and the Establishment of England in the Year 1688.* London, 1725.

Evelyn, John. *The Diary of John Evelyn.* Edited by E. S. de Beer. Vol. IV. Oxford, 1955.

Foxcroft, Helen C. *A Supplement to Burnet's History of My Own Time.* Oxford, 1902.

Great News from Nottingham. The Fifth of December, 1688. Nottingham?, 1688.

Gutch, John. *Collectanea Curiosa.* Oxford, 1781.

Historical Manuscripts Commission
Series 4, 5th Report. *Cholmondeley; Ellacombe; Pine-Coffin.*
Series 5, 6th Report. *Frank.*
Series 6, 7th Report. Appendix I. *Sir F. Graham; Verney.*
Series 8, 9th Report. Part II. *H. C. Pole-Gell; Morrison.*
Series 20, 11th Report, Appendix V. *Dartmouth*, I.
Series 22, 11th Report, Appendix VII. *Leeds; Waterford.*
Series 23, 12th Report, Appendices II-III. *Cowper*, II-III.
Series 24, 12th Report, Appendix V. *Rutland*, II.
Series 25, 12th Report, Appendix VII. *Le Fleming.*
Series 29, 14th Report, Appendix II. *Portland*, III.
Series 33, 13th Report, Appendix VII. *Lonsdale.*
Series 35, 14th Report, Appendix IV. *Kenyon.*
Series 36, New Series, *Ormonde*, VIII.
Series 38, 14th Report, Appendix IX. *Lindsey.*
Series 39, 15th Report, Appendix II. *Hodgkin.*
Series 45. *Buccleugh*, II.
Series 75. *Downshire*, I.

Series 78. *Hastings*, II.

Howell, Thomas B., ed. *A Collection of State Trials*. Vol. XI. London, 1811.

Japikse, Nicolaas, ed. *Correspondentie van Willem III en Hans Willem Bentinck, eersten graaf van Portland*. The Hague, 1927-37.

Journal of the House of Lords, vol. XIV.

Kennet, White. *Complete History of England*. Vol. III. London, 1706.

—————. *Memoirs of the Family of Cavendish*. London, 1708.

—————. *Sermon Preach'd at the Funeral of the Right Noble William, Duke of Devonshire*. London, 1707.

Laughton, John Knox, ed. *Memoirs Relating to the Lord Torrington*. London, 1889.

Lee, Matthew Henry, ed. *Diaries and Letters of Philip Henry, M.S. of Broad Oak, Flintshire*. London, 1882.

[Leeds, Thomas Osborne, Duke of]. *Copies and Extracts of Some Letters Written to and from the Earl of Danby (now Duke of Leeds) in the Years 1676, 1677, and 1678*. London, 1710.

Letters of Philip, Second Earl of Chesterfield. London, 1835.

Letters Written by Eminent Persons in the Seventeenth and Eighteenth Centuries. Vol. I. London, 1813.

London Gazette, 1687, 1688.

Lonsdale, John Lowther, Viscount. *Memoir of the Reign of James II*. Reprinted in Carrel, Armand. *History of the Counter-Revolution in England*. London, 1857.

Luttrell, Narcissus. *A Brief Historical Relation of State Affairs*. Vol. I. Oxford, 1857.

Macpherson, James, ed. *Original Papers*. Vol. I. London, 1775.

[Mainwaring, Arthur]. *The King of Hearts*. London, 1690.

[Marlborough, Sarah Churchill, Duchess of]. *An Account of the Conduct of the Dowager Duchess of Marlborough, From Her First Coming to Court, to the Year 1710*. London, 1742.

Morris, Christopher, ed. *The Journeys of Celia Fiennes*. London, 1947.

Nuttal, Geoffrey, ed. *Letters of John Pinney, 1679-1699*. London, 1939.

Oldmixon, John. *The History of England During the Reign of the Royal House of Stuart*. London, 1730.

Reresby, John. *Memoirs of Sir John Reresby*. Edited by Andrew Browning, Glasgow, 1936.

Rogers, James E. Thorold, ed. *A Complete Collection of the Protests of the Lords*. Vol. I. Oxford, 1875.

Sacheverell, William. *The Case of the Corporation of Nottingham*. Reprinted in Deering, Charles. *Nottinghamia Vetus et Nova*. Nottingham, 1757.

Scott, Walter, ed. *A Collection of Scarce and Valuable Tracts*. Vols. IX-X. London, 1813.

Singer, Sameuel Weller, ed. *The Correspondence of Henry Hyde, Earl of Clarendon, and of his Brother, Laurence Hyde, Earl of Rochester; with the Diary of Lord Clarendon from 1687 to 1690*. Vol. II. London, 1828.

A Sixth Collection of Papers Relating to the Present Juncture of Affairs. London, 1689.

Steele, Richard. *Memoirs of the Life of the Most Noble Thomas, Late Marquess of Wharton*. London, 1715.

Stocks, Helen, ed. *Records of the Borough of Leicester, 1603-1688*. Cambridge, 1923.

Strong, S. Arthur, ed. *A Catalogue of Letters and Other Historical Documents Exhibited in the Library at Welbeck*. London, 1903.

Thoresby, Ralph. *The Diary of Ralph Thoresby, F. R. S.* Edited by Joseph Hunter. Vol. I. London, 1830.

True Copy of a Paper delivered by the Lord De—shire to the Mayor of Darby, where he Quarter'd the One and Twentieth November, 1688. London, 1688.

Tryall of Henry Baron Delamere for High-Treason. London, 1686.

Turner, G. Lyon, ed. *Original Records of Early Nonconformity under Persecution and Indulgence*. Vol. II. London, 1911.

Verney, Frances P. and Margaret M. Verney, eds. *Memoirs of the Verney Family*. Vol. II. London, 1907.

Warrington, Henry Booth, Earl of. *The Works of the Right Honourable Henry, Late Lord Delamer and Earl of Warrington*. London, 1694.

Wood, Anthony à. *The Life and Times of Anthony of Wood,*

Antiquary, at Oxford, 1632-1695, Described by Himself.
Edited by Andrew Clark. Vol. III. Oxford, 1895.

B. *Secondary*

Ashley, Maurice. *The Glorious Revolution of 1688.* London, 1966.

Bailey, Thomas. *Annals of Nottinghamshire.* Vol. III. London, n. d.

Baxter, Stephen B. *William III and the Defense of European Liberty, 1650-1702.* New York, 1966.

Blackner, John. *The History of Nottingham.* Nottingham, 1815.

Brand, John. *The History and Antiquities of the Town and County of the Town of Newcastle upon Tyne.* Vol. II. London, 1789.

Brown, Cornelius. *The Annals of Newark-Upon-Trent.* London, 1879.

Browning, Andrew. *Thomas Osborne, Earl of Danby and Duke of Leeds, 1632-1712.* Glasgow, 1944.

Carpenter, Edward. *The Protestant Bishop, Being the Life of Henry Compton, 1632-1713, Bishop of London.* London, 1956.

Carswell, John. *The Descent on England.* New York, 1969.

Chambers, Jonathan D. *Nottinghamshire in the Eighteenth Century.* London, 1966.

Cherry, George L. *The Convention Parliament, 1689.* New York, 1966.

Churchill, Winston S. *Marlborough, His Life and Times.* Vol. I. London, 1933.

Clark, George N. *The Later Stuarts, 1660-1714.* Oxford, 1961.

[Cokayne, George Edward]. *The Complete Peerage of England, Scotland, Ireland, Great Britain and the United Kingdom, Extant, Extinct, or Dormant.* Edited by Vicary Gibbs. London, 1910-59.

Collins, Arthur. *The Peerage of England.* London, 1756.

Cummingl, P. "The Revolution House at Whittington, Derbyshire." *The Everyday Book and Table Books.* Edited by William Hone, III: 514-20. London, 1838.

Darby, H. C., ed. *An Historical Geography of England.* Cambridge, 1951.

Deering, Charles, *Nottinghamia Vetus et Nova*. Nottingham, 1757.

Dickinson, William. *The History and Antiquities of the Town of Newark*. London, 1819.

Feiling, Keith. *A History of the Tory Party, 1640-1714*. Oxford, 1959.

Fortesque, John William. *A History of the British Army*. Vol. I. London, 1899.

Fox, Charles James. *A History of the Early Part of the Reign of James the Second*. Philadelphia, 1808.

Foxcroft, Helen C. *The Life and Letters of Sir George Savile, Bart., First Marquis of Halifax*. London, 1898.

Glover, Stephen. *The History of the County of Derby*. Edited by Thomas Noble. Vol. II. Derby, 1829.

Gray, Duncan. *Nottingham Through 500 Years*. Nottingham, 1960.

Hart, A. Tindal. *William Lloyd, 1627-1717, Bishop, Politician, Author, and Prophet*. London, 1952.

Helm, P. J. *Jeffreys*. London, 1966.

Horwitz, Henry. *Revolution Politicks: The Career of Daniel Finch, Second Earl of Nottingham, 1647-1730*. Cambridge, 1968.

Hutton, William. *The History of Derby*. London, 1791.

Jacobsen, Gertrude Ann. *William Blathwayt*. New Haven, 1932.

Jones, G. F. Trevallyn. *Saw-Pit Wharton: The Political Career from 1640 to 1691 of Philip, Fourth Lord Wharton*. Sydney, 1967.

Jones, George Hilton. *Charles Middleton: The Life and Times of a Restoration Politician*. Chicago, 1967.

Jones, James R. *The Revolution of 1688 in England*. London, 1972.

Kenyon, John P. *The Nobility in the Revolution of 1688*. Hull, 1963.

————. *Robert Spencer, Earl of Sunderland, 1641-1702*. London, 1958.

Lacey, Douglas R. *Dissent and Parliamentary Politics in England, 1661-1689*. New Brunswick, N.J., 1969.

Macaulay, Thomas Babington, Lord. *The History of England*. Edited by Charles Harding Firth. Vols. II-III. London, 1914.

Mackintosh, James. *History of the Revolution in England in 1688*. London, 1834.

Matthews, Arnold G. *Calamy Revised. Being a Revision of Edward Calamy's Account of the Ministers and Others Ejected and Silenced, 1660-62*. Oxford, 1934.

Mazure, François A. J. *Histoire de la Revolution de 1688 en Angleterre*. Paris, 1825.

Mingay, Gerald E. *English Landed Society in the Eighteenth Century*. London, 1963.

Nichols, John. *The History and Antiquities of the County of Leicester*. London, 1748.

Nicholson, Thomas C. and Arthur Stanley Turberville. *Charles Talbot, Duke of Shrewsbury*. Cambridge, 1930.

Ogg, David. *England in the Reigns of James II and William III*. Oxford, 1955.

Ormerod, George. *The History of the County Palatine and City of Chester*. Vol. I. London, 1819.

Pegge, Samuel. *A Narrative of What Passed at the Revolution House at Whittington, County of Derby, in the Year 1688*. Nottingham, 1788.

Piercy, John S. *The History of Retford*. Retford, 1828.

Pinkham, Lucile. *William III and the Respectable Revolution*. Cambridge, Mass., 1954.

Plumb, J. H. *The Growth of Political Stability in England, 1675-1725*. London, 1967.

Powley, Edward B. *The English Navy in the Revolution of 1688*. Cambridge, Mass., 1928.

Prall, Stuart E. *The Bloodless Revolution in England*. New York, 1972.

Ranke, Leopold von. *A History of England Principally in the Seventeenth Century*. Vol. IV. Oxford, 1875.

Seacome, John. *The History of the House of Stanley*. Preston, 1793.

Simpson, Robert. *The History and Antiquities of Derby*. Derby, 1826.

Sitwell, George. *The First Whig*. Scarborough, 1894.

Somerville, Dorothy H. *The King of Hearts*. London, 1962.

Stone, Lawrence. *The Crisis of the Aristocracy, 1558-1641*. Oxford, 1965.

Straka, Gerald. *The Revolution of 1688: Whig Triumph or Palace Revolution?* Boston, 1963.

Trevelyan, George M. *The English Revolution, 1688-1689.* Oxford, 1965.

Turberville, Arthur Stanley. *A History of Welbeck Abbey and Its Owners.* Vol. I. London, 1938.

_____. *The House of Lords in the Reign of William III.* Oxford, 1913.

Turner, Francis C. *James II.* London, 1948.

The Victoria History of the Counties of Cumberland, Derby, Leicester, and Nottingham.

Western, John R. *The English Militia in the Eighteenth Century.* London, 1965.

_____. *Monarchy and Revolution: The English State in the 1680's.* London, 1972.

Wood, Alfred C. *A History of Nottinghamshire.* Nottingham, 1947.

III. PERIODICALS

Atkinson, Christopher T. "Two Hundred and Fifty Years Ago: James II and His Army," *Journal of the Society for Army Historical Research* XIV (1935):1-11.

Barlow, T. Worthington, ed. "Memoires of the Family of Finney of Fulshaw, (Near Wilmslow), By Samuel Finney of Fulshaw, Esquire." *Cheshire and Lancashire Historical Collector* I (1853):40-53.

Briscoe, John Potter. "History of the Trent Bridges at Nottingham." *Transactions of the Royal Historical Society,* New Series II (1873):212-21.

Brooke, Thomas, ed. "Extracts from the Journal of Castilion Morris." *Yorkshire Archaeological and Topographical Journal* X (1889):159-64.

Browning, Andrew. "Parties and Party Organization in the Reign of Charles II." *Transactions of the Royal Historical Society,* Fourth Series XXX (1948):21-36.

Browning, Andrew and Doreen Milne. "An Exclusion Bill Division List." *Bulletin of the Institute of Historical Research* XXIII (1950):205-25.

Cherry, George L. "The Legal and Philosophical Position of the Jacobites, 1688-1689." *Journal of Modern History* XXII (1950):309-21.

173

Clarke, A. Bernard. "Notes on the Mayors of Nottingham, 1600-1775." *Transactions of the Thoroton Society* XLI (1937):35-75.

Davies, Godfrey. "Letters on the Administration of James II's Army." *Journal of the Society for Army Historical Research* XXIX (1951):69-84.

De Beer, Esmond S. "The House of Lords in the Parliament of 1680." *Bulletin of the Institute of Historical Research* XX (1943-45):22-37.

Duckett, George, "King James the Second's Proposed Repeal of the Penal Laws and Test Act in 1688." *Yorkshire Archaeological and Topographical Journal* V (1879): 433-73.

Furley, O. W. "The Whig Exclusionists: Pamphlet Literature in the Exclusion Campaign, 1679-81." *Cambridge Historical Journal* XIII (1957):19-36.

George, Robert H. "The Charters Granted to English Parliamentary Corporations in 1688." *English Historical Review* LV (1940):47-56.

————. "Parliamentary Elections and Electioneering in 1685." *Transactions of the Royal Historical Society,* Fourth Series XIX (1936):167-95.

Guilford, Everard L. "Nottinghamshire in 1676." *Transactions of the Thoroton Society* XXVIII (1924):106-13.

Habakkuk, H. John. "English Landownership, 1680-1740." *Economic History Review* X (1939-40):2-17.

Haley, Kenneth H. D. "A List of the English Peers, c. May 1687." *English Historical Review* LXIX (1954):304-6.

Hosford, David. "The Peerage and the Test Act: a List, c. November 1687." *Bulletin of the Institute of Historical Research* XLII (1969):116-20.

————. "Bishop Compton and the Revolution of 1688." *Journal of Ecclesiastical History* XXIII (1972): 209-18.

Huskinson, G. N. B. "The Howe Family and Langar Hall, 1650-1800." *Transactions of the Thoroton Society* LVI (1952):54-60.

Jewitt, Llewellyn. "The Booths or Bothes, Archbishops and Bishops, and the Derbyshire Family to which they Belonged." *The Reliquary* XXV (1884-85):33-41.

Jones, James R. "Shaftesbury's Worthy Men." *Bulletin of the Institute of Historical Research* XXX (1957):232-41.

————. "James II's Whig Collaborators." *The Historical Journal* III (1960):65-73.

Kenyon, John P. "The Reign of Charles II." *Cambridge Historical Journal* XIII (1957):82-6.

Kirke, Henry, ed. "Dr. Clegg, Minister and Physician in the 17th and 18th Centuries." *Journal of the Derbyshire Archaelogical and Natural History Society* XXXV (1913): 1-74

————. "The Revolution House at Whitington." *Journal of the Derbyshire Archaeological and Natural History Society* XXXVI (1914):1-8.

Milne, Doreen J. "The Results of the Rye House Plot and Their Influence upon the Revolution of 1688." *Transactions of the Royal Historical Society*, Fifth Series I (1951):81-108.

Mitchell, A. A. "The Revolution of 1688 and the Flight of James II." *History Today* XV (1965):496-504.

Muilenburg, James. "The Embassy of Everaard van Weede, Lord of Dykvelt, to England in 1687." *The University Studies of the University of Nebraska* XX (1920):85-161.

Mullet, Charles F. "The Legal Position of English Protestant Dissenters, 1660-1689." *Virginia Law Review* XXII (1936):495-526.

Norling, Bernard. "Contemporary English Catholics and the Policies of James II." *Mid-America* XXXVII (1955):215-28.

Notes and Queries, Seventh Series V (1888):316-7; 436.

Parsloe, C. Guy. "The Growth of a Borough Constitution: Newark-on-Trent, 1549-1688." *Transactions of the Royal Historical Society*, Fourth Series XXII (1940):199-224.

Plumb, J. H. "Elections to the Convention Parliament of 1688-9." *Cambridge Historical Journal* V (1937):235-54.

Prior, Charles. "The Spatemans of Roadnook," *Journal of the Derbyshire Archaelogical and Natural History Society* XXXVII (1915):43-54.

Rowen, Herbert H. "A Second Thought on Locke's *First Treatise*." *Journal of the History of Ideas* XVII (1956): 130-3.

Sachse, William L. "The Mob and the Revolution of 1688." *Journal of British Studies* IV (1964):23-40.

Sacret, Joseph H. "The Restoration Government and Municipal Corporations." *English Historical Review* XLV (1930): 232-59.
175

Swift, William. "Staveley Hall and its Occupants." *The Reliquary* III (1862-63):149-57.

Vellacott, Paul C. "The Diary of a Country Gentleman in 1688." *Cambridge Historical Journal* II (1926):48-62.

Walker, Violet W., ed. "The Confiscation of Firearms in Nottingham in Charles Harvey's Mayoralty, 1689-1690." *Thoroton Society Record Series* XXI (1962):21-7.

Wood, Alfred C. "A Note on the Population of Nottingham in the Seventeenth Century." *Transactions of the Thoroton Society* XL (1936):109-13.

_____. "A Note on the Population of Six Nottinghamshire Towns in the Seventeenth Century." *Transactions of the Thoroton Society* XLI (1937):18-26.

_____. "The Revolution of 1688 in the North of England." *Transactions of the Thoroton Society of Nottinghamshire* XLIV (1940):72-104.

INDEX

177

178

berland, 8, 46, 82

Newport, Francis, Viscount, 15, 20

Nobility, 8-9, 11, 20, 22, 108-09, 121-24; and Test Act, 10, 19, 68; opposition to James II, 12, 17, 23-24

Nonconformists, 42, 49, 59, 61, 63-64, 74, 76, 93, 96; *see also* Dissenters

Norfolk, Henry Howard, Duke of, 22-23

Northampton, George Compton, Earl of, 17, 21, 39, 97, 103, 110

Northampton, Northamptonshire, 8, 97, 116

Northamptonshire, 97, 102, 110-11, 114-16, 122

Northern landing, 31-32, 36

Northumberland, 82, 104, 113

Nottingham, Daniel Finch, Earl of, 12, 17-18, 29, 32-34, 79, 97, 99

Nottingham, Nottinghamshire, 54, 59, 61, 63, 76, 82; regulation of, 45, 47, 49-53; rising at, 3-8, 36-37, 39-41, 44, 80-81, 84-86, 89-92, 95-96, 98-99, 101, 103, 108-19, 122-25

Nottinghamshire, 45, 54, 59-60, 62, 68, 70, 72-73, 75-76, 96, 98-99, 109, 111, 117, 124

Ormonde, James Butler, Duke of, 20, 33, 36, 38, 117

Oxford, Aubrey de Vere, Earl of, 22

Oxford, Oxfordshire, 90, 108, 114-18

Oxford University, 36, 115

Oxfordshire, 22, 97

Palmes, Francis, 96

Parliament, 20, 23, 121; sessions in 1685, 10-11, 13, 16, 18; Convention, 66-67, 118-19; free, 106-07; *see also* House of Commons *and*

House of Lords

Penal laws, 10, 18, 24, 47, 49, 59, 67, 70

Penn, William, 16, 49

Peterborough, Henry Mordaunt, Earl of, 22, 79

Plymouth, Thomas, Windsor, Earl of, 22

Presbyterians, 59, 61-62

Preston, Richard Graham, Viscount, 83, 87

Prime, Philip, 96

Protestants, 18, 39

Quakers, 59

Reresby, Sir John, 8, 41, 83-85

Rippon, Gervas, 48

Rochester, Laurence Hyde, Earl of, 15, 22

Rose Tavern club, 35, 42-43

Russell, Admiral Edward, 17, 29, 39

Russell, Sir William, 91

Russell, William, Lord, 17, 43

Rutland, 22

Rutland, John Manners, Earl of, 13, 21, 40, 65-66, 68, 77, 110, 116

Sacheverell, William, 46, 50, 71, 73, 96

Sadd, Leonard, 56

St. Albans, Charles Beauclerk, Duke of, 21

Salisbury, Wiltshire, 35, 82-83, 94-95, 123

Savile, Henry, 15

Scarborough castle, 81, 112

Scarsdale, Robert Leke, Earl of, 21, 36-37, 66, 68-69, 70, 97, 99, 109

Scotland, 13, 83-84, 120

Seven bishops, 28-29, 38, 52, 63

Seven signatories, 31-33, 38, 39, 44

Shakerley, Peter, 88, 105

Sharp, Dr. John, 14

Sherard, Bennett, Baron, 110